D0806317

William Edward Dodd

Minds of the New South

William Edward Dodd

The South's Yeoman Scholar

Fred Arthur Bailey

University Press of Virginia

Charlottesville & London

Acknowledgment for previously published material appears on p. xi.

THE UNIVERSITY PRESS OF VIRGINIA
© 1997 by the Rector and Visitors of the University of Virginia

Printed in the United States of America

First published 1997

⊗ The paper used in this publication meets the minimum requirements
of the American National Standard for Information Sciences—
Permanence of Paper for Printed Library Materials, ANSI Z39.48-1984.

Library of Congress Cataloging-in-Publication Data
Bailey, Fred Arthur.
    William Edward Dodd : the South's yeoman scholar / Fred Arthur
Bailey.
        p.   cm.—(Minds of the new South)
    Includes bibliographical references and index.
    ISBN 0-8139-1708-5 (cloth : alk. paper)
    1. Dodd, William Edward, 1869–1940.   2. Historians—Southern
States—Biography.   3. Southern States—Social conditions.
4. Social classes—Southern States—History.   I. Title.
II. Series.
E175.5.D63B35   1997
975.04'092—dc21
    [B]   96-47667
                                                               CIP

Dedicated to the memory of
Norman Hogan, Raymond Muncy,
LeRoy P. Graf, and Richard Hepler.
Caring scholars greatly missed.

CONTENTS

PREFACE

An overmastering rage characterized William Edward Dodd's intellect. Born into a North Carolina culture in which a privileged few prospered from the labor of the dispossessed many, he would emerge from his youthful poverty to become a path-breaking historian of the American South as well as a political activist and eventually the American ambassador to Adolf Hitler's Germany. He was the South's "yeoman scholar," a rarity among intellectuals, a man who rose from among the inarticulate masses to voice their fundamental frustrations. He lashed out at the South's oppressive class structure, embraced Jeffersonian idealism, and longed to be the the catalyst who would infuse an egalitarian spirit into his native region.

This study of Dodd's mind assumes his essential uniqueness. At the opening of the twentieth century most southern men and women of letters were the scions of the region's "better families" and thus were inclined to defend the Old South, with its high-minded aristocracy and sharply articulated social structure. Having viewed life from the bottom up during his youth, Dodd saw little virtue in a society dominated by patricians, and he deeply resented the easy successes of the privileged. His lectures, articles, and books are studied critiques of the South's class system, powerful condemnations of the region's self-centered aristocracy. Dodd left the narrow confines of Clayton, North Carolina, to become the friend and intellectual peer of the historians Frederick Jackson Turner, John Spencer Bassett, and Carl Becker, to develop an intimate association with Presidents Theodore Roosevelt, Woodrow Wilson, and Franklin Delano Roosevelt, and to observe and experience the villainy of Adolf Hitler, Joseph Goebbels, and Hermann Goering. Imbued with values honed in his youth in the South, Dodd easily added Prussian Junkers, capitalist exploiters, and German Nazis to his list of rapscallions oppressing the common folk.

A man of intellect and accomplishment, Dodd has merited his share of interpreters. Those interested in his character development would do well to read the chapter on Dodd in Wendell H. Stephenson's book *The South Lives in History: Southern Historians and Their Legacy* (1955) and Robert Dallek's biography *Democrat and Diplomat: The Life of William Edward Dodd* (1968).[1] The two works focus on different aspects of Dodd's career. Whereas Stephenson was principally interested in assessing Dodd's place among the chronicler's of the South's past, Dallek was drawn to him "primarily out of an interest in his diplomatic career, or, more specifically, out of a desire to understand why someone as perceptive about Nazism as Dodd should have a reputation as a poor diplomat."[2] Both scholars were impressed by Dodd's infatuation with democracy and stressed the positive nature of his Jeffersonian beliefs. Neither, however, fully appreciated the origins and evolution of Dodd as a southern thinker. Writing during the height of consensus historiography, they did not adequately grasp the importance of conflict in southern life or how that conflict led to the lifelong bitterness that so influenced Dodd's thinking.

This study explores the darker side of Dodd's intellect and also suggests an essential ignominy in southern historiography. The judgment of history, after all, depends on who writes it. From the opening of this century until the civil rights crusade of the 1960s the chronicling of southern history was almost exclusively the domain of individuals born into its upper class. They were apologists for the Old South, presenting a felicitous image of southern aristocratic order in contrast to northern democratic anarchy, of contented slaves loyal to their solicitous masters, and of hardworking yeomen residing in harmony with their social betters. In their model an ignorant and aggressive Yankee culture thrust the Civil War upon the South, subjugated the region by overpowering force, and then imposed corrupt Reconstruction. The South's postbellum saga became the courageous struggle of its "better folk" to regain their rightful dominion over its social, economic, and political weal, to rightly order class and race relationships, and to create a model worthy of American society as a whole. Having risen from the mudsill of southern society, Dodd stood as a lonely foil to that saccharine paradigm. His life and his thoughts reveal the unrequited longings of the southern masses, a people who endured while a fortunate few prospered.

This study would have been impossible without the kindness and support of others. I am grateful to John Inscoe and Jack Roper for encouraging me to expand my article on Dodd's historical assumptions into a longer manuscript. John David Smith and Charles Bryan Jr. scrutinized different versions of the work in progress, making cogent and appreciated suggestions. I am especially thankful for John Robinson, who is not only a colleague and department chair but also a friend. He has always been willing to critique my style, suggest a better word or phrase, and in general mold my stilted prose into something more readable. I am likewise appreciative of Joanne Allen for her thorough reading of the book in manuscript and for her many positive suggestions. Without the kindness of all of these individuals this project would not have been possible.

Portions of chapter 3 appeared in a different form in "William Edward Dodd: The South's Yeoman Historian," *North Carolina Historical Review* 66 (July 1989): 301–20; and "A Virginia Scholar in Hitler's Court: The Tragic Ambassadorship of William Edward Dodd," *Virginia Magazine of History and Biography* 100 (July 1992): 323–42, yielded some of the ideas expanded here on Dodd as a diplomat.

Abilene Christian University strongly encourages its faculty to pursue their creative urges, and its Cullen Research Fund has most generously provided summer grants for travel to archives and libraries. Every historian owes a debt to dedicated librarians and archivists, and I am no exception. The staffs at the Library of Congress, the University of Chicago, the Franklin Delano Roosevelt Presidential Library, the Virginia Historical Society, the Virginia State Library and Archives, and Duke University exemplify the hospitality and professionalism that promote scholarship. I would be remiss if I did not also thank the librarians at my home institution. I am especially thankful for the efforts of Ellen Schoenrock, whose tenacity secured for me rare volumes on interlibrary loan. W. Kirk Wood, Richard Hepler, and Jackie Goggins graciously shared with me Dodd materials gathered by them in the course of their own research projects.

Bonnie, my wife and soul mate of many years, has stood by me through each crisis of this work and much more. Her love and solace are always a comfort and a refuge. Eternity is not long enough to express how much I cherish and adore her.

ABBREVIATIONS

Dodd Papers, LC | William E. Dodd Papers. Library of Congress, Washington D.C.

Dodd Papers, RM | William E. Dodd Papers. Randolph-Macon College Library, Ashland VA.

Dodd Papers, SHC | William E. Dodd Papers. Southern Historical Collection, University of North Carolina, Chapel Hill.

Roosevelt Papers, POF | Franklin Delano Roosevelt, President's Official Files. Franklin Delano Roosevelt Presidential Library, Hyde Park NY.

Roosevelt Papers, PPF | Franklin Delano Roosevelt, President's Personal Files. Franklin Delano Roosevelt Presidential Library, Hyde Park NY.

Roosevelt Papers, PSF | Franklin Delano Roosevelt, President's Secretaries Files. Franklin Delano Roosevelt Presidential Library, Hyde Park NY.

Turner Papers, HEH | Frederick Jackson Turner Papers. Henry E. Huntington Library, San Marino CA.

Turner Papers, HU | Frederick Jackson Turner Papers. Houghton Library, Harvard University, Cambridge MA.

William Edward Dodd

CHAPTER ONE

The Genesis of a Class-Conscious Scholar

William Edward Dodd met the offer of a prestigious award with amiable restraint. When in 1920 Emory University proffered an honorary doctorate in recognition of his "notable contributions to Southern history," the University of Chicago history professor was "greatly obliged for the expression of approval" but surprised "that Southern universities would feel disposed to endorse the kind of work I try to do."[1] The North Carolina native grounded his skepticism in a rigorous critique of the South's class system and the wealthy elite that controlled the region's social, political, and economic life.

One year earlier Yale University Press had published his book *The Cotton Kingdom: A Chronicle of the Old South,* a work with broad ramifications. To Emory's council of deans Dodd suggested that "any man who reads twenty years hence such books as I have . . . published will find something to commend . . . in the spirit manifested. It represents my whole method." He warned, however, that he would continue in this direction in future writings and said that should Emory "still wish to endorse me, then I shall be very happy indeed."[2]

Emory granted the degree, but far more than twenty years would pass before southern scholars dealt seriously with the ideas Dodd articulated in 1919. *The Cotton Kingdom* portrayed a South deeply divided along class lines in which dominating planters hoarded wealth, oppressed small farmers, and sought national preeminence. "What the South really desired in 1860," he explained to a colleague, "was control of the government and [Southerners] would [have been] as national as any body. . . . Only it would have been a distinctly aristocratic nationality." [3]

Historiographers have generally overlooked the seminal role that class consciousness played in Dodd's scholarly constructions, grasping his emphasis on the American democratic ideal without appreciating its distinctively southern roots.[4] Intensely aware of his heritage, Dodd believed that history must "always reflect . . . the mind of the historian, and the mind of the historian will reflect the thinking of the group, social group, to which he belongs." [5] His understanding of southern social-class strife was a product of his North Carolina yeoman origins.

Dodd was among the South's important intellectuals in the early part of the century. First as a historian of the American South, then as a respected advocate of Woodrow Wilson's internationalism, and finally as the American ambassador to Hitler's Germany, he was not only a radical proponent of democracy but also a strident critic of those he marked as its enemies. With remorseless energy he savaged southern aristocrats, northern industrialists, and German Nazis alike. Through it all he never strayed far from his roots; his interpretation of the broader world drew upon his infatuation with his native soil. "The tale of the South is an epic," he wrote in 1908, "it lends itself to the dramatic and all her leaders of eminence play their roles on its great stage." [6]

By the time of his death, in 1940, Dodd had become one of those "leaders of eminence" whose personal epic had interwoven with those of many of the century's luminaries. By profession he was a peer of the historians Frederick Jackson Turner, John Spencer Bassett, Frederic Bancroft, and Carl Becker; as a graduate professor he honed the scholarship of such important academicians as Frank Lawrence Owsley, Herman C. Nixon, Walter Prescott Webb, and Henry Steele Commager. But Dodd chafed in the role of a passive interpreter of the past; driven by almost fanatical democratic beliefs, he longed to stand as an ideological adviser to a great twentieth-century statesman, to play John the Baptist to a democratic Messiah.

The swirling events of the Great War drew Dodd into Woodrow Wilson's circle and propelled him into the role of an apostle of the president's vision for world peace and democracy in the 1920s. The Democratic Party rewarded his devotion with an ambassadorial posting to Berlin in 1933, but there his life's drama turned to tragedy. Appalled by Nazi totalitarianism, he determined to expose its autocracy, but his diplomatic staff, patrician career officers who neither shared nor appreciated his egalitarian philosophy, constantly undermined him. They joined the other elites who had been his antagonists in both his personal and his professional life. Born into a southern culture dominated by an aristocracy, he remembered both the folk of his origins and the privileged groups who had frustrated the ambitions of the masses.

Dodd's historical interpretations reveal a barely suppressed rage leveled at a southern social structure founded on the premise of man's innate inequality. He crafted his writings as extended sermons in praise of common-man democracy, urging the people to rise up against their aristocratic oppressors. During the antebellum epoch, he wrote, "the piney-woods men, the farmers and tenants of the hills, were all dependents of their greater neighbors, willing hangers-on of a system which, if they but knew it, could give them no promise of better things."[7] Such words flowed naturally from one who saw life from the perspective of the lower stratum of the social environment of nineteenth-century North Carolina.

Growing up near the Johnston County community of Clayton, Dodd knew firsthand the complex class distinctions grounded in the pre–Civil War epoch. Although North Carolina lacked the sophistication associated with neighboring Virginia and South Carolina and the wealth characteristic of the Deep South's cotton and sugar regions, it evolved a class structure whose essential elements corresponded to those of the South as a whole. Ensconced at the top was a small, powerful elite of planters, manufacturers, merchants, attorneys, and physicians, all hostile to democratic inclinations. They dominated local and state government, protecting their wealth and power, fearing its use by resentful nonaffluent whites, and feeling little inclination to share its emoluments with the common folk.[8]

Largely untouched by the Jacksonian democratic reforms of the 1830s, North Carolina's governmental system vested power in a favored few. As late as 1857 only men who owned at least fifty acres of land could vote for state senators. Candidacy for the state legislature was restricted to those holding one hundred acres or more, and the property requirements were even higher for those who wished to run for the offices of governor and U.S. senator. Legislative districting secured slaveowner supremacy by defining state senate districts according to taxable wealth, thus ensuring overrepresentation of more affluent regions. The lower house apportioned its members by population, using the federal ratio, which counted a slave as three-fifths of a person, again protecting slaveholder dominance. In 1860 85 percent of North Carolina's legislators owned human chattel, the highest percentage in the South.

Elites controlled local government as well. Except for sheriffs and county court clerks, all county officials were appointed. Nominated by state legislators and confirmed by the governor, the powerful justices of the peace held life tenures. Virtually omnipotent in local affairs, they selected most other county officials, set tax rates, determined road-building policies, established schools, and provided for aid to the poor. In their judicial capacity they issued all writs necessary for legal activities. Selected from the "best families" of each county and secure in the values of their social class, the justices of the peace benefited their own kind in the conduct of local affairs.

Yet the overwhelming majority of North Carolina antebellum whites constituted an underclass to whom access to economic advancement and political power was largely denied. In 1860 almost 70 percent of the state's farmers had landholdings of fewer than one hundred acres, and 42 percent owned fewer than fifty acres, only enough for subsistence farming. Excluded from viable political activity and thereby isolated from the nation-splitting issues of state rights and slavery, these farmers valued their tenuous economic independence, focusing upon annual crop cycles and the life cycle of birth, baptism, marriage, and death.

Landless whites, constituting just under 30 percent of adult white males in 1860, were located still lower on the social scale. They struggled as tenant farmers, common laborers, and farm hands—all dependent for their income upon the patronage of more affluent whites. Small landholders and propertyless whites rarely looked to local government for their needs; even more rarely did they seek justice from the elite-controlled legal system. Each family took care of its own, more often than not resolving quarrels through personal confrontation.[9]

Southern patricians led their region out of the Union in 1861, confident that their fellow whites would follow in a heroic crusade against the iniquitous North. Initially this was the case, but the malign realities of death, disease, and war-induced poverty slowly eroded Confederate loyalty and disrupted traditional social relationships. Gradually disillusioned, nonelite whites saw little reason to fight so that the wealthy might own slaves. Discontented North Carolinians protested, joining the Union army, forming peace societies, and deserting the Confederate forces. At war's end the rest of the South reflected North Carolina's disunity and class hostility.[10]

The flight of nonelite whites from the Confederate banner dealt southern aristocrats a severe ideological blow. If "proper" social order mandated subordination of most men—white as well as black—to the patricians, then the desertion of common soldiers raised a serious challenge to traditional class relationships. This threat intensified during the postwar decades as discontented agrarians, whites now joined by blacks, repeatedly denounced the elites' governance. Although the patricians rapidly reestablished their personal fortunes and, following the demise of Reconstruction, their political authority, they could no longer count on the meek acquiescence of small farmers and artisans. The Granger Movement, the Farmers' Alliance, and the Populist Party crusade in turn evidenced powerful discontent with the southern oligarchy.[11]

Agrarian protests were but outward manifestations of economic disenchantment. Across the South yeomen returning from the war found their farms in dire need of attention. Both armies had confiscated farm animals, especially mules; fences had been burned for firewood; and homesteads stripped of men of military age had fallen into disrepair. The common farmer without financial reserves had to sacrifice his valued economic independence, mortgaging his crops to merchants and bankers, who demanded that farmers cultivate cotton and other revenue-producing crops. No longer free to engage in subsistence agriculture, the yeomen relied on the general store for credit and for the foodstuffs, clothing, and supplies they had once produced for themselves. At century's end the once tenuously autonomous yeomen found themselves heavily in debt, and they often lashed out against businessmen and large landowners, who now controlled not only wealth and political influence but also the very pattern of small farmers' life.[12]

Growing up in Clayton, North Carolina, Dodd was keenly aware of this yeoman dilemma. Founded in the mid-1850s, Clayton, located twenty miles southeast of Raleigh, received its charter in 1869.[13] Dodd remembered it as a "dirty" little community "with negroes loitering on every public place."[14] Most citizens farmed cotton, trapped in the crop-lien system that left them heavily in debt to the community's three principal merchants, W. H. McCullers, J. G. Barbours, and Ashley Horne.[15] Dodd's great-uncle Ashley Horne was by far the most powerful. Scion of a moderately wealthy Johnston County farm family, he returned from the Confederate army in 1867 and opened a dry-goods store, extending generous credit to his neighbors; and in concert with his brothers Samuel and Hardee he invested in banking and manufacturing concerns. By 1900 he was an acknowledged millionaire, a power broker in the Democratic Party and former state senator, president of the Clayton Banking Company, and a patron of the local Methodist church and Confederate patriotic associations. As was typical in such cases in small towns in the South, he was an important man, accustomed to the honorific title "colonel" and gracious in his acceptance of the deference extended by his community's less exalted members.[16]

In 1918 Dodd looked back fondly on the egalitarianism of the yeomen in his boyhood community; toward the few individuals who had held economic sway he was acrimonious. "Everybody except three families was on an equality," he recorded in his diary. The exceptions were "my great uncle Ashley Horne, W. H. McCullers, and J. G. Barbours." All three "merchant[s] and lender[s] of money" on farm mortgages, they were "hard men, those traders and aristocratic masters of their dependents! They were by no means aristocrats in the old South sense, but they were respected or feared by everyone I knew." His other "boyhood acquaintances" were "poor people, small farmers who owned their homes but paid interest on loans from one or another of these three men." Everyone in Clayton "worked in the fields with their own hands," he remembered, all but the merchants and their clerks. Their daughters and sons "were the only people I ever knew who drove or rode summer evenings for their health or pleasure."[17]

These musings reveal Dodd's understanding of the reasons for his own success. Born into poverty, he escaped the almost predestined lot of his peers by suppressing his feelings toward the Horne family, deferring to these local patricians, and accepting their patronage. Putting behind him the mind-numbing drudgery of the farm, he built his future largely on an exceptional education and in time parlayed his intellectual ability into fame, influence, and financial comfort. This suggests the essential irony, or more correctly, contradiction, of Dodd's life. Although in promoting radical social egalitarianism he condemned the elite's unearned advantages in the quest for society's honors and rewards, at the same time he recognized his dependence upon the approval and acceptance of privileged individuals in order to achieve his own ambitions. Dodd reconciled his distaste for upper-class dominance and his frequent courting of these people by intellectually dividing them into two distinct categories. In his mind the vast majority were insensitive exploiters of the masses, individuals who wore their wealth and power as the natural perquisites of their class. An enlightened minority, however, looked beyond the narrow interest of their class, grasped the virtues of democracy, and extended the hand of fellowship to unprivileged men of ability. As a historian, Dodd cast his heroes in the latter mold; thus, he saw Thomas Jefferson, Woodrow Wilson, and Franklin Delano Roosevelt as supreme examples of men born to advantage who recognized the virtues of democracy. In turn, those who assisted Dodd, who opened for him the doors to advancement and enabled him to move among the intellectual and political elites of his time, were classed with society's exemplars. Most, however, fell short and earned his scorn.

Throughout Dodd's formative years two imperfect models shaped his early intellect and set before him alternative life choices. The first, his father, John D. Dodd, had cultivated his small farm west of Clayton and dreamed of the economic independence sometimes attainable in the antebellum generation. But he was trapped by indebtedness to Ashley Horne's general store and dissolved into a frustrated and morose figure resentful of the power brokers. The Horne family served as an alternate model. Although Dodd was offended by their oppression of Clayton's less affluent citizens, he envied his kinsmen's association with the politicians who charted society's course, imagining that in time he also could wield similar influence, but in a manner more sympathetic to the common man.

Dodd's disdain for aristocratic privilege sprung from his plebeian origins. Descended from an undistinguished paternal ancestry and a maternal line that twice married down in status, young William grew up among simple country folk for whom the biblical injunction to sweat for one's bread gave life its mission.[18] Largely reliant upon familial labor, his people made a virtue of necessity; even their recreations—corn shuckings, barn raisings, and quilting bees—served utilitarian purposes. For them the Civil War was a cultural disaster, robbing them of their cherished economic independence, imposing intense poverty, and forcing them into restrictive, demeaning debt.

Immersed in North Carolina's yeoman culture, John Dodd, William's grandfather, desperately clung to his modest holdings west of the line separating Wake and Johnston Counties. Deemed illiterate by the census marshal, he owned real estate valued at only $340 in 1850 and had little prospect of accumulating anything beyond independence. In fact his personal fortune had declined slightly by the eve of the Civil War.[19] Since he was too poor to own slaves, his family's weal depended upon each member's physical effort; there was little time or money available for his children's schooling. John D., the oldest son, showed a certain native intelligence, but a limited education gained him only the most minimal reading skills. In 1868 he left home to wed Evelyn Creech and to earn his living on land given to the couple by Evelyn's father. On 21 October 1869 his wife gave birth to the first of their seven children, William Edward.[20]

John D. Dodd instilled in William and his other children reverence for labor. He focused his attention on the gritty necessity of wrenching sustenance from the soil and insisted that his sons work from morning's first light to dusk, hoping that such effort would free his family from debt. Locked in perpetual penury, he could ill afford even the simplest luxuries, and his children grew up unaccustomed to amenities.[21] Impotent before his debtors, John D. Dodd grew sullen and disrespectful of his social betters. "I never knew any person anywhere who did not either love or like [mother]," William Dodd reflected late in life. "My father was not so possessed of such appealing traits. He distrusted other people and paid the penalty."[22]

Although William's father lacked social standing in the Clayton community, his wife Evelyn was directly related to the prestigious Horne family.[23] Her grandfather Benajah Horne, the clan patriarch, accumulated an estate that was worth fifteen thousand dollars in 1860, which placed him among the neighborhood's wealthier inhabitants and opened for his children opportunities that were denied to less well endowed Southerners. Expansive in personality and charitable toward others, he served forty years as a county magistrate. Grateful neighbors remembered his sense of noblesse oblige; they especially recalled his using his personal carriage to transport sick, wounded, and dying soldiers from Clayton's railroad station to their homes during the war.[24]

Benajah Horne wanted his children, particularly his six sons, to move beyond Clayton's limited boundaries and associate with the elite of North Carolina. The Civil War nearly destroyed that vision. Needham, his eldest son, who studied medicine in Philadelphia, volunteered as a surgeon in the Confederate army and disappeared, his fate undetermined; two other

boys died fighting for the South. When the war ended, Ashley Horne returned from Appomattox and Samuel and Hardee drifted back from
Union prisons. Buttressed by education, contacts, and family position,
these men met the New South's challenges with entrepreneurial courage,
investing in mercantile and industrial enterprises. By the end of the century all three had gained the status their father had hoped for.[25]

Whereas Benajah Horne's sons enhanced the family's stature, his eldest
daughter married beneath her station. In 1848 Martha Horne choose as
her consort Stanford Creech, a yeoman of modest background. Two years
later the census listed their real-estate holdings at no more than three
hundred dollars, which placed them on the economic plane of the nearby
Dodd family. Over the next decade their status improved somewhat,
doubtless aided by Benajah Horne. In 1860 Stanford Creech valued his
total estate at just over forty-four hundred dollars; what was more significant, he classed himself as a slaveowner, having invested most of his
personal worth in a twenty-seven-year-old woman and her three children.
Although emancipation cost him this luxury, Creech emerged from the
Civil War a respectable though not wealthy farmer.[26] Little is known
about the Creech household or the parents' aspirations for their sons and
daughters. When Evelyn, their oldest, allied with John D. Dodd, she followed her mother by marrying down in status.

A committed patriarch, Benajah Horne concerned himself with the
welfare of his and his children's progeny. Unfortunately, their numbers
diluted his final beneficence. He died in 1878; when his widow succumbed two years later, most of his estate was partitioned into six equal
parts, one for each of his five surviving offspring and the remaining one
divided among the six children of his late daughter, Martha. Among
them, Evelyn Dodd, and by rights her husband, received a small, appreciated inheritance, but one that was insufficient to relieve them of their
chronic debt.[27] More important for William Dodd, Benajah Horne had
imbued his successful sons with a sense of familial duty, a commitment
both to embrace the needs of their immediate families and to encourage
their less fortunate relations.

Throughout the 1880s young William Dodd increasingly came to understand the complicated dynamics of his immediate world. Family tension, class prejudice, and alienation fostered by the war shaped an emotionally charged environment that troubled his evolving intellect. While
other boys sat enthralled by the heroic remembrances of aging veterans

and echoed their invectives against the "damnyankees," young Dodd anguished with those who had lost dear ones in the conflict, felt the crushing poverty of his parents and his neighbors, and wondered at the paradox of Southerners raining curses upon the North for a war he believed the South had brought upon itself.

To a great extent William reflected his mother's complex values. Beneath Evelyn Dodd's cheery disposition rested a troubled awareness that her impoverished state was a step down from her parents' comfortable household and well below her maternal grandparents' affluent station. Had it not been for the Yankees, she told her children, she "would have inherited a number of negroes," and she added wistfully that in her childhood she had been given the use of a young slave. But on other occasions she lectured William and his siblings that "slavery had been a great wrong" and praised Lincoln for his courage in freeing an oppressed people. Years later Dodd confided to J. Franklin Jameson, editor of the *American Historical Review,* that he had difficulty understanding how his mother "could teach her son that emancipation had been right and according to God's will" and at the same time be "in all the essential acts of her life, conformed to the economic and social forces which held fast her community." Upon reflection, he added: "I am conscious that some of these things . . . influenced my thinking if not my writing. Yet, I believe it is not a wholly unfortunate influence."[28]

Surrounded by vestiges of the Old South—former slaves, Confederate veterans, dispirited civilians—Dodd felt the first stirrings of his historical inclinations. Early mated to the plow, he attacked the soil of his father's farm, churning up corroded rifles and broken swords, detritus from William T. Sherman's last furious campaign against Joseph E. Johnston. Intrigued as he was by the material culture of war, its human wreckage fascinated him even more. Claytonians rarely spoke of chivalry or romantic crusades; they more often related acid memories of personal loss. Harry Durham, a neighboring farmer, had suffered the indignity of having Sherman occupy his house; had the general not been "under guard day and night," the old man often swore, he would have killed him. Having lost family members in the war, Durham "never saw two sides to the conflict," Dodd remembered. Whenever a little snow dusted Clayton, he inevitably hoped that "it was 40 feet deep all over the North."[29]

Dodd's family cherished its own bitter memories. His mother had witnessed the Union army's violent thrust through her community and its impounding of Benajah Horne's homestead, leaving the land bare of stock, produce, and fences. Family tradition held that soldiers had ransacked Horne's property, searching the "house from top to bottom," dismantling "the wood pile," and driving "long steel pikes into the ground . . . in search of buried treasures." Throughout the neighborhood, farmers had watched helplessly as soldiers despoiled crops, slaughtered horses, and hanged defiant Southerners. William remembered that his mother had "unceasingly denounced General Sherman for the cruelties of the spring of . . . 1865." Yet she was ambivalent in her wrath, pointing to those in her community who shared equal guilt. "Slaveholders," she declared, "were wholly to blame for the great war."[30]

Another important family member, Dodd's great-uncle Samuel Horne, almost never spoke kindly of the North. An alumnus of the Johnson Island prison in Ohio, he talked "of Lee and Gettysburg and Appomattox like an unreconstructed rebel."[31] Reflecting on such passions in 1919, Dodd mused that it "would have been a great thing if the Southerners could have forgotten that they were Southerners at the close of the Civil War; . . . the one thing they remembered best was the wrongs that had been done them, but none of the wrongs they did the North or themselves in their attempt to set up a reactionary and aristocratic system in this country."[32]

Although William generally dismissed the Hornes as emblematic of the aristocratic class's negative influence, he was genuinely fond of his Uncle Samuel. An aging bachelor, the old soldier frequently visited the Dodd household, considered Evelyn a favorite niece, and took great joy in encouraging her precocious son William. The historian pleasured in describing his uncle as "a unique man, . . . industrious and painstaking in all that he did." Since Samuel Horne lived in distant Morrisville, the youth knew little of his business practices and rarely associated his general-store ethics with those of Ashley and Hardee Horne, whose Clayton enterprises gave them visible power over their clients. William's admiration resulted in part from the fact that Samuel Horne revered learning. Having briefly attended Wake Forest College and later taught in an academy, Samuel counseled his grand-nephew to embrace education as a surety against poverty. In large measure, however, William's positive recollections sprang from Samuel Horne's devotion to physical labor, a trait the boy identified as more plebeian than patrician. With deepest respect Dodd recounted that his uncle toiled at his business "from early morning till ten o'clock at night" and delighted as well in the workings of his huge farm. Dodd later recalled that he had "often seen" his Uncle Samuel "following one of his own plows in the field."[33]

Young William, although less entranced by farming, spent far more time behind the plow than he did at the classroom desk. He summed up his earliest education with the comment that "there was so little time to be in school." During the 1880s William's father did manage a few months' tuition for William to study at Clayton's "moderately priced" academy. Among the boy's teachers were the school's superintendent, E. G. Beckworth, and the superintendent's young sister, Rena.[34] Dodd's senior by only three years, Rena soon married the recently widowed Ashley Horne. After her brother left to teach mathematics at Wake Forest College in the autumn of 1888, she may have been responsible for the school's employing the nineteen-year-old William Dodd and a Miss Ellington to run the school from January to June 1889. Late in life Dodd recalled with satisfaction that "we managed it successfully. . . . That was my first experience as a teacher."[35]

Dodd's experience as a schoolmaster represented a major turning point in his life. But for that experience he probably would have followed the agrarian path charted by his father and grandfather, bound inextricably to the North Carolina soil. However, during the first six months of 1889 he enjoyed his role as a respected schoolmaster responsible for the intellectual development of others. Bereft of the monetary wealth associated with the patrician Hornes, he had discovered another negotiable asset—his intellect. Although he had no clear concept of how to convert this asset into an enhanced status, he knew that he had to enrich his mind before he could achieve any level of success. Dodd immediately began a decade-long quest that eventually led him far from his Clayton home and into the halls of one of Germany's most prestigious universities.

In the summer of 1889 Dodd decided to pursue the goals that would take him from his Johnston County roots. From his father he had inherited a yeoman's sense of pride, a desire for economic independence, and an austere reverence for labor. His mother had given him optimism, in contrast to the fatalism that often plagued the southern common man. The Horne brothers served him as examples of success. Dodd admired their vitality and their power to influence the course of affairs, but he would not emulate their entrepreneurial activities or their oppression of yeomen.

Although Dodd's aspirations led him into a world in which people were judged according to their ancestry, their wealth, and their education, his affinity for the common folk and his identification with the inarticulate masses undergirded all he would accomplish as an adult. Born of undistinguished parents in impoverished circumstances, he could breech the formidable barriers of class only by means of his intellect. It was imperative that he cultivate his mind; he had to secure an impressive education, to attain degrees that commanded respect from those who monitored the avenues to success. Deterred chiefly by his lack of financial resources, Dodd initially resisted help offered by the Hornes, preferring to chart his own course unfettered by debts to his affluent kinsmen. Yet he willingly accepted his relatives' influence. As a courtesy to the politically powerful Ashley Horne, two state senators, the Johnston County sheriff, and the ambitious newspaper editor Josephus Daniels endorsed Dodd's West Point application. He stood for the competitive examination and tied with another candidate for the appointment but in the end had to settle for the empty honor of being designated an alternate.[36]

Although Dodd scored well on the test, his failure to gain the appointment highlighted his educational deficiencies. Thus warned, Dodd entered Winston-Salem's Oak Ridge Academy, a school noted for its college-preparatory curriculum. Paying for his tuition with money saved from his teaching in Clayton, he had worked out a method of financing his undergraduate education. Each summer he would teach in North Carolina's rural common schools, setting aside his earnings to pay for college tuition.[37]

Barely into his twenties and fresh from a year's preparation at the Oak Ridge Academy, he accepted an appointment in the tiny mountain community of Glenn Alpine. A budding intellectual, Dodd brought to the school unique attributes, readily appreciating that country youths preferred the plow to the teacher's podium and admired physical prowess far more than scholarly discourse. One of the local merchants who met Dodd shortly after he stepped from the train found the young pedagogue self-assured, enthusiastic, and physically impressive. The storekeeper warned him that his predecessors had been terrorized by a gang of seven youths who bragged that they would thrash the incoming teacher. In fact a thrashing occurred, but Dodd was the victor, laying into each of the boys with a hickory cane. He won their respect, even their friendship, and left for college with a ringing endorsement from the Glenn Alpine populace—an invitation to return the following summer. He did so, and he later taught in Clayton's common schools as well, sandwiching these appointments between his studies at the Virginia Polytechnic Institute in Blacksburg.[38]

Dodd enrolled at VPI in 1891, the year "John M. McBryde . . . had just been made President." Recently emancipated from the farm, he may have been drawn to Blacksburg by McBryde's reputation as a pioneering southern agronomist. First as a professor of agriculture at the University of Tennessee and then as chief administrator of the University of South Carolina, McBryde promoted a scientific curriculum over the liberal arts and expected to emphasize this same philosophy in Virginia.[39] Ironically, Dodd soon discovered that he did much better in English, history, and political science than he did in mathematics, chemistry, and mechanics. Although he was an honor student, Dodd's grades in the practical arts hurt his standing, limiting him to the distinction "proficient" and not allowing him to attain one of the school's higher designations, "distinguished" or "highly distinguished."[40]

Dodd's innocent eagerness and nonelite class status intrigued English Professor Edward E. Sheib, who had left the University of South Carolina in company with McBryde. Having earned his doctoral degree from Germany's Leipzig University, a far more prestigious degree than those of his Virginia colleagues, Sheib held in contempt the pretensions of the South's educated elites. Returning from Germany in 1885 to begin his career as the founding president of the Louisiana State Normal School in Natchitoches, he had soon rebelled against an education system disadvantageous to the poor. His campaign for the expansion of the public-school program and for the certification of teachers by professional pedagogues had met with resistance from the state's social elites, who had little interest in instructing those whose status was below their own. Wrapped in controversy, he left in 1888 to become dean of the University of South Carolina's normal school and three years later moved on to Virginia.[41] Sheib found Dodd a kindred spirit, and Dodd in turn relished the professor's classes, spellbound by Sheib's vivid descriptions of Shakespearean England and fascinated by his dictum that "history, like a faithful mirror, reflects all the phases of human character and all types of human relations."[42]

Dodd embraced college resolutely as a way to extricate himself from poverty and social impotence. He budgeted little time for extracurricular activities, and with a sobriety that reflected his religious upbringing he forswore the sophomoric, often drunken antics characteristic of less determined undergraduates.[43] Although he had been raised in a Baptist household and had been a lifelong communicant, Dodd was not inclined to religious fervor, but he had inherited the faith's reverence for labor, sternness, and intense patriotism. Thus, he limited his out-of-class activities to involvement with the school's chapter of the Young Men's Christian Association, eventually serving as president. He valued this fellowship more for its supportive philosophy than for its piety. "Experience has taught all close observers," Dodd wrote in the school's literary magazine, "that long sermons lose . . . their influence over our young active minds." He was happy that the association's twice-weekly meetings lasted only thirty minutes and concentrated on admonishing members to "draw closer to one another, to learn each other's troubles, and to [become] stronger by binding . . . together."[44]

Dodd's association with the YMCA awakened in him a class-based distaste for formal religion. Decades later he recalled that he had come "slowly to recognize the insincerity of people who call themselves Christians and I have been compelled out of honesty to cease attending church services, save on certain official occasions. If men were Christians there would be no war, also one of the terrible exploitations which our business men have applied to our people."[45]

Blessed with scant humor and little tolerance of juvenile follies, Dodd took his academic studies seriously. His stern bearing occasionally irritated his fellow students. Like many southern colleges in the nineteenth century, VPI imposed strict military discipline upon its young charges. Dodd did well in his military classes; he willingly joined in the daily drills and enjoyed marching to and from each meal. Commissioned a lieutenant of cadets, he carried out his duties with gravity, although his peers scarcely appreciated such solemnity. Charged with inspecting the dormitories, an assignment Dodd followed to the strictest rule, he was enraged when a disgruntled student doused him with a bucket of water. When the administration refused to punish the malcontent, Dodd felt slighted, recalling the inequities and favoritisms characteristic of southern society. He resigned his commission, serving the last few months of his college career as a private rather than hold an office devoid of respect.[46]

Dodd received his bachelor's degree in June 1895 and immediately returned to Clayton. Although he was employed once more to teach a sum-

mer's common school, he felt adrift. He had earned a measure of community adulation as that rare local boy to earn a college degree, and the
townsfolk gladly entrusted their children to him. Even the Hornes extended him a more open fellowship than when he had been merely the
unlettered son of their downwardly mobile niece. Samuel Horne remained
friendly and encouraging, Ashley Horne's wife brought him into her literary circle, and Hardee Horne's son Herman became one of his best
friends. Five years Dodd's junior and a recent graduate of the University
of North Carolina, Herman looked up to his distant cousin, shared his
interest in things intellectual, and in time copied Dodd's eventual academic success by becoming a nationally respected scholar in psychology.[47]
For the moment, however, none of this satisfied Dodd. After years of
study he was still in Clayton, important by his community's standards but
far from his goal of renown in the broader world.

Dodd's fortunes soon changed. Probably at the insistence of VPI's English professor, President McBryde asked Dodd to return to the school to
serve as an "assistant in history" and pursue a master's degree. For the
next two years, Sheib tutored Dodd in English literature and in German
and French. At the same time, Dodd taught "general history," a course
designed to supplement Sheib's English classes.[48]

In the summer and fall of 1896 Dodd first confronted a dilemma that
would plague him ever afterward. Although he was committed to the academic world, he harbored a passion for the political realm, thirsting to
wield influence in the domain of statesmen. Captivated by William Jennings Bryan's agrarian rhetoric, Dodd defied McBryde's opposition to the
"Great Commoner" and his presidential crusade. Dodd campaigned for
Bryan throughout the Blacksburg area; when Bryan lost, the North Carolina farmer's son blamed the nation's "industrial-financial" interests, adding them to his growing list of enemies of the masses.[49]

Sheib admired Dodd's spirit. He not only esteemed his student's intellectual potential but also saw in his open conflict with McBryde a courage
worthy of cultivation. The professor complimented Dodd, urging him to
look beyond his graduate work at VPI and consider attending Leipzig
University.[50] Dodd's career goals then came into focus; he longed for the
honor accorded the university professor, the opportunity to commune
with serious-minded students, and the privilege of being consulted by society's power brokers. The fact that these visions might not accord with
the normal realities of academic life perhaps escaped Dodd. When VPI

awarded him the master's degree in 1897, he was already thinking about Germany and about an undefined but luminous future.[51]

Whatever Dodd's dreams, he faced the simple reality that their cost surpassed his financial reserves. Forced by poverty into parsimonious habits, he had set aside a small but insufficient sum. For once aspiration overcame yeoman pride, and he petitioned Samuel Horne for assistance. The aging merchant enjoyed advancing moneys to ambitious young men and gladly granted Dodd an open-ended loan at reasonable interest. In time totaling over fifteen hundred dollars, a considerable amount in the late nineteenth century, it sped Dodd on his way to Leipzig.[52]

For Dodd the two and a half years in Germany were a matchless adventure. Not only did he experience the wonder of living in an exotic land that before had existed only in books and lectures but he was freed from the social constraints that had always bound his status in the American South. He was an aspiring intellectual, one of the many young men who had come to polish their education in an Old World seat of learning. He thus attained a measure of respect never accorded southern yeomen. Leipzig's townsfolk deferred to him as an aspiring man of future influence, professors honored him as a worthy disciple, and his fellow graduate students welcomed him into their circle as a searcher for truth and sufferer in the inevitable crises of advanced study.

Eager for the task before him, Dodd left for Europe with a determined sense of mission. He was sure that just as his degree from VPI had facilitated his rise in social status in Clayton, his training in Leipzig would ensure even greater rewards. With good fortune, it could thrust him into the rarefied world of the distinguished.

Although the university's classes would not commence until November, Sheib advised Dodd to depart for Germany in early June. Booking passage on a Dutch liner, he docked in Rotterdam, bought a sturdy bicycle, and peddled eastward. By July he had located suitable quarters and begun acclimating himself.[53] In spite of his Baptist aversion to alcohol, Dodd warmed to the conviviality of the beer table and developed a taste for pale Munich brew. In the gregarious company of German friends he shed some of the inhibitions that had narrowed his personal relationships. With their help he became fluent in German, though he always spoke it with a soft southern drawl.[54]

Dodd thrived in the European university. The embryonic intellectual relished his impressive professors' classes, pored happily over original documents, and delighted in stimulating conversations with fellow graduate students both German and American. He matriculated under the direction of Erich Marcks and Karl Lamprecht, who tutored him in the "scientific method" of historical investigation.[55] Reacting to the romantic historians' propensity toward an uncritical chauvinism, the scientific scholars preached an unrelenting faithfulness to documented fact and a careful construction and unbiased interpretation of past events. In consequence they published massive, spiritless tomes focusing primarily on political events, constitutional developments, and military campaigns.

Although Dodd's professors trained him as a disciplined observer, their style scarcely prepared him for the innovative historical methods developing in the United States at the time. While he was studying at Leipzig, such American scholars as James Harvey Robinson, Frederick Jackson Turner, and Charles A. Beard were producing their first tentative contributions to the "New History," presentation of the past strongly emphasizing theme or thesis. Advocates of the New History searched for deterministic forces—economic, environmental, or class-conflict—which they believed explained society's evolution.[56] In time Dodd would embrace their method. Even though his graduate training little prepared him for the emerging methodology, his personal experiences in Germany reenforced the convictions of his youth and laid the foundation for his future interpretations of the American South.

Alone among his German professors, Lamprecht moved Dodd toward his future themes. A full professor at the early age of thirty-six, Lamprecht broke with Germany's historical establishment and challenged the idea of history as largely a chronicle of past politics. He stressed instead the importance of cultural history, *Kulturgeschichte.* He first investigated the social conditions of Rhineland peasants, later turning to economic and social forces, relegating wars and politics to elements—rarely the most important ones—in a people's development. Dodd noted proudly that with Lamprecht the "common man" became "a guiding force in society, the very corner-stone of the building." In Dodd's mind, *Kulturgeschichte* was a "practical, if unspoken, declaration that the aristocratic portion of the country should occupy only a part of the pages of history."[57]

A class-conscious Dodd viewed the German social structure through the jaundiced eyes of a southern yeoman, finding in the Prussian Junkers uncanny parallels to southern aristocrats. Both oppressed the poor, both shared a martial spirit, both focused on narrow economic interests. Dodd's experience outside the classroom reenforced these views. Often strapped for money, he frequently slipped away from the university to milk cows for German farmers, which allowed him to gain some understanding of the German yeoman.[58] Looking back on this experience during World War I, he assured a correspondent: "I am one who believes the plain German peasant peoples do not share the enthusiasm of [their] overlords for militarism. Some experiences I had as a student among the poorer folk cause me to think that, with a fair chance, they would break away from the unnatural leadership of the present."[59]

During his Leipzig sojourn Dodd witnessed an incident that underscored his negative impression of patricians in general and of the German upper classes in particular. He watched with intense interest an American-born theology professor's unsuccessful campaign for election to the Reichstag. Word of the professor's defeat reached Dodd's seminar class, and to his dismay the students cheered because "a real German and an aristocrat" had been elected. Dodd wrote later that although he never met the professor, his "reputation and defeat in Leipzig left an indelible impression on my mind."[60]

Troubled by aristocratic ascendancy at home and abroad, as a historian Dodd longed for a people's hero. Virginia's Thomas Jefferson met his criteria, becoming the subject of his earliest research and remaining a lifelong preoccupation. Dodd believed that the Sage of Monticello possessed a "boundless faith in the masses," and he made Jefferson the foundation of his initial articles and lectures, as well as the standard by which he judged other political figures both historical and contemporary. Had Jefferson been a contemporary, Dodd later told a Chicago audience, he "would have been a populist in 1892 or an insurgent in 1910."[61] When Erich Marcks approved Dodd's dissertation topic, an investigation into Jefferson's challenge to Alexander Hamilton and John Adams in 1796, the young scholar commenced his first serious effort to write history.[62]

Dodd tore enthusiastically into the project. In late summer 1898 he traveled to London, where for six weeks he explored the archives of the British Museum, searching for materials on Jefferson, Hamilton, and Adams. On weekends he roamed the English countryside, fascinated by a land he had once viewed only through the vivid descriptions of his favorite professor at VPI. Once he stood spiritually awed by Stratford-upon-Avon, "trying to understand the miracle of William Shakespeare about which Dr. Sheib had lectured so frequently." He left the bard's home and hiked across the landscape, immersed in the "wondrous reminders of medieval England." Exhausted, Dodd boarded his London-bound train satisfied that he had spent one of the "most delightful and stimulating week-ends" of his life. By the end of October, judging that he had enough material for his dissertation, he reluctantly departed for Leipzig, concluding the happiest days of his European adventure. He left England with "a sense of English life and tradition which made me long to see more of the country of Alfred the Great and Queen Elizabeth."[63]

Dodd soon had an opportunity to contrast English and German cultural dynamics. Shortly after returning to Leipzig, he realized that he needed additional information from the American State Papers, a complete set of which existed in Berlin. He bicycled to the great capital intent upon serious research but quickly gave in to the temptations of the city's grand museums and public monuments. Everywhere he was struck by an oppressive martial spirit. At the gold depository of Spandau his guide told tourists that it contained two hundred fifty million dollars in bullion, reparations from the Franco-Prussian War held in reserve to finance the next conflict with France. Days later, upon leaving the magnificent German War Museum, he witnessed a ceremonial greeting of Kaiser Wilhelm II by his army officers. "Swords rattled and heils echoed in true Prussian style. The impression left on my mind was not favorable. There was too much war spirit everywhere."[64]

Although Dodd had enjoyed cadet training at VPI, German bellicosity weighed heavily upon him. One memorable evening Professor Marcks held informal court at a Leipzig beer table, theorizing with Dodd and his other students about an invasion of France through Belgium and speculating whether it would result in war with England. On another occasion Dodd watched as several English students walked out during a psychology lecture after hearing the professor's Anglophobic invectives. Even Lamprecht proved himself a "Grossedeutser," intent upon assessing which peoples deserved accolades as true Germans and which were lesser beings, worthy only of subjugation.[65]

Caught up in all this, Dodd spent the winter of 1898 and the spring of 1899 writing his dissertation, "Jefferson's Return to Politics in 1796," and preparing for the dreaded oral examinations. During these months he developed a close and enduring friendship with Eliot H. Goodwin, a fellow doctoral candidate and the nephew of Charles W. Eliot, Harvard's innovative president. They encouraged and comforted each other, developing practice questions for the examination and sharing the stresses imposed by their devotion to graduate training.[66] Tension became all the more acute when a mutual German friend committed suicide following his failure to pass the examinations.[67]

Throughout these difficulties the dissertation gradually took shape. Required to write in acceptable German, Dodd limited the effort to eighty-three tightly composed pages. Marcks scrutinized the manuscript, making the requisite critiques of a conscientious professor and questioning Dodd's evident bias against Alexander Hamilton. By the end of July Marcks deemed the dissertation advanced enough to waive the requirement that it be completed before the oral examination.[68]

At the appointed hour in late August Dodd descended into the seminar room somewhat affectionately known as "die Hölle" (Hell). For three hours Marcks, Lamprecht, and others grilled him about modern European history, German politics, and historical philosophy. At its conclusion, Marcks scribbled "cum laude" in the record book and a dazed but elated Dodd stumbled out of the room, welcomed by his friend Goodwin, who would be examined the following afternoon.[69]

That evening the two comrades escaped to a local theater seeking relief from their shared tensions. To Dodd's consternation, one of his recent inquisitors met them in the hallway. The austere professor had metamorphosed, however, and was now most encouraging. He assured Dodd that he would "soon find a college position in America [because] everything [was] expanding over there." Dodd felt less hopeful. In contrast to Goodwin, who hailed from an established New England family with powerful connections in university circles, Dodd had few influential friends and no relatives with academic standing; he even worried that southern college administrators might not respect his German diploma. "Being here," he lamented to a North Carolina intimate, "I can not know" of employment opportunities, "and being totally unknown in my state, no position would be offered me unless some friend first made the suggestion."[70]

Dodd plodded through a postexamination depression, making suggested changes in his dissertation, feeling happiest whenever Marcks complimented him on a passage that was especially well written. By October 1899 he had satisfied all his requirements, but he had missed the deadline for graduation: his degree would not be awarded until the spring of 1900.[71]

Dodd packed his small library, sold his dependable bicycle, and "bade farewell to friends and the ancient city where I had learned what real study and research" were like. He dallied a week in Paris and then made for the port of Antwerp and home. That November the Atlantic Ocean was unusually calm, and Dodd enjoyed a time of relaxed contemplation before he reached home.[72]

Dodd had to secure a teaching post as entry into his chosen profession. He was counting on Edward Sheib, his VPI mentor, to guide him to an appropriate placement; he did not know that his teacher and friend had been at least temporarily forced out of academia.[73] Dodd also planned to make his mark among the leading lights of America's history community, to bask in the acceptance of men who might respect his Leipzig degree but honored solid research and impressive publications more.

Dodd recognized with accustomed honesty that his dissertation had been little more than an academic exercise. Perhaps at some future point he might become an important student of Jefferson, but the Virginia statesman was too imposing a figure, too vast a subject, for a beginning intellectual. The first endeavor should be more modest, more attainable, and Dodd had in mind the ideal project: a biography of Nathaniel Macon. In examining Jefferson's clash with his fellow titans Hamilton and Adams, Dodd had noted the importance of Macon, a rising star from North Carolina. Like Jefferson a southern aristocrat, Macon mixed a democratic faith with common-folk values. Now that he was on American soil again, Dodd felt ready to explore Macon's life and to present his findings to critical audiences.[74]

Dodd had attained a level of education rarely reached by those of his class, but in the process he had become a man divided. He retained his strong affinity for the South's common folk even as his ambitions moved him into the society of those he identified as their oppressors. His education had cost him more than tuition and hard work; it had taken him from his roots and stirred personal tensions that would haunt him during his entire career.

A family incident immediately drew Dodd back into the cruel social realities of his North Carolina origins. While he was studying in Europe, Samuel and Ashley Horne pressured his father into selling the farm he had cultivated for over three decades; they wanted it for a cotton mill. Although Dodd's father subsequently purchased a farm near Wake Forest, his family suffered. He found himself overwhelmed by new debts, and his wife sank into an intense depression, lonely for friends and family left behind in Clayton. The whole affair showed afresh how the financial exactments of the state's economic elite transcended family loyalty, constantly threatening the fragile contentment of North Carolina's small farmers.[75]

Despondent over these family problems and despairing of employment, Dodd sought counsel from his old mentor at VPI. But the years had not been kind to Sheib. Involved in a conflict with the school's board, he had submitted his resignation, confident that he could secure another appointment. But no position opened up, and he suffered the humiliation of returning home to Norfolk to clerk in his father's hardware store. "I do sigh for my books and the surroundings of the class room," he confessed to Dodd. "I made a mistake in leaving that atmosphere."[76]

Sheib hoped that Dodd could learn from his error. Knowing that his former student had "breathed the liberal air of Continental Universities," Sheib predicted that he had "a difficult road" before him. In America, the older man warned, "there is an immense amount of sham in the so called educational field," but "you are young, and within the next ten or fifteen years you will find things . . . more in harmony with the ideas you would like to proclaim to-day." He urged Dodd to secure a post, even if it was imperfect, because "it will probably be the stepping stone to something better." He advised Dodd to set aside his "better convictions" until he had become an established scholar. "You may well laugh at me," Sheib concluded, "but I can see, how, had I used a little more policy, I might have accomplished more."[77]

Sheib's melancholy letter forecast Dodd's immediate future. He stood at the threshold of a notable pilgrimage, but one marked by controversy and struggle. Following a brief but harrowing search, Dodd accepted his only firm offer of employment, a chair at Randolph-Macon College in Ashland, Virginia. There he forgot Sheib's counsel to set aside his "better convictions" and in consequence passed through a time of trial that robbed him of his youthful innocence and hardened his views toward those he identified as class oppressors. For the next eight years Dodd held firm to his faith, boldly confronting his critics, and he emerged from his initial academic appointment as one of the nation's more respected historians.

CHAPTER TWO

A Plebeian Scholar
in the Old Dominion

In September 1900 William Edward Dodd assumed his academic appointment at Virginia's Randolph-Macon College. His irrepressible ambition and firm conviction that historical truth must be boldly proclaimed ensured that controversy as well as recognition would mark his early career. Even though he was teaching at an elite southern college, Dodd unreservedly articulated his plebeian values. His distrust of the southern ruling classes led him to challenge their comfortable dominance with ideas that were unacceptable to them.

At Randolph-Macon Dodd defied the mind-set cultivated by an entrenched aristocracy. "As a Southerner teaching young Southern men," he declared, "I endeavored to quiet and still that attitude in the heart of old Virginia." Looking back upon the consternation caused by his views, he reflected wistfully that he "rather enjoyed the distress of certain classes of people, especially those who maintained that all Southerners of 'any account' are descended from noble followers of Charles I."[1]

Virginia's first families came to regard Dodd as a threat to their social order. These patricians marched in the vanguard of a regional movement dedicated to the creation of a historical paradigm that justified slavery, sanctified the southern cause in 1861, cleansed the upper classes of the onus of war guilt, and legitimized the patricians' postwar dominance. Determined to inoculate young minds against ideas detrimental to their elite rule, they established the Confederate patriotic societies to create and guard "historical truth." The United Confederate Veterans, the Sons of the Confederate Veterans, and the United Daughters of the Confederacy denounced the sectionalism of northern historians, established lists of approved and condemned books, and fostered literature more congenial to their perception of history. Once established as the arbiters of southern thought, they silenced dissident teachers and indoctrinated children with patrician values unchanged since the antebellum era. Feeling their wrath firsthand, Dodd reported to the American Historical Association (AHA) convention in 1903 that a "man who [takes] a perfectly dispassionate attitude" toward the South's past is "apt to be met not only with disapproval, but with things even more disagreeable."[2]

Dodd knew of course that history stirred passion and that its interpretation profoundly influenced contemporary values. He naively thought that his writings would expose the corruption of the South's oligarchy, leading to a democratic outcry from the masses. He shared this task with a small circle of like-minded scholars, among them his friend and fellow historian John Spencer Bassett, of Trinity College, now Duke University. "Let us write history," Bassett admonished Dodd in 1902, "and . . . stir up the fellows—both of which you are already doing well."[3]

Dodd and Bassett involved themselves in a dangerous game played within the context of a South then deep in the process of restructuring the Civil War. More than sectional honor was at stake; having just defeated the Populist Party's challenge to Redeemer rule, the South's elites brooked no threat to their suzerainty. They understood the importance of history as an intellectual bulwark of the *ancien régime,* and they dealt swiftly and harshly with any scholar who threatened their status.

Dodd's conflict with the Confederate societies reflects his broader struggle to maintain professional integrity and personal idealism in a culture that demanded social orthodoxy. From his simple quest for employment in 1900 to his elevation to a prestigious University of Chicago chair in 1908, he strove for acceptance in a southern society that valued birth, status, and conformity above ability and achievement.

Upon his return from Germany in November 1899 Dodd had commenced the daunting task of securing an appointment commensurate with his Leipzig degree. Since he had neither family stature nor important patrons, his queries were answered by polite refusals at best. The lukewarm responses of North Carolina schools disappointed him intensely. "The colleges of the state would not have me," he later grumbled, pointing especially to the University of North Carolina, which "maintained the policy of not getting a man from the wrong pew." He concluded sadly that the ordinary southern people had "so many would-be aristocrats among them they never get to show their greatest qualities."[4]

Hope turned into frustration and then to desperation. Only the University of Tennessee offered Dodd a position, an appointment with the inadequate salary of six hundred dollars annually, and even that offer was soon rescinded due to budget reductions.[5] By the spring of 1900 Dodd feared that his career would abort even before it came into being.

In despair, Dodd turned to historical research, hoping both to forget his employment troubles and to enhance his scholarly reputation. His project, a biography of Nathaniel Macon, grew out of his dissertation research and provided him his first opportunity to employ history as social commentary. Because Dodd saw Macon as a southern aristocrat sympathetic to the values of the common folk, he envisioned the biography as a parable that would summon his state back to its democratic past.

Throughout the spring and early summer of 1900 Dodd corresponded with various scholars in his search for leads to Macon manuscripts, explored the North Carolina state library for newspaper files, legislative journals, and other documents, and then journeyed across the state hoping to obtain letters still held by prominent families. Then in July he scraped together enough money for a hurried trip to the Library of Congress in Washington D.C.[6]

In the nation's capital Dodd's fortunes changed when a chance encounter netted Dodd the patron so necessary to secure employment in the South. James Hammond, a Southern Methodist minister and amateur historian, met Dodd at the library and was impressed by the scholar's interest in Macon and by his obvious enthusiasm for his discipline. An alumnus of Randolph-Macon College (named in part for Dodd's subject), he directed a discreet inquiry to its president asking whether the school might employ the exuberant young historian.[7] Unaware of Hammond's letter and the positive response it would eventually produce, Dodd anguished through more fruitless weeks of search for a job.

Dodd meanwhile sought work in fields only tangential to that for which he had trained. In Washington he wrote Herbert Baxter Adams, the august graduate professor of history at The Johns Hopkins University. Rather than seeking a posting to this impressive American institution, Dodd expressed interest in the "Boys Country School near Baltimore." Having learned that it needed a teacher of modern languages and knowing of Adams's connection with the school, Dodd asked for his aid in securing the position. He told Baxter of his degree from Leipzig but chose not to reveal that his emphasis had been in history, stressing instead his fluency in German and French.[8] There is no evidence that Adams responded to this petition. At the end of July Dodd returned to North Carolina convinced that he had little prospect for future employment.

Dodd's family concerns added to his woes. Living with his parents in Wake Forest, he lamented his own lack of achievement, worried over his fifteen-hundred-dollar debt to Samuel Horne, and raged that his parents had been forced out of Clayton by Ashley and Samuel Hornes's entrepreneurial ambitions. He also grieved about his mother's weakened constitution. "Mother was not in good health. . . . She was only 51 years old, but . . . bore the signs of a hard life."[9]

In spite of all this, the spring and summer of 1900 had happier moments. During that time Dodd began what became two lifelong associations. During his trips to Raleigh he frequented the newspaper office of Josephus Daniels, an ambitious liberal politician whose opinions national Democratic Party officials sought. Although the two had been acquaintances since 1888, their friendship ripened after Dodd returned to North Carolina. Ever the pragmatic politico, Daniels also possessed a lively intellect and thoroughly enjoyed listening to Dodd's excited musings about Nathaniel Macon. As the summer progressed, Daniels encouraged Dodd to complete his projected biography, offered help in its publication, and promised to assist Dodd in his quest for a North Carolina professorship. Both men agreed that just as elites had subverted the Democratic Party following Macon's death, in contemporary North Carolina the upper classes remained in control. Macon deserved a biography, Daniels wrote that fall, because his name "stands for liberty, equality, and democracy." It would be a "valuable book, not only historically, but politically."[10]

That same summer Martha Johns captured much of Dodd's attention; she shared both his interest in things intellectual and his desire for a life's companion. Six years his junior and a recent graduate of Salem Female College, she was the daughter of Thomas Johns, "a distinguished country gentleman of the old South type." The family owned a thousand acres of poor-quality cotton land just five miles north of Clayton, a bequest of "John Bunyan Johns a great slave holder of the prewar days." A gentleman of local substance, Thomas Johns served as a Wake County commissioner, took seriously his duties as a trustee of a private academy in nearby Auburn, and cherished his family's long association with the Mount Moriah Baptist Church. True to his status as a southern patriarch, he eyed his daughter's suitor carefully and judged that his earned doctorate and scholarly potential compensated for his family's low status.[11]

Having met in the spring of 1896, William and "Mattie" nurtured their friendship by writing letters throughout his Leipzig sojourn. She became Dodd's most frequent correspondent, entertaining him with news from his home community and encouraging his quest for a German degree. In turn, Dodd catered to her interest in classical music by sending her postcards portraying noted German composers, and appealed to her own taste for adventure by describing in detail his excursions on the Continent. Much to his delight, Mattie remained single, and on his return their mutual affection ripened into a deeper commitment.[12]

Dodd reveled in Sunday visits with his beloved Mattie. In company with her family they strolled to the large grove surrounding the Mount Moriah Church and with friends exchanged preworship greetings and gossip "after the manner of 17th Century Virginia." Neither he nor Mattie appreciated the sermons, finding in Baptist homilies "a want of content"; they preferred the leisurely afternoons "under the ample shade of the great spreading oaks," discussing the possibility of marriage. Mattie demurred, however, vowing her deep affection for William but postponing a final commitment until he found stable employment.[13]

His felicity initially blighted, Dodd rejoiced when in early August his attractiveness dramatically improved. Intrigued by James Hammond's recommendation, Randolph-Macon's president offered Dodd the school's newly created position of instructor in history and economics. Dodd responded immediately, dashed to Ashland for an interview, and by the middle of the month had began preparing for classes, which were to commence in five weeks. Although the appointment paid a modest seven hundred dollars for the entire year, it thrust him into academia.[14] Faithful to the admonition of Professor Sheib to secure a position however imperfect, Dodd recognized this as a "stepping stone" to something better; it would also prove an important crucible. For the next eight years Dodd polished his skills as a teacher, confronted powerful forces dedicated to the restriction of southern academic freedom, and established his reputation as a scholar worthy of national respect.

Dodd arrived in Ashland proud to be Randolph-Macon's first professor of history, his discipline having only recently emerged as a subject deemed worthy of special consideration. Since 1890 the college's board had debated adding history to its curriculum; a gift of thirty thousand dollars from the estate of Isaac Newton Vaughan allowed them to endow the position that Dodd filled.[15]

Although he was a professed Baptist, Dodd had few qualms about teaching in a school faithful to its Methodist heritage. Chartered in 1830 by the Virginia legislature, it had commenced classes in 1832, making it one of the state's older institutions of higher learning. Three years after the Civil War the school had settled permanently in Ashland, and by 1900 it had expanded into a small system of campuses. The Ashland school was reserved for men only, women matriculated at Randolph-Macon College in Lynchburg, and both divisions received graduates from allied academies in Bedford City, Port Royal, and Danville. The men's college enrolled 130 students, who were taught by eight professors, four of whom possessed doctorates.[16]

Grateful for employment at Randolph-Macon, Dodd was more fortunate still in its location. Situated in a resort area twenty-five miles north of Virginia's capital, Ashland sat astride the principal railroad leading to Washington. The college's stately buildings formed three corners of a quadrangle whose open west end fronted the railway, and scant yards to the south stood the town's small, picturesque depot. From there Dodd regularly traveled by train to Richmond, where his prestige as a Randolph-Macon professor earned him respect within the city's intellectual community. He admitted, however, that "I was counted slightly un-Southern in my treatment of American history."[17] Dodd just as often traveled to Washington to do research at the Library of Congress or dine with influential political and intellectual figures. From there he ventured outward to appointments in the northern states. In turn, prominent historians and other intellectuals often interrupted their sojourns southward at Ashland to enjoy his fellowship. But such experiences lay in the future. In the fall of 1900 Dodd arrived in Ashland facing the immediate tasks of establishing his reputation as a Randolph-Macon teacher and laying the foundations for a successful scholarly career.

Robert Blackwell, the college's senior faculty member and professor of English, welcomed Dodd into the school's fellowship. Also possessing a Leipzig doctorate, Blackwell quickly began a lasting friendship with Dodd and guided him through the inevitable problems associated with a first appointment. Privileged to draft his own curriculum, Dodd created a three-year course of study opening with lectures on ancient history and covering up to the death of Charlemagne in the first year, moving to a study of European history from A.D. 812 to the close of the French Revolution in the second year, and concluding with a survey of English and American history in the third year. Deficient in his understanding of Greek and Roman history, Dodd spent twelve to fourteen hours each day in class preparations and took pride in meeting with his students "exactly at the appointed hour every morning."

This demanding schedule distracted Dodd from his biography of Macon, and other college responsibilities made further demands upon his time. At best lukewarm in his own faith, Dodd nonetheless felt guilty when he declined invitations to teach Sunday school for the local Methodist and Baptist congregations. "I could not very well say the plain truth that I worked on my *Macon* every Sunday."

Dodd felt ill-suited for the "solemn Chapel services in the leading Methodist institution in the Old South." Taking his first turn in the rotation of professors who oversaw chapel, he floundered, having no concept of how to organize a devotional, select hymns, choose scriptures, lead prayers, or deliver a homily. His colleagues looked on with bemusement as the students barely suppressed their laughter. Taking pity on Dodd, the older professors made allowances for his "mudsill Baptist" breeding and then more fully instructed him about the appropriate formalities.

In subsequent chapels Dodd muddled through the rituals with but little conviction, and he retained a lifelong suspicion of religion as an antiintellectual force. "I was reared in the South," he wrote two decades after leaving Ashland, "and personally observed, while at Randolph-Macon, the effects of revivals designed to excite the emotions of young people."[18] However much such things improved student morals, Dodd reasoned, they detracted from a proper focus on education.

Dodd entered the classroom determined to create a positive learning environment. As a result of his recent exposure to European universities and his earlier disciplinary experiences in North Carolina's common schools, he resolved to maintain rigid control over his charges. Dodd's years at VPI had taught him the sad truth that southern students did not always share his conviction, and he soon confronted a class of twenty young men determined to take the measure of the new instructor. One in particular ridiculed Dodd's lectures, cracked jokes in class, and gave impudent responses to his questions. Having tolerated such behavior for two periods, on the day of the third assembly Dodd marched to the room's door and ushered the malefactor out. Unknown to Dodd, a student's removal from class also meant his dismissal from the college; to complicate matters, this individual was the son of a prominent trustee. Confronted with a minor crisis, the administration offered the student a face-saving opportunity to apologize and be reinstated, but the willful youth refused to muffle his pride, preferring instead to sit out the remainder of the semester. The incident briefly shook Dodd's confidence, but his fellow professors applauded his actions, and he gained the respect of the remaining students. "Never again in my eight years at Randolph-Macon did I have any disorder in class," Dodd remembered late in his career. Indeed, Dodd's obvious love for history and his intense concern for his students soon made him the school's most popular teacher.[19]

Having established his reputation at Randolph-Macon, Dodd craved recognition from the larger community of historians. At the end of the first semester he returned briefly to North Carolina to visit his family and his beloved Mattie, and then on 26 December he left for the AHA convention in Detroit. A minim among the mighty, Dodd met for the first time Albert Bushnell Hart, J. Franklin Jameson, and Andrew C. McLaughlin, men who would soon play major roles in his career. Dodd loved the convention's ambience and relished the camaraderie of his fellow historians, and he listened intently to the presentation of scholarly papers. When the convention ended, the careful Dodd returned to Virginia; calculating the trip's heavy expense, he judged it a worthy investment.[20]

Apparently Dodd hinted to his new acquaintances that he too was engaged in a valuable study, a biography of the important North Carolina Democrat Nathaniel Macon. Shortly after he settled back in Ashland, Trinity College's John Spencer Bassett arrived in the community, wanting to meet Dodd. During this genesis of a long personal and professional friendship Bassett told Dodd of his intent to edit a new periodical, the *South Atlantic Quarterly;* he was seeking forward-looking southern liberals like Dodd as potential contributors. More to the point, Bassett, who was a member of the program committee for the next AHA convention, asked Dodd to present a paper on Macon. "I could hardly decline," Dodd remembered, "even though it added to my heavy load."[21]

Emboldened by this small recognition and believing himself qualified for a more distinguished appointment than the one he had at Randolph-Macon, Dodd devoted his spring semester to correspondence with other schools. Although he sent inquiries to several colleges in Kansas and Virginia, he focused his principal attention on the open chair of economics and history at the University of North Carolina. A Randolph-Macon colleague sent President F. P. Venable a letter extolling Dodd; more importantly, Josephus Daniels met with the university's chief executive, adding his considerable influence to Dodd's cause. In spite of a correspondence that consumed six months, Venable was little impressed with Dodd's merits and recommended instead Charles Lee Raper, a graduate of Columbia University and, like Dodd, a native North Carolinian. "Mr. Raper is a man of capacity & stuff," Daniels assured Dodd, "not unlike you in antecedents and feelings."[22] Such condolences did little to assuage Dodd's disappointment.

More troubling, however, were Dodd's emotions as Randolph-Macon's board assembled for its spring meeting. Reflecting on his run-in with the trustee's son, his reputation as a liberal on a conservative campus, and his known desire to seek other employment, he feared that his reappointment was in jeopardy. But Dodd had developed a rapport with key trustees, among them Benjamin Franklin Lipscomb, a prominent Methodist minister, and John P. Branch, a millionaire contributor. Lipscomb proposed Dodd's permanent appointment even though he noted with amusement that he had caught Dodd reading a recently published biography of Thomas Paine, the American Revolutionary War radical and notorious atheist. The board concurred, increasing Dodd's annual salary to one thousand dollars.[23]

Secure in his position at Randolph-Macon, Dodd turned his attention to other goals. To be sure, his income remained inadequate to reduce his debt to Samuel Horne, but it did encourage Dodd to pursue with more vigor his marriage proposal to Martha Johns and to defeat her parent's objections. They committed to a December wedding.[24]

Dodd began the fall semester of 1901 with renewed enthusiasm. Having assessed their professor, his second-year students accorded him the respect he desperately craved, and several shared his passion for history, or at least for things intellectual. Dodd found that "young Methodist preachers wanted to learn . . . medieval church history as given by a German doctor," and he would eventually take pleasure in the memory of several who followed his path, receiving their doctoral degrees from Johns Hopkins, Leipzig, and other noted universities. But that autumn more immediate objectives warmed the professor's heart. He looked forward to his forthcoming marriage, regretting daily the distance separating him from Mattie. Fortunately his teaching obligations and his preparations for the AHA's Washington meeting diverted his mind, filling the lonely days until the eventful Christmas season.[25]

Having recorded the last of his grades, Dodd excitedly left for Auburn, North Carolina, where on the morning of 24 December he stood in Thomas Johns's commodious parlor. Dodd's entourage included only Randolph-Macon Latin professor Edwin P. Bowers as best man and one of his brothers as a family representative. Twenty or so others joined with the bride's relatives to witness the couple's union. That afternoon the newlyweds boarded a train bound for Washington, where they settled into a tasteful but not expensive hotel to await the convention scheduled for 28 December.[26]

Although few of the assembled scholars knew Dodd, the sight of an obviously affectionate couple among the staid historians attracted notice, and a brief rain shower confirmed what many already suspected. When Dodd gallantly lifted his umbrella to protect his young spouse, rice covered his bride, producing good-natured laughter from his dignified colleagues. Thereafter William and Mattie were the object of sly glances and whispered comments, all of which assured that when Dodd ascended the speaker's rostrum he would be accorded attention rarely given a beginning scholar.[27]

Bassett advised Dodd to keep his initial paper short, an admonition he followed by preparing a competent, unpretentious fifteen-minute presentation. Seated on the stage anxiously waiting his turn, Dodd surveyed his audience. Albert Bushnell Hart positioned himself before the podium, notebook in hand; J. Franklin Jameson and Andrew C. McLaughlin stared at Dodd, assessing his character; and John Spencer Bassett sat among them as Dodd's one sure friend in the profession. Mattie diffidently took a chair, confident that her husband would prove his mettle.[28]

"Many who are well acquainted with Southern history are almost entirely unfamiliar with the historical character of Nathaniel Macon," Dodd informed his audience. He then enlightened them, outlining the political career of Thomas Jefferson's North Carolina protégé, noting his patrician origins, and extolling his democratic virtues. Encapsulated in his short address were ideas Dodd would reiterate throughout his career. Macon entered the North Carolina legislature in 1781, he explained, and immediately allied himself with the radical party opposed to "the prominent leaders of the old regime," wealthy conservatives critical of democracy.

Elected Speaker of the United States House of Representatives in 1801, Macon supported Jeffersonian reforms, opposed John Marshall's autocratic Supreme Court, and authored the famous Macon's Bill No. 2, designed to avert war. In every respect but one Macon functioned as a democratic saint. Unfortunately, Dodd noted, he remained true to his southern origins, espousing the cause of slavery, and thus gave to a future generation "a weapon with which to fight the free states."[29]

Dodd's speech was well received. Bassett offered his heartiest congratulations, McLaughlin, recently made editor of the *American Historical Review,* solicited an expanded paper for publication, and Mattie dutifully assured him that the audience had listened respectfully.[30] That evening the contented couple headed southward to their little cottage adjacent to the Randolph-Macon campus. Both assumed that they would establish a quiet, comfortable home, living as a respected scholar and his supportive wife. They were mistaken: controversy soon enveloped Dodd, adding unwanted stress to his Randolph-Macon years.

In their anticipation of a tranquil professorial life in a small college town the newlyweds failed to take into account William Dodd's irresistible propensity to march boldly into discord. Even as he labored to expand his Macon paper into an acceptable article and to polish an even larger manuscript into a publishable biography, he launched an attack upon southern elites that would make him an anathema among prominent elements of Virginia society even as it marked him as a daring scholar worthy of note in the history profession.[31] Dodd publicly challenged the powerful Confederate patriotic organizations, condemned their prescribed interpretation of the Civil War epoch, and exposed their crusade to censor scholars. In turn, the societies, especially the United Confederate Veterans, branded him an unpatriotic Southerner and demanded his dismissal from Randolph-Macon College.

Having established their home just north of the capital of the Confederacy, the Dodds lived among the leaders of a southern movement dedicated to rewriting history in order to justify a stratified society. With the creation of the United Confederate Veterans and their collateral associations, the Sons of Confederate Veterans and the United Daughters of the Confederacy, southern patricians devised an effective network through which they supervised the intellectual development of future generations. Prominent in the Richmond area movement were the real-estate developer

John Cussons, the physician Hunter Holmes McGuire, and the attorney George L. Christian. McGuire and Christian had impressive links to Virginia's first families, and Cussons, an English immigrant who had worked as a journalist before the Civil War and risen to the rank of colonel in the Confederate army, had invested his considerable wealth after the war in the creation of the resort community Glen Allen, a village situated on the rail link between Richmond and Ashland.[32]

Cussons, Holmes, and Christian cooperated in writing scathing critiques of northern histories and dominating the history committee of Virginia's Grand Camp of Confederate Veterans. In 1898 they succeeded in a reorganization of the state school board, whereupon they presented to the board a list of condemned books and had the satisfaction of seeing those works banished from the classroom. Holmes died shortly after this victory, and Cussons became immersed in legal problems that consumed his final years, but Christian remained zealous as an arbiter of historical truth. Until his death in 1924 he continued as an active member of the history committee of the Virginia United Confederate Veterans and served as a prominent trustee of the Virginia State Historical Society. "I fear," Christian wrote in 1898, "that some of our children, misled by the false teachings of certain histories . . . may have some misgivings" concerning the South's righteousness in 1861.[33]

Dodd declared himself an enemy of such formidable opponents in an article in the 7 August 1902 issue of *Nation* magazine. As a southern plebeian, he bridled at the upper class's cavalier manipulation of the past, and as a professional historian he took umbrage at their restrictions on the free investigation of truth. Aware of pressure focused on the Virginia State Board of Education to implement further restrictions on textbook adoptions, Dodd bristled especially at the crusade of Virginia's Grand Camp of Confederate Veterans crusade to banish John Fiske's American-history textbook from the classrooms. In May 1902 the board approved these censorship policies, which went into effect on 1 August. Brooding over these events for several months, Dodd finally attacked the state officials and the Confederate societies' obvious bias against Fiske. They simply asked "'Who is the author?'" he charged. "This being answered, 'A Yankee,' the matter was settled and the public made no protest."[34]

A more personal affront inspired his initial contribution to the *Nation*. Dodd had offered his Macon biography to Richmond's B. F. Johnson Publishing Company, a firm noted for its close association with the Confederate societies, and the company rejected it out of hand. Dodd seethed at the fact that a "representative of the largest publishing house in the South [had] recently refused so much as to read the manuscript of a piece of investigation in Southern history, though posing all the while as the champion" of it, and he denounced those southern publishers who felt "the pulse of the Confederate veteran" before accepting a book for publication.[35]

Whatever Dodd's ancillary motives for the *Nation* essay, he clearly saw the question of free speech as bound inextricably to the South's pervasive class struggle. "The ruling classes of society are usually responsible for the kind of training the young receive," Dodd explained, and in the modern South "public sentiment has been and is still controlled by men who were either participants in the great Civil War or whose fathers were." These veterans and their sons demanded that all history teachers pledge themselves to two oaths: "(1) that the South was altogether right in seceding from the Union in 1861; and (2) that the war was not waged about the negro." No investigation, he proclaimed, "no honest unbiased work can ever be hoped for when such a faith is made a sine qua non of fitness for teaching or writing history." Confederate veterans, he charged, gathered "in great assemblies, and, without critical knowledge or even careful examination of the books used in schools and colleges," prepared lists of acceptable and unacceptable texts and authors. "It is not difficult," he told his readers, "to say what class of writers are commended." Dodd maintained that such efforts clearly retarded "the educational and intellectual advancement of the South."[36]

Dodd's article gained widespread notice, eliciting criticism from some, praise from others, and curiosity from still more. One Virginia professor read into Dodd's article an unpatriotic attack upon the South, inferring from it ideas Dodd had not fully articulated. "Any Southern man," wrote the indignant correspondent, "who would say that . . . he would not have followed Lee and Jackson, ought to be kicked out of a Southern School." Closer to home, George L. Christian demanded that the Randolph-Macon board dismiss Dodd for putting forth ideas the Confederate veterans could not countenance. In campaigns to be repeated several times over the next six years Christian pressured individual trustees, condemned Dodd in meetings of the veterans' camps, and fired off letters to local newspapers.[37]

Fortunately, Dodd had advocates as well. Among them was the editor of the *Richmond News,* who enthusiastically championed Dodd's views by joining in his proclamation that the time had come to cease equating fidelity to the Confederacy with faith in "the Christian Religion or democratic principles." Virginians, he continued, had too long been denied "the intellectual exercises and development that comes from comparing and weighing different points of view and the luxury of choice and discrimination. We hope Professor Dodd will find many followers." In a private correspondence, Bassett encouraged his friend's crusade and invited Dodd to join with him in creating an intellectually honest "scientific history of the South."[38]

Heartened by such endorsements and comforted by unanimous faculty and student support for Dodd, the board deemed the controversy a threat to academic freedom, reaffirmed his appointment, and refused to reprimand him. Nonetheless, the affair unsettled Dodd. "Many subjects which everyday come before the mind of the historian may not with safety even so much as be discussed," he reflected months later. To do so invites "an enforced resignation."[39] Dodd's own difficulties, together with controversies that soon engulfed Randolph-Macon alumnus Andrew Sledd and Dodd's friend Bassett, prompted this observation.

At the same time that readers were considering Dodd's *Nation* article, Sledd, a humane and bookish Latin professor at Emory College, in Georgia, was feeling the full wrath of southern close-mindedness. Horrified by the animal ferocity with which the white mob at an exceptionally brutal Georgia lynching literally dismembered its black victim, he raged against a southern culture that employed such violence to compel "the negro . . . 'to know and keep his place.'" In the July issue of the *Atlantic Monthly* Sledd berated those members of his own race who deemed African Americans "utterly worthless and depraved." Those "whose skins are white," he wrote, "need to remember that our color, too, has its number of the ignorant, lecherous, and wholly bad." Many blacks, "well educated, courteous, God-fearing," are equal to or "superior to many white men," he said. Stung by Sledd's imprecations, southern forces of orthodoxy clamored for his expulsion from Emory and were gratified when he voluntarily resigned. Only his link by marriage to Atlanta's powerful Candler family enabled him to remain in the region and in time quietly to rebuild his career.[40]

Shortly after the article's publication, Dodd wrote the embattled Sledd praising his insight and imploring him to stand firm against elite southern proscriptions. "Your words are very gratifying and encouraging to me," responded a grateful Sledd. "I appreciate your support in proportion as your attitude is, like mine, divergent from the Southern norm."[41]

In November an optimistic correspondent to the *Richmond News* professed to see the publications of Dodd and Sledd as signs of growing southern toleration. Detecting what he considered a more charitable attitude in the South than in earlier times, he explained that only a few years before "Prof. Dodd and Dr. Sledd would have been ostracized" and forced into northern exile. The writer knew little of the pressures weighing upon Dodd to conform and of Sledd's sad fate in Georgia. In fact, Virginia newspapers, especially the *Richmond Times,* had been among Sledd's foremost detractors. Having learned of the Emory professor's resignation, the *Times* editorialized that the "southern man who holds any view . . . not entirely orthodox on the all-important question [of race] is not the man to teach southern youth, and Professor Sledd ought either to change his views or stop teaching in southern schools." Having chastised Sledd, the newspaper advised him to refrain from going "to the North and figure as a 'martyr to southern prejudice.'"[42]

At the same time that Sledd temporarily departed academe, Dodd found himself allied with Bassett in a similar controversy. Together the two friends challenged the forces of southern convention in battles for free speech, from which they came away badly scarred in the end. The campaign commenced when Dodd's *Nation* article and Bassett's growing reputation as a southern iconoclast captured the attention of Columbia University's William Dunning. He invited both to sit on an AHA panel to discuss "Study and Teaching of History in the South, Past, Present, and Future." Dodd and Bassett were to join four other Southerners in presenting fifteen-minute addresses at the New Orleans convention. "Take your own line," Bassett encouraged Dodd with enthusiasm, "hew it out just as you choose and let others 'report' what they like. There'd be the two of us at any rate & and we will be just as 'sassy' as we choose."[43] Ebullient at the moment, both Bassett and Dodd soon learned that crusades for uncensored expression arouse powerful opposition.

By the fall of 1903 Bassett's newly inaugurated *South Atlantic Quarterly* had already developed a reputation as a progressive southern journal. In the October issue Bassett printed one of his own articles, a provocative commentary on southern race relations. Appealing for moderation, he praised black educational and economic successes since the Civil War and described Booker T. Washington as "the greatest man, save General Lee, born in the South in a hundred years."[44] The state's conservatives exploded, vilifying Bassett in the press, showering him with menacing letters, and pledging to boycott his school.

When a disenchanted Bassett tendered his resignation from Trinity College, Dodd plunged into the conflict. Appealing to Randolph-Macon and Trinity's close relationship as sister Methodist schools, he encouraged faculty and students to sign a resolution supporting Bassett's retention; he then sent a strongly worded personal letter to the Trinity board. When the trustees met in early December they weighed negative public opinion against the policy of academic freedom and refused to accept Bassett's resignation.[45] But the damage was done, and Bassett had learned the bitter lesson that southern elites were quick to challenge threats to their cherished cultural traditions.

In the tumultuous weeks separating the publication of Bassett's article and the Trinity board's supportive vote, Bassett anguished over the forthcoming panel before the AHA and began to draw back. Chastened by the storm swirling about him, he admitted to Dodd that his paper would have to be considerably less controversial than planned and might indeed conform to acceptable values. "I fancy," he told his friend, "that I can see your good face pass from a smile to a grin to a full broad chuckle as I thread the maze of so dangerous a subject." On a more sober note, he concluded: "I don't know what I shall say, and if I could get out of it I should not say anything at all." And get out of it he did; pleading a severe attack of rheumatism, the fearful Bassett missed the New Orleans meeting, leaving Dodd momentarily alone in the crusade for southern free speech.[46]

Less intimidated by events in North Carolina, Dodd headed for the convention recklessly determined to expose the Confederate societies. In a wholly negative address he condemned the South's failure adequately to train or pay history teachers, to provide students sufficient classrooms and equipment, and most of all, to allow any semblance of academic freedom. On those rare occasions when a college graduate taught high-school history, Dodd proclaimed, he had just enough knowledge "to prove conclusively to . . . every pupil, and more particularly to their parents, that the South was entirely right . . . in 1860 and that slavery was not the cause for which its people were contending." Such instructors followed a prudent course because "our grand confederate camps fear what they call 'false history' . . . and have history committees to keep watch and put out of the schools any and all books which do not come up to their standard of local patriotism." Under these conditions, Dodd argued, to "speak out boldly means . . . to destroy one's usefulness; to remain silent is out of the question for a strong and honest man; and to follow the smooth via media means failure to influence anybody or anything." [47]

The speech attracted broad and favorable attention at the convention and even more notice, with less approval, when it was published in the *South Atlantic Quarterly* the following April. Dodd endured another round of incessant criticism from Confederate loyalists. Months later Bassett reported unhappily that Dodd had been immediately branded "a traitor to the South and a flatterer of all those who were not in sympathy with the section in which he lives." Pressured once again to purge Randolph-Macon of this "unSouthern" professor, its board reviewed the controversy and choose to followed Trinity's example, retaining Dodd in the name of academic freedom. [48]

In spite of their reprieves, both Bassett and Dodd recognized that their freedom to criticize came at the cost of constant harassment, a price that grew ever more burdensome, and one that lesser men refused to bear. "I must write cautiously," Dodd explained to J. Franklin Jameson in 1906, "for a certain class of good patriotic folk would oppose anything I stood for." Certainly Bassett appreciated this southern equation. That year he left North Carolina for the more open climate of Smith College in Massachusetts, where he soon observed the irony that he, "the son of a confederate soldier," was "teaching the daughters of union soldiers the true story of the civil war and reconstruction." [49]

From the comfortable safety of exile Bassett initially encouraged Dodd to remain in Virginia and prolong his liberal crusade. "Do not allow yourself to become alienated," he cautioned in April 1907, adding a few weeks later that "I shall watch your battle with interest; and I believe you will not lose your life in it." [50] Bassett's concern stemmed from a recent article by Dodd in the 25 April *Nation*, "Freedom of Speech in the South."

Hoping to inspire like-minded reformers, Dodd praised his generation of "younger Southerners, teachers especially," who "recognized that the restoration of absolute freedom of speech . . . is the first step toward the emancipation of our section from the trammels of a bygone age." Optimistically pointing to examples of other southern leaders who had vocalized their aversion to longstanding race and class oppression, he nonetheless acknowledged the strictures that muted their voices. In the past, he reasoned, the South had suppressed free speech to protect slavery, and even in his own age "the presence of the negro among us . . . reconciles many to" the repression of ideas.[51]

According to Dodd, the attacks on his speech sprang from the common folk's ancient conflict with the aristocracy, now augmented by new forces that continued the suppression of nonelites. He maintained that in the first decade of the twentieth century the old slave power had been supplanted by a "new industrial slavery which gradually [replaced] negro servitude." Influencing state legislatures and college boards, modern capitalists showed no more tolerance than their slave-owning predecessors. Fearing the loss of academic liberty, Dodd appealed to scholars throughout his region to "unite in a great cause," that of restoring freedom of expression in the South.[52]

Predictably, Dodd evoked both applause and condemnation. Praising his boldness, one elderly southern expatriate proclaimed that the South was too "much devoted to tradition." He said that there was "certainly less freedom of thought and freedom of speech than in the north; indeed this fact was the chief cause of my moving to the north in 1877." Bassett echoed these sentiments: "We Southern men cannot too well insist on freedom of thought in the South," he admonished Dodd from his northern sanctuary, adding that his friend should not "get discouraged if some of the fellows don't keep step properly."[53]

As Bassett had suggested, southern academicians sympathetic to the South's patrician culture condemned the Randolph-Macon professor. "If you wished to warn . . . the Southern college world . . . against the dangers of industrial slavery," lectured a teacher at Washington and Lee University, then "the very fact that your warning appeared in a medium so often unfriendly to the South as the Nation" arouses "a prejudice . . . against your words." This correspondent shared with others the belief that Dodd was less interested in real reform than in groveling before northern leaders in order to gain favor in their circles.[54]

Doubtless the Washington and Lee detractor and Dodd's other critics felt vindicated when he accepted a posting to the University of Chicago the following year. For his part, Dodd agonized over the move. "I have been disposed to stand my ground" in Virginia, he commented in December 1907, to be "of service to the common cause in the South." But his effectiveness at Randolph-Macon had reached its limits. Perhaps the act of leaving his beloved South, he mused, "might after all be conducive of real results in the purpose for which I am striving." Bassett bolstered Dodd's resolve: "Don't linger in Va. on account of any sentimental attachment to the South," he warned. "I have never regretted my own change."[55]

Certainly Dodd had courted recognition from leading northern and liberal scholars, but his Chicago appointment was an acknowledgment of evident scholarship over the last eight years. As early as 1905 Harvard's Albert Bushnell Hart had congratulated Dodd on his liberalizing influence in the South and expressed confidence in his future as a historian. "I have not the same opportunity of knowing your reputation in Virginia that I have of knowing it in other parts of the country," wrote the respected scholar, "but I assure you [that] you have many warm friends who are watching your career with interest and who expect you to be a powerful influence."[56] Emboldened by such encouragements, Dodd not only grappled with the defenders of southern aristocracy and critiqued their prescriptions for history writing but also generated his own impressive record, delving into themes that were unacceptable to the patrician class.

During the Randolph-Macon years Dodd dueled with the commanding forces of southern oppression and struggled intellectually with historical methodology. Trained in the German style of scientific investigation, he undertook at first to present the past in precise, detail-laden prose, describing events but avoiding interpretation. But he lived and wrote in the context of the Progressive Era, an epoch entirely hospitable to reform. Believing himself the product of an oppressed social class, Dodd immersed himself in the spirit of his age, gradually modifying his methodology to produce historical literature tinged with social commentary. In the process his approach to his discipline evolved from the scientific strictures of his Leipzig professors to an interpretive daring more akin to the work of Frederick Jackson Turner, Charles Beard, and Carl Becker.

Dodd particularly acknowledged his debt to Turner and his epochal work "The Significance of the Frontier in American History." Writing to Turner in 1919, he admitted that his Leipzig training had not prepared him for the emerging American techniques. "I was never brought into touch with an American historian until 1901," he commented ruefully, noting with regret that Turner's essay had not begun "to count with" him until he commenced "teaching American history [in] 1903 and 1904." By that time he had published his Macon biography, and although he had stumbled upon many of the themes Turner articulated, Dodd understood that he had then lacked the intellectual maturity to express his ideas effectively.[57]

Although Turner and Dodd shared a devotion to American democracy, their appreciation of it sprang from far different origins. Raised on the Wisconsin frontier, Turner matured in an environment congenial to the free exchange of ideas. On frequent campaign trips with his politically active father Turner was stirred by the spirited debates common to the rustic environs of the general store, and he concluded that his region more fervently reverenced democratic values than did the older, stratified societies to the east. In 1893 Turner proclaimed that the frontier, "the meeting point between savagery and civilization," had created the uniquely American institutions of democracy. There the basic struggle for survival made social distinctions based upon education and ancestry irrelevant, prompting instead a social leveling that valued individual worth most highly. From this environment sprang a culture that was perhaps crude and even lawless but ineluctably democratic.[58]

Dodd, by contrast, emerged from the South's stratified culture. He understood the requisite customs of a differentiated society, and as a member of the South's underclass he decried its most demeaning features. To his mind, the South's white masses revered democracy and African Americans strove for it, but the region's upper classes just as fervently suppressed it.[59] Even as he labored over his Macon biography, minutely delineating his subject in the careful prose of the scientific school, Dodd evidenced his worship of liberty and his distaste for those who denied it. Although his first monograph lacked the strong, thesis-oriented thrust characteristic of a Beard or a Becker, it broached themes and introduced concepts that Dodd would explicate more forcefully in future works.

Dodd's friend Josephus Daniels valued the manuscript as an able depiction of North Carolina's past and an insightful commentary upon the state's present condition. At his suggestion, Dodd submitted the work to the Raleigh printing firm of Edwards and Broughton, but to the author's great consternation, they demanded a surety of six hundred dollars, half his annual salary. Daniels rushed to Dodd's aid, contributing a portion of the payment himself and soliciting the balance from political cohorts. With this crisis passed, *The Life of Nathaniel Macon* appeared in September 1903, affectionately dedicated to "Mattie Johns Dodd."[60]

Although it was descriptive in style, the biography did provide glimpses of Dodd's perception of the southern class struggle. Although he later professed little knowledge of Turner's frontier paradigm, Dodd divided late-eighteenth-century North Carolina into dichotomous, warring regions. Whereas the east was "divided into plantations . . . cultivated by negro slaves," the west "was composed of small farms" worked by industrious husbandmen. The aristocratic east jousted with the democratic west as the "East persisted in domineering and exploiting the West." Always a champion of the oppressed, Dodd identified with the latter, empathizing with colonial Regulators who opposed unjust taxation imposed by the east, identifying with western patriots arrayed against the Tory east, and commiserating with democrats fighting oligarchs.[61]

In this extended parable Nathaniel Macon marched boldly into the conflict, allied with liberty-loving folk. Born into aristocratic comfort in 1758, he entered the College of New Jersey (now Princeton) at age fifteen but left three years later to fight for the patriot cause. Imbued with the democratic fervor of the American Revolution, Macon returned to North Carolina, entered the state senate in 1781, and joined the radical forces organizing against patrician rule. He was then elected to the United States House of Representatives in 1790, arriving at precisely "the first pass of arms between Jefferson and Hamilton, the representatives of the antagonistic forces of the new nation." A Jefferson ally, he opposed Hamilton's efforts to secure the "attachment of the wealthy class." Remaining true to his democratic convictions, Macon grew in stature, gaining the House Speakership in 1801 and moving on in 1815 to the Senate, where he challenged Henry Clay's neo-Hamiltonian policies. Macon retired to his North Carolina estate in 1828, affecting the quiet lifestyle of a true republican. "Like Washington and Jefferson," wrote an admiring Dodd, "he thought the most fitting close to a long political career was on a plantation far removed from the centres of life." Excepting Macon's strong defense of slavery, Dodd pronounced the man an exemplar. The work closed with a powerful benediction summarizing Macon's dynamic life. Macon, he eulogized, "was no great man in the ordinary sense of the word, but no taint of corruption ever touched his garments, and he served his constituents, the people of North Carolina, more faithfully and more satisfactorily by far than any other man who ever represented them. *He actually believed in democracy.*"[62]

Far from excited by the volume, most reviewers assessed the work as little more than a welcome, competent account "of a little-known Southern leader." All noted Dodd's obvious admiration for democracy, and most found him reasonably objective in his presentation, but the book editor for the *Nation* doubted the author's open-mindedness. He admitted Dodd's forthrightness in acknowledging Macon's "mistakes [and] some of his limitations," but he found in Dodd's prose a too obvious identification with his subject. Like Macon, Dodd had little sympathy for New England Federalists, Alexander Hamilton, John Marshall, or Henry Clay. "One cannot but feel," mused the writer, "that some of the limitations of Macon are shared by his biographer."[63]

Not yet fully mature in his acceptance of criticism, Dodd raged at the review, sharing his indignation with Andrew C. McLaughlin, a recent houseguest. The older, veteran scholar urged Dodd to regard such critiques with judicious remoteness. "Reviewers are apt to be severe and the writer always thinks a review severer than it really is," he soothed. "I do not think that anyone reading . . . the Nation would judge that you had done unprofitable and unsatisfactory work."[64]

The *Nation's* instructive rebuke was helpful to Dodd, who in 1903 had begun to publish his own assessments of other people's books. For the most part he wrote long narrative pieces for the *New York Times* and shorter notices for the Minor Reviews section of the *American Historical Review*. On the whole these early efforts were little more than descriptive analyses laced together with a few mild comments on the book's importance in the larger historical literature. One volume, however, stirred his wrath. Offended by the patrician slant of John H. Claiborne's memoir *Seventy-five Years in Old Virginia*, Dodd proclaimed that whatever value the work might have to students of Virginia's history, the author was "uncompromisingly Southern"; Claiborne, he charged, "believes in and defends the caste system which slavery engendered."[65]

Claiborne's aristocratic hauteur provoked Dodd's emotional response, a reaction rooted in his yeoman origins. From his youth Dodd had despised the slave-rich antebellum regime, and his early career conflicts with the Confederate patriotic societies had intensified his distaste for their ethics. He did share with southern patricians a profound appreciation for the past as a source of social enlightenment, an affirmation that historical interpretation impacts present values and future beliefs. But as Dodd wrote his histories and developed his grand view of the southern chronicle, he fashioned an image of the past designed to move the region toward a future far different from that sought by the apologists for the old order.

Whereas his Macon biography revealed the South's lost heritage of democracy, Dodd envisioned his new project, a biography of Confederate president Jefferson Davis, as a means to denounce that class of Southerners who he believed subverted the rights of their less affluent peers.[66]

Already committed to the Davis study, Dodd was delighted when the Philadelphia publishing house George W. Jacobs commissioned him to write it for its American Crisis Biography series.[67] Like Dodd, Jacobs anticipated that the looming centennial of Davis's birth and the not too distant semicentennial of the Civil War would create a lucrative market for a well-written volume about Davis. The controversial nature of the subject demanded a skilled southern author, but one whose commitment to regional mores would not offend northern readers. The Macon biography impressed the Philadelphia publishers, who quickly signed the Virginia professor.

Dodd's small salary meant that the Davis project's advantages transcended any possible ideological objectives. He recognized the financial convenience of having Richmond and Washington libraries nearby and anticipated only brief excursions to Pennsylvania, where the papers of James Buchanan were located, and to the Franklin Pierce home in New Hampshire. A somewhat longer journey to repositories in South Carolina, Alabama, and Mississippi should round out the essential research trips.[68]

Although most southern archivists welcomed Dodd's interest in their Confederate hero, at least one, the director of the Confederate Memorial Hall in New Orleans, denied him access to the institution's Davis collection. This action outraged the history committee of the Sons of Confederate Veterans. Not yet aware of Dodd's convictions, they condemned the Confederate Memorial Hall's obstruction of "so worthy a purpose as the presentation of an authentic biography" of Jefferson Davis. "The failure to permit the . . . examination of these papers can hardly be defended." Working around this one setback, Dodd devoted the summers of 1904 and 1905 to research and then spent some eighteen months writing and polishing the manuscript, presenting it for publication in October 1907.[69]

At first Dodd found much to admire in Davis and his contemporaries. By the 1850s, he explained, the South had created "an excellent civilization . . . built upon the black and apparently impregnable foundation of negro slavery." The Davis home and similar dwellings produced "thoughtful students of things political and literary [who] were then, and would be now, an honor to their day and generation." In Dodd's view, Davis possessed the finest characteristics of an aristocrat: an appreciation for life's quality, a thirst for useful knowledge, and a nobleman's concern for the wards, both black and white, entrusted to him.[70] But Dodd loathed other traits of the aristocracy, and the book soon turned to a vigorous critique of the planters' civilization.

Dodd thoroughly catalogued and condemned the abuses associated with the South's patrician culture. He indicted the great planters—chief among them Jefferson Davis—for instigating the tragic Civil War. Endowed with "concentrated wealth," slaves, and land, these "monopolists of 1860" embraced war rather than "surrender . . . their privileges." The most powerful of them lived in the opulent environs of Charleston, South Carolina, and along the banks of the Mississippi River "from Wilkerson County, Mississippi, to a point about one hundred miles above Vicksburg." There the "great plantation lords" plotted secession and courted as "allies and lieutenants . . . the less wealthy planters who lived in the 'black belt,' beginning about Washington city and extending to New Orleans." Living on but one-tenth of the South's land and constituting less than one-twentieth of its population, the members of "this ruling, monopolistic class" plotted the lamentable fate of their less favored contemporaries.

Slavery, Dodd assured his readers, undergirded the South's patrician civilization. Like any good patrician, Davis daily made the rounds of his plantation, "supervising his broad Mississippi acres," whose work force of "slave-laborers increased annually." It "was not difficult to 'make money' in those 'flush times,'" Dodd explained, and "the income was mainly spent in improvements, new houses, and thoroughbred horses. No Southern gentleman was content with less than a half-dozen of the most expensive thoroughbreds; Davis kept a dozen." From Richmond to New Orleans, "the whole social fabric rested upon negro servitude," and the South's "handsome if not luxurious country houses . . . were filled with picked and trained servants who stood ready at all times to do the slightest bidding of their masters."

Southern colleges and universities also served the master class. From the philosophical reflections of Thomas R. Dew at William and Mary to the sturdy maxims of William A. Smith at Dodd's own Randolph-Macon, instructors dutifully taught the doctrines of human inequality to wealthy students whose personal property at school typically included body ser-

vants. Confirmed in their dedication to a slave-based culture, Jefferson
Davis and the South's elites brooked no compromise in 1861, departing
the Union confident in their cause's virtue.

Davis's world, however, nourished the seeds of its own destruction.
The Confederate president soon learned that aristocrats demanded privileged considerations. "The great South Carolina families expected to receive high stations and special rewards," Dodd wrote. "The 'first families'
of Virginia could not be neglected; [and] the large slave proprietors demanded in thousands of cases special exemptions from military service."
As these patricians in their thousands sought either position or safety, the
southern masses in their hundreds of thousands bore the war's ghastly
burdens. By 1864 they had grown weary, deserted the southern armies,
formed peace societies, and flocked to anti-Davis politicians who promised relief to the common folk—Zebulon Vance of North Carolina and
Joseph E. Brown of Georgia.

Reflecting on the essential themes of his Davis biography, Dodd confessed to the New England Brahmin Charles Francis Adams Jr. that it "is
a conceit of mine that a Southern man who feels and thinks nationally
must write the true story of our fearful Civil War." Certainly the salient
elements of Dodd's "true story" varied significantly from those of the
story propounded by the Confederate societies. Reviewing Dodd's work,
the historian-general of Virginia's United Daughters of the Confederacy
dismissed the volume, noting that "in his efforts to be unsectarian, the
author has not done President Davis justice."[71] She could not grasp the
insights of a scholar whose understanding of his native region derived
from social circumstances unfamiliar to those descended from the "best
families."

Professional reviewers praised Dodd's biography of the Confederate
president as a major contribution to the field of Civil War literature and
saw in it evidence of the author's considerable talent. In spite of his inclu-
sion in his text of several minor factual errors, they pronounced him a
master of his craft. "Whether the biographer praises, defends, or criti-
cizes" Davis, editorialized the *Nation*'s anonymous reviewer, he "displays
that most important but really rare quality in a historian—a passion for
truth and a certain mental delight in compelling its acceptance." Charles
Francis Adams Jr. complimented Dodd more succinctly in the *American
Historical Review*, proclaiming that he was "thoroughly sympathetic with
his subject; yet throughout judicial in tone."[72]

Pleased as Dodd was by these comments, he recognized the controversial nature of his subject. In the introduction he urged both northern and southern partisans to be circumspect in their reading, to accept the book as a work remaining "as close to the sources as possible." In a private note Dodd prayed that "my 'Davis' will not bear the criticism that it is apologetic [for the South] or that it attempts to unduly blame the Northern spokesmen for misfortunes or bad tendencies." To Dodd's intense disappointment, he was sharply rebuked in southern newspapers and rejected by some northern commentators as well. One southern editor particularly disappointed him since it "was one of those [from] whom I had expected to receive praise . . . he knows the war is over." Equally dissatisfying, the New York–based *Outlook* twice rejected Dodd's offer to write articles commemorating the centennial of Davis's birth.[73]

Believing that some northern publications would rebuff anyone from the South and that most southern editors catered to the patrician class, Dodd consoled himself with the thought that in spite of such obstructionism the Davis biography found grateful readers. "Strange to say," he explained to the historian Frederic Bancroft, "the people of the South—the average readers, in so far as I have been able to find out what they think—are enthusiastic" in their approval of the book's themes, and in the North "I have found a great many friends on account of it."[74] However valid Dodd's judgment of the work's popularity with the inarticulate masses, the biography certainly won him warm acceptance into the historical fraternity, and two short articles published in the scientific style further enhanced his reputation among this fellowship.

While working on his Macon and Davis biographies, Dodd wrote "The Principle of Instructing United States Senators" for the October 1902 *South Atlantic Quarterly* and "Chief Justice Marshall and Virginia, 1813–1821" for the July 1907 *American Historical Review*. These articles stand alone as competent, descriptive pieces working through episodes in the political history of the early national period and reveal Dodd's essential sympathy with the Jeffersonian ideal. More importantly, both hint that the United States Senate and the Supreme Court were the instruments of aristocratic control, points that would be stated more explicitly when Dodd became a player in national politics, first as a friend and proponent of Woodrow Wilson and then as a diplomat appointed by Franklin Delano Roosevelt. "I am . . . 'raiding' the country for Marshall letters," he told a North Carolina judge in 1906. Based on preliminary research, he postulated that "the power of the Supreme Court is derived from Judge Marshall and that power is akin to the Divine Rights theory."[75]

If the precise prose of the scientific historian marked these two articles and *The Life of Nathaniel Macon,* the Davis biography evidenced a stylistic transition moving Dodd toward the Progressive school, carefully tying the past to present conditions. Having criticized Jefferson Davis and his fellow "slave lords," Dodd pontificated that their circumstance was "similar to that which we observe in the industrial system of the United States at the present day. . . . The lords of industry and transportation of the year 1906 are as loath to surrender any of their monopoly rights as were those of 1861; and, according to the view of many acute students, there is as much slavery connected with the latter as with the earlier system."[76] Born too late to challenge the antebellum aristocrats, Dodd mounted his own crusade against those he identified as his generation's oppressors, and in his developing career this impulse was increasingly at war with his historical objectivity.

By 1906 Dodd had begun to move from chronicling past affairs toward actively participating with the power elites of his own generation. He sought the role of policy adviser to a great democratic leader, convinced that the "duty of all scholars and students" was to enlighten the masses of society, to instruct their representatives, and to guide them all when they began "drifting in the wrong way." In his early career he often left the comforts of his Ashland home for the company of important men who would listen to his views on things political. Dodd substituted the pragmatics of politics for the metaphysics of religion. Initially his passion for statecraft served as handmaiden to his history vocation, but in the course of a lifetime it first competed with and then overwhelmed his scholarship. In reflective moments Dodd admitted that his love of politics had drawn him from his "real task in life which is history." But, he mused, "what will history be worth if we lose our democratic and idealistic life!"[77]

Dodd knew firsthand the frustrating, destructive stresses of an authoritarian society. His father's fatalism, his mother's wistfulness for her family's faded status, and the Hornes' autocratic dominance stirred in Dodd a longing for a brighter, more democratic society. Embarking for Germany in 1897, Dodd had left behind the oppressive debt system according to which privileged Southerners lived by the sweat of other men's brows, but its memory drove his aspirations for the rest of his life.

In Leipzig Dodd had sought to understand the means by which elites imposed their collective will upon others. However, although his education had honed his skills as a researcher and excited in him the stirrings of scholarship, it had provided no ideological paradigm to satisfy his personal cravings. To his dismay, the aristocratic tyranny that he so despised in Clayton was echoed in Europe, particularly Germany, his professors more often praising than criticizing the devices of upper-class order. Disappointed by Old World despotism, he had at last found an icon in the New World's Thomas Jefferson. This well-born Virginian became Dodd's secular saint, the embodiment of democratic virtue.

Shortly after returning to America Dodd had visited Clayton; he noted how little its society had changed and was aware of the vast gulf that separated its unlettered inhabitants from his own enlightenment. He was saddened by the small farmers' poverty as well as by their complaisance. Religion, he decided, was the ally of the aristocracy, robbing the masses of their will and soothing them into passivity. The "people still went to church in great numbers," he remembered, "and the preachers still held their positions; but, I was far less interested than I had been when our home was there."[78] Dodd left in sorrow and would not return for eight years. He commenced his own spiritual quest, a search for a living Jefferson—a great and powerful man with whom he could share his democratic faith and his passion to uplift the exploited.

Witness to oppression, Dodd was intensely committed to change. "I should be a Liberal in England and perhaps a socialist in Germany," he explained in 1908. "I am constitutionally a reformer in feeling and thought and therefore more nearly a follower of Rousseau and Jefferson than of Burke and Alexander Hamilton."[79] Yet Dodd had no inclination to run for public office. Even if he had been so inclined, he lacked the status and wealth that empowered the elites; nor did he possess the demagogic skills that enabled the less well born to court the masses. But as a scholar he might seek entry to the inner circle of a democratic idol.

Ashland's location astride the railway between Richmond and Washington favored Dodd's quest. Secure in his Randolph-Macon chair and growing in stature as an intellectual, in 1906 he broadened his world to include notable acquaintances among the most influential figures of both capitals, chief among them President Theodore Roosevelt and Governor

Andrew Jackson Montague. Honored by the recognition extended to him by these executives, Dodd idolized both, seeing in them the outward manifestations of Jefferson. They shared with his hero birth into an aristocratic class—Roosevelt a scion of New York's Dutch patroons and Montague a descendent of Virginia's tidewater gentry—and like Jefferson, they both rejected the will of the elites in order to pursue reforms congenial to the masses. Dodd initially deemed Roosevelt and Montague living Jeffersons, but gradually and regretfully he found in each debilitating flaws.

A trivial incident led to Dodd's initial meeting with the Republican Roosevelt. Angered over the postmaster's dismissal in nearby Hanover, Virginia, Dodd boldly requested an interview with the president. Having recently survived a major scandal in the postal department, Roosevelt granted Dodd a few moments in May 1906. Although little inclined to interfere in the matter in question, the chief executive was intrigued with the bookish petitioner and immediately scheduled a second and longer appointment, intent upon cultivating Dodd's acquaintance. As the two talked at length on topics ranging from local Virginia politics to philosophical approaches to contemporary society, they discovered that they had many interests in common. A man of letters in his own right, Roosevelt flattered Dodd by adding him to his list of regular correspondents. Several months after their initial meeting he confided to Dodd his belief that there were "plenty of very wealthy men who think that if they can get rid of me and my ideas, their troubles in this country [would be] over."[80]

Exhilarated by this attention from such an exalted personage and momentarily impressed by Roosevelt's goals, Dodd gushed in his praise of him. "Mr. Roosevelt is a good man[,] a great one," he wrote shortly after their first meetings. "I sincerely hope he may win many of the important struggles—He has already done so to a remarkable extent considering the array of adverse power." Roosevelt in turn admired the reform rhetoric in Dodd's writings and was particularly struck by his biography of Jefferson Davis. To honor Dodd, he invited him to the White House on 14 February 1908 to lunch with Lord and Lady Bryce and Lyman Abbott, the publisher of *Outlook* magazine.[81]

In a meal lasting just over ninety minutes the guests shared a literary feast, enjoying one another's knowledge of and interest in contemporary historical literature. Unhappily for Dodd, it ended on a discordant note. The president reacted positively to a recent biography of Alexander Hamilton and praised the first secretary of the treasury as "the greatest of our statesmen." Lord Bryce gave his heartiest endorsement, but, Dodd explained to a friend, "you can be sure he did not have mine."[82]

Dodd remained friendly with the president, and their correspondence and visits continued for several years, but the idealistic scholar had lost his awe of Roosevelt. "The man who believes in and admires Alexander Hamilton is not democratic." Roosevelt, he affirmed, "does not believe in democracy, but good government administered from above." By the time of the elections of 1908 Dodd regretted that he had "been an admirer and supporter of President Roosevelt," a lament compounded by the chief executive's unrestrained sponsorship of William Howard Taft. The professor supported William Jennings Bryan. For all his faults, Dodd later remarked in a letter to Virginia's former governor Montague, "I think more highly of [Bryan] now than ever before. He is a radical; he is surely our Tiberius Gracchus and . . . history loves the first Gracchus as it does few other figures." Claiming fellowship with both the ancient patrician advocate of plebeian rights and the crusading "Great Commoner," Dodd proclaimed himself "a radical," though he admitted that "what suits me can not suit others," not even "my best friends."[83]

Dodd's friendship with Andrew Jackson Montague established a pattern for relationships with promising political figures that Dodd would repeat in the decades to follow. Craving the company of powerful men, he still searched for that one individual who might at some auspicious moment achieve great importance and lean upon Dodd as his personal adviser. Seizing such an opportunity, Dodd might then alter the fundamental political equation in favor of the masses.

Enamored with the Jeffersonian image, Dodd judged Montague to be a reincarnation of his historical hero. Although born into a Virginia first family, Montague matured with a stringent distaste for rule by a single class. In large measure his political education developed through long conflict with U.S. Senator Thomas S. Martin, whose corrupt machine dominated state politics from the 1890s until Martin's death in 1919. Heavily subsidized by Virginia railroad entrepreneurs and by the New York rail titan Thomas F. Ryan, Martin loyally supported their monopolistic interests, using their funds liberally to bribe both the Virginia legislature and the state's supreme court. Only the governor's chair remained untainted by Martin's machinations.[84]

As governor from 1902 to 1906 Montague clashed continually with

Martin. Championing a progressive program of party primary elections, employer-liability laws, improved roads, and better schools, the chief executive secured these reforms in spite of the Martin machine's opposition. Montague then challenged Martin directly, running against him in the Democratic primary for the United States Senate in 1905. Dodd, among those cheering the governor, canvassed for Montague in the Ashland environs. But Montague lacked Martin's solid political organization and could not match the goodwill generated by the senator's procurement of national appropriations for Virginia's waterways and port systems. On 22 August Montague suffered defeat in the very primary system he had so diligently fought to establish.[85]

Montague left the governor's mansion in early 1906, but he remained in the capital as the dean of the Richmond College law school. Over the next two years he and Dodd developed a regular correspondence, and Montague frequently invited the professor and his wife to dine. On one such occasion the former governor expressed his sincere gratitude for Dodd's "views and the friendship which inspired them. Whatever you say has great weight with me always, as I value the sincerity which prompts them and the ability with which they are expressed."[86]

Honored by such compliments, Dodd continued to cultivate Montague's company even after the historian had moved away from Virginia. In 1913 Montague entered the United States House of Representatives, and he remained there until he died in 1937. But he eventually disappointed Dodd. Although Montague was competent as a national legislator, he never seized a leadership role, and time eroded much of his passion for reform. Following a brief visit with Congressman Montague in 1919, Dodd lamented that "he does not know the world is going forward. . . . This saddened me. I used to find him rather forward-looking. He is of course high-minded and honorable, but he does not see the course of things in the least."[87]

But in 1906 such regrets lay years ahead. For the moment both Dodd and Montague shared a reforming zeal based on their opposition to the Martin machine. The incident that had drawn Dodd briefly into Theodore Roosevelt's circle had been the firing of the postmaster in nearby Hanover, which had been instigated by Martin supporters. Dodd's strident opposition to such flagrant abuses of power continued for the next two years, expressed in public speeches, private letters, and occasional letters to the editor of the *Hanover Herald*. Ever alert to potential threats, however small, Martin's henchmen noted the professor's opposition and quietly suggested to the Randolph-Macon College administration that such behavior was inappropriate for a man dedicated to the academic world.[88]

The Martin machine's mild harassments did not seriously threaten Dodd's tenure at Randolph-Macon, but they did serve to remind Dodd that free speech in the South might court negative reactions. By 1908 he longed for a more open, freer environment, one congenial to his controversial bent. Fortunately he had established a solid record of scholarship and nurtured contacts among the more eminent historians of his era, which soon prompted invitations from three prominent institutions. In 1908 Dodd savored the luxury of choosing from offers tendered by the universities of Wisconsin, California, and Chicago.

Dodd's Randolph-Macon years had been characterized by conspicuous personal and academic growth. He had emerged from obscurity to become a respected, if controversial, scholar, an intellectual communing with a state's governor and the nation's president. Impressed by his books and articles, his fellow historians accorded him high respect, viewing him as a coming name in their profession. Another measure of success was that he had acquired prominent enemies, important personages who considered him a threat to the social order. Leaders of the Confederate patriotic societies and partisans of Thomas S. Martin's political machine eyed him suspiciously and stood ready to challenge Dodd at the first misstep.

Conscious of his enhanced stature as an academician and his vulnerability as a professor in a small Virginia school, but burdened by the recently assumed responsibilities of fatherhood—William Jr. had been born in 1905—Dodd and his wife considered a career move. The stubborn professor longed to remain in the South, to confront his foes and to campaign for reform, but in the end the promise of academic freedom, improved professional status, and a higher salary lured him from his native land.[89]

Late in the autumn of 1907 Dodd had learned that the University of Chicago's Edward E. Sparks would be leaving the history department to assume the presidency of Pennsylvania State College. Remembering that Harvard's Albert Bushnell Hart twice had promised to "advance [his] interests as a teacher and student of American history," Dodd asked the noted historian to nominate him as Sparks's successor. Endowed by Standard Oil money, the Chicago institution had rapidly emerged as one of the nation's leading universities. "I think the work there would suit me," Dodd reasoned, "with the single exception that I would be grazing in Rockefeller's pasture." But, he considered, "[Andrew C.] McLaughlin is there and that would mean much for me and I take it that he is absolutely free or he would not be there."[90]

Well established as an authority on the colonial and early national periods of American history, McLaughlin had recently left the University of Michigan to chair Chicago's history department. First impressed by Dodd's 1901 address before the AHA, he had appraised the younger scholar's potential and quickly established a lasting acquaintance. In 1904 McLaughlin visited in the Dodd home, and a fond rapport developed between the two scholars. McLaughlin was delighted by Dodd's interest in Chicago but was soon frustrated by the meandrous university bureaucracy. Although by early April he still lacked permission to replace Sparks, McLaughlin had at least gained President Harry P. Judson's approval to interview Dodd. "We are still uncertain as to what we ought to do to fill the vacancy," McLaughlin explained to Dodd, "but at all events, we should be glad to talk the matter over somewhat seriously with you without committing any of us to any future steps."[91]

Dodd immediately traveled to Illinois. In several intense interviews he fulfilled McLaughlin's expectations by impressing Judson. Even so, both Dodd and the Chicago officials had some misgivings. Dodd had little wish to break ties with the South but was intrigued by the university's suggestion that he would attract southern students. Far from leaving the South, they argued, he would teach southern and western history, and he would be encouraged to write about the South, to purchase southern research materials for the library, and to develop closer ties between Chicago's graduate school and southern colleges and universities. For his part, Judson considered Dodd a worthy candidate but worried that because of his lack of graduate teaching experience he might not measure up to Chicago standards.[92]

Home again in Virginia, Dodd immediately declared his willingness to "come to Chicago as a professor permanently at $3,500 per year. . . . With the additional understanding . . . that the salary will within a reasonable time be increased to $4,000 or $4,500." His boldness surprised Chicago, and although McLaughlin was eager for Dodd to join him at Chicago, he had to tell Dodd of Judson's restricted commitment. The position could pay no more than three thousand dollars a year and would be a one-year trial appointment. The chairman implored Dodd "to bring your family and your household goods and household gods" and establish himself at the school.[93]

Throughout May and early June Dodd anguished over the decision. He feared leaving the secure tenure at Randolph-Macon for an uncertain posting. At the same time, he remained acutely aware of his southern foes. "I should like to hear your opinion on the question of whether I ought to accept a chair in a Chicago university," he wrote to his friend Frederic Bancroft on 20 June. "Keep in mind my position as I see it in the South."[94] Even as Dodd sent this query the University of Chicago trustees formally endorsed Judson's proposal for Dodd's appointment to take effect at the beginning of the fall quarter, with no teaching responsibilities until 1 January. The open months were to be dedicated to research and preparation of lectures and to locating southern primary documents and newspaper files for purchase by Chicago's library. When Randolph-Macon's board graciously granted him a year's leave of absence, Dodd focused his attention upon the northern institution.[95]

Just when the terms of the Chicago appointment were being finalized, Frederick Jackson Turner briefly courted Dodd, offering him a chair of southern history at the University of Wisconsin. Famous for his emphasis upon frontier themes, Turner staffed his department with scholars dedicated to sectional studies, notable among them the young Georgian Ulrich B. Phillips. But Phillips longed to return to the South, and in 1908 he accepted a position at Tulane University in New Orleans.[96] Turner thought Dodd would make an ideal replacement.

Still mulling over the Chicago offer, Dodd accepted Turner's invitation to visit the "library and the lake" at the University of Wisconsin. Dodd took the train to Madison and spent a delightful weekend with Turner discussing southern history, philosophical approaches to the discipline, Virginia and national politics, and, most importantly, teaching responsibilities at the university. Enticed by Turner's hospitality, Dodd requested additional information about teaching loads and salary, adding that although he was "impressed with Chicago and . . . positively fond of Prof. McLaughlin," he had no commitment beyond a few month's residence. By the end of July, however, Dodd had decided on Chicago.[97]

Looking upon the fall quarter as "a gift from Chicago," Dodd remained in Virginia until December.[98] He fulfilled the university's expectations by preparing his lectures and by searching rare materials for purchase. These activities, coupled with the sundry tasks associated with leaving their Ashland home, consumed his and Mattie's days. Then, in addition to these affairs, Dodd was presented with yet another career opportunity: Harry Morris Stephens, of the University of California, invited Dodd to become chairman of the history department and settle in Berkeley. A native of Scotland and an eminent European authority, Stephen knew Dodd well through conversations at the AHA conventions and admired his scholarship, his energy, and his ambition. "We can offer you as much or more salary than Chicago," Stephens wrote on 5 November, "and I venture to think that you will find Berkeley a more desirable place of residence than Chicago. . . . You are the only man I want and . . . I want you badly." Weeks later Stephens confided to John Spencer Bassett his interest in Dodd, and Bassett encouraged Dodd to accept the California post. Citing his own migration, the former North Carolinian expressed few regrets about moving. "My work is lighter, specialized, and the surroundings more pleasant," he testified. "I would not be back in Trinity teaching everything from Mycene to the treaty of Plymouth—not for a great deal." [99]

Dodd was tempted by the California offer, which he found far more appealing than the one from Wisconsin. In early December he traveled through Clayton—it was only his second visit since returning from Leipzig—and spent a long Sunday in conversation with Ashley Horne. Proud of his successful nephew, Horne listened intently as Dodd requested his counsel concerning his opportunities in both Chicago and California. The two also talked at length about their different perspectives on southern social life, during which the aging patrician expressed his appreciation for Dodd's frankness. "Many of us would be greater friends," he assured his kinsman, "if only we knew each other better." As for Dodd's career, the old Civil War veteran admonished: "Keep your eye on California and if not entirely satisfied with Chicago I would go to that section as soon as I could. Chicago is a cold and undesirable location for Southern people." [100]

Dodd finally chose Chicago, with all its uncertainties. Wisconsin, he knew, had proved less than satisfactory to Phillips, and California, though more enticing, lay far to the west and seemed unlikely to attract southern-born graduate students. [101] Firm in their decision, the Dodds prepared for the journey to a new academic home.

Before leaving the South, however, Dodd fired a parting volley at one of Virginia's more important intellectual nabobs. In a review of Thomas Nelson Page's book *The Old Dominion: Her Making and Her Manners* for the *American Historical Review* he censured the author's class assumptions. Dodd found in the book "nothing new or fresh"; rather, it was a panegyric celebrating a "traditional Virginia" populated by "colonial lords and ladies, or their close imitators." Dodd appreciated Page's analysis of the American Revolution, "with all its bitterness, class hatred and shrewd political manoeuvres," but pointed out that the author's heroes were "gentlemen [and his] villains . . . outside the charmed circle." In his original manuscript Dodd had personalized his attack, saying that "through all Mr. Page has ever written [runs] the judgement and the language . . . too frequently akin to those of a confirmed snob," but chided gently by the *Review*'s editor, Dodd softened the offending passage to read, "too frequently those of one who supposes character to be absolutely determined by status."[102]

Filled with a passion to right the historical wrongs of Page and like-thinking patricians, Dodd looked forward to Chicago's academic environment. In short order his classroom would become a mecca for aspiring southern historians, and his publications candid expressions of his class values. The next decade would witness his most productive work in academia, but they would also see him continue to drift into the eddies of politics. In the end Dodd would find his living Jefferson and radically redirect his life's goals.

CHAPTER THREE

A Southern Scholar
in Chicago

"To be a historian," William Edward Dodd mused in 1913, "one must feel the same devotion to truth, the same courage to speak and write the truth that marked . . . the martyrs to early Christianity; for there are many powerful men today who do not care to have the facts of our life made known, and there are some who would gladly return to the methods of the sixteenth century in order to get rid of disagreeable persons who will not perjure or stultify themselves." This sort of rhetoric flowed easily from the mind of a scholar reared in Southern Baptist tradition. But Dodd little admired formal Christianity; he considered organized religion the domain of plutocrats, with clergymen their doting minions. "Churches," he wrote in 1911, are "on the side of the 'biggest battalions,' of wealth and power." [1]

Indeed, a secular faith comforted Dodd, one grounded in the vision of a democratic society and emboldened by a firm belief that "the study and teaching of history" constituted a form of "mission work." If "a man is a Christian he cannot avoid being a democrat," Dodd argued, not a democrat "who swears by Jefferson and then talks of the fallacies of the Declaration of Independence, but a democrat who believes in equality." [2]

In Chicago Dodd sought the intellectual freedom for his "mission," a freedom that had been lacking during his tumultuous years as an academician in the South. When one of his Chicago students, Mary Shannon Smith, chose North Carolina's Confederate Governor Zebulon B. Vance as her dissertation subject, Dodd warned her that "being a woman of northern birth, you will be attacked unless you find a verdict already reached," and he added gravely, "I was attacked severely."[3]

Although the Chicago appointment liberated Dodd from distinctively southern historical shackles, he found the North no more friendly to his yeoman leanings than his homeland had been. Union veterans nurtured Civil War passions as intensely as did their Confederate peers, and northern industrial leaders shared many of the social values of the southern aristocrats. Throughout his long tenure at Chicago Dodd dwelt uneasily in an alien culture, for he discovered that the postbellum North lacked the egalitarianism he sought.

Northerners influenced by the racist dogma of Social Darwinism looked disdainfully on the southern and eastern Europeans who flooded into the United States each year. Intellectual leaders blamed these immigrants for increased poverty, labor violence, and political corruption. Literary figures such as Henry Adams, Herman Melville, and Henry James yearned for a more stable, orderly America; ironically, they turned to the antebellum South for a cultural model. In their minds the southern aristocrat, no longer a slaveowner, with his sense of tradition and social deference, furnished the perfect alternative to northern instability.[4]

Such beliefs appalled Dodd, who painfully endured his closest colleagues' antiegalitarian, racist discourses. He cringed whenever University of Chicago President Harry P. Judson warmed to a favorite theme, that "slavery was the only proper way to manage and work the negroes in the Old South." Dodd found it peculiar that a man who had served in the Union army would hold such a view, but in time he concluded that the people of the North had developed "a social philosophy like that of the South." By 1919 he had wearied of hearing "in the so-called best circles, most frequent approval of negro slavery and constant apologies of the North's breaking down of a social system that ought to have been left alone." In his view, that attitude stemmed from the North's striking industrial expansion. "We threw off a feudalism in which the negro was the 'mud-sill,'" Dodd reflected, only to accept "another in which industrial workers [took] the dependent's place. Turning our back . . . upon one system of serfdom we walked boldly into another."[5]

But these disappointments lay in the future. In 1909 Dodd began his twenty-four-year tenure at the University of Chicago. The first decade was his most intense period of academic accomplishment. He wrote two important books and authored a widely acclaimed textbook; he composed challenging, insightful articles textured by his critiques of Old South elites and their oppression of whites and blacks alike. He became a major force in the history profession, was applauded as a trendsetter in historical interpretation, and developed graduate classes that attracted earnest students appreciative of the quiet enthusiasm of his lectures and seminars and anxious to explore the South's dynamic past.

In the shadow of these successes, however, Dodd struggled with personal discomforts. He adjusted to the Chicago environment with difficulty, chilled by its frigid climate and and distressed by its urban frenzy. The painful departure of old friends saddened him, and he developed new attachments with difficulty. Throughout his Randolph-Macon years he had received continual encouragement from the nation's best historians, but once he matured into the equal of his discipline's finest practitioners and emerged as a force in the American Historical Association he was caught up in the profession's power struggles, compelled to choose between warring friends and to weigh his democratic idealism against the pragmatic needs of his closest associates. And throughout this period he retained a warm zeal for social reform and a personal ambition that eventually led him into a close relationship with President Woodrow Wilson. Entranced by the Wilson mystique, Dodd gradually turned away from his academic interests to join those who were dedicated to the implementation of political ideas.

The Dodd family—William, Mattie, young Will, and infant Martha— arrived in Chicago at the height of a January freeze. Settling into a small house four blocks from the university, one of the first things William and Mattie did was buy warmer clothing for their family; then William concentrated upon his class assignments. Dodd delighted in his first experience of teaching graduate students, guiding them through a seminar devoted to the "religious, social and political conditions in the Old South prior to 1820." He appreciated their "considerable knowledge and ability" and pleasured in sitting around the table with them. "I think the students will help me," he confided to one of his closest friends, "quite as much as I help them."[6]

Dodd was less pleased with the city itself. Chicago had "a sooty dark-looking" countenance, he grumbled; it was "no suitable place for humans." Lonely for "the little group of friends" he had left in Virginia, he wrote to former Governor Montague in 1909 that both he and Mattie felt "daily how great a loss" they had sustained. "Yet," he admitted, "it seemed necessary for us to leave, though of this, time will be the judge." Dodd remembered the crushing pressure to conform to the southern elite's historical judgments that had driven him from Randolph-Macon. "One of the primary reasons for my move to Chicago," he reflected a year later, "was the hope that the change might bring relief." That "had been realized to a great extent."[7]

Peace of mind, however, proved relative. Dodd had only a year's contract at Chicago, with renewal by no means assured. When the University of California contacted him again, Dodd weighed the offer carefully. Invited to Berkeley between the winter and spring quarters, he hesitated, fearing that receiving expenses might imply acceptance of the position. Deferring to this concern, the university paid Dodd an honorarium in exchanged for lectures on Old South political philosophy. He returned to Chicago from the two-week trip impressed by California's program and tempted by a salary of four thousand dollars. But he knew that the western school offered few opportunities for research on southern topics, and when the Chicago trustees renewed his contract with a substantial raise, he stayed.[8]

Yet Chicago was only marginally equipped for researching southern history. University administrators had promised to acquire southern materials—manuscripts, newspaper files, rare books—but had only partially fulfilled their pledge; by early 1910 Dodd was unhappy with their efforts. McLaughlin supported his colleague's insistence and shared Dodd's disenchantment with the library's refusal to purchase a moderately priced set of the *National Intelligencer.*[9]

A dearth of primary materials not only frustrated Dodd's efforts to teach graduate seminars in southern history but also threatened a project just taking shape in his mind. He confessed his discontent to his friend Frederic Bancroft, explaining that "I have a plan, long nursed, which I am now convinced Chicago will not aid me to carry out: I mean to write a history of the Old South some day—covering the period of 1763 to 1833 and the area of Virginia, North and South Carolina with their hinterland."[10] This project would consume a large portion of Dodd's academic energies for the rest of his life. Although multiple interests often took him away from this enterprise, Dodd always considered its completion his primary scholarly goal, envisioning it as his chief legacy.

Hearing that The Johns Hopkins University needed a new history chairman, Dodd asked Bancroft, who lived in Washington D.C., to discreetly inquire about his prospects for the position. At Chicago, Dodd explained, his graduate students had only a "meager supply of materials," but in "Baltimore it would be an easy matter . . . to work out subjects" for student research, and being there would "help me to get at some work I have in mind." Would "the headship at Johns Hopkins be an agreeable bent?" he asked, adding that "the nearness of Baltimore to Washington [and] the great resources for Southern history . . . are attractions to me."[11]

Even though Bancroft was skeptical of Dodd's chances, considering him a bit too young and his attachment to a major university too short, he discussed the matter with friends at Johns Hopkins and was initially encouraged, but the position went to another. Dodd was intensely disappointed. "I had an idea," he said at the matter's conclusion, "that as a Southern American interested both in the Old South and American History . . . I might . . . start up some fresh lines of study there." Under the circumstances, he gloomily resigned himself to Chicago, far from his southern roots.[12]

Dodd longed to be near the Library of Congress and other repositories of southern documents as strongly as he longed to return to a rural South untainted by urban blight. When in the fall Bancroft complained of overwork and fatigue, Dodd urged him to purchase a few acres outside Washington, where he could enjoy the restorative benefits of bucolic reflection. "I imagine [it] would be a great thing for you," he suggested, "as it certainly would be for me."[13]

Although such advice was wasted on Bancroft, Dodd meant to follow his own prescription. When he was asked to deliver an address near Richmond in July 1911, he spent a few days vacationing in Virginia's Blue Ridge Mountains accompanied only by his six-year-old son beforehand. A man of intense work habits and no hobbies, he relished this brief period of recreation. Together he and Will enjoyed carriage excursions across the tranquil countryside, unmindful of Dodd's pressing obligations. "I am having a pleasant time," he wrote his beloved Mattie, remarking that the "weather is not so hard on me here as in Chicago."[14]

Raised with the yeoman's respect for productive labor, Dodd had little appreciation of the necessity for leisure. The brief Virginia interlude not only reminded him of the need to lessen the pace of his own life but also stirred a desire to own a small farm where his city-bred children could "get something of outdoor life." With this in mind, he and Mattie spent two weeks of the following summer exploring the region south of Harper's Ferry until they located an ideal spot, a picturesque tract near Round Hill in Loudoun County. Well suited to wheat and diary cattle, the land surrounded a comfortable antebellum stone house, tenants' quarters, and several substantial outbuildings. Equally important, it was within easy walking distance of the rail line to Washington; in ninety minutes Dodd could be at the Library of Congress. Anticipating a six months' annual leave from the University of Chicago beginning in the fall of 1913, Dodd envisioned this as the perfect haven, a refuge where he could withdraw, Jefferson-like, combining rural pleasures with active scholarship.[15]

Unfortunately, the price of the farm—seven thousand dollars—exceeded the Dodds' means. After considerable negotiation, Dodd paid three hundred dollars in earnest money and pledged to pay fourteen hundred dollars on 1 January 1913. All other sources exhausted, he reluctantly asked Ashley Horne for a loan of one thousand dollars. In spite of their philosophical differences, Horne admired his nephew and gladly complied. The farm, costly both in money and wounded pride, was now Dodd's piece of the southern soil, a yeoman's paradise and a refuge from the tensions of his career. Within two years he happily reported to a colleague, "I am . . . so absorbed in making things grow . . . that I can not discuss even so interesting a subject as history intelligently." He added with a rare twinkle, "You must not take seriously anything I may say."[16]

The farm was Dodd's tonic, his antidote to stress-induced ailments. Throughout the summer of 1913 he excitedly counted the days until his first prolonged stay at Round Hill. In mid-August the Dodds shipped furniture to Virginia and boarded a train for their country retreat. Although Dodd packed boxes of books, note cards, and writing materials, he concentrated his initial energies on the farm, milking cows, baling hay, and planting fruit trees. After receiving an ebullient report from farmer Dodd, McLaughlin joined in his friend's joyous experience. "I picture you sitting on top of Round Hill as monarch of all you survey," McLaughlin wrote. "I have no doubt you embrace in your view acres of corn and grapes and apples and pumpkins. . . . I wish I were there with you." A few weeks' fresh air, pleasant walks, and physical labor refreshed Dodd and improved his digestion. "I eat anything I want without evil effects," he rejoiced. "This sojourn . . . in the Blue Ridge mountains has wrought a change as unexpected as it is welcome."[17]

Dodd had begun a dual life. From January through July he devoted himself to his classes and related university assignments, trusting the management of his farm to his live-in tenant, but in midsummer he would hasten to his Virginia haven, with its satisfying physical activities interspersed with research excursions to the Library of Congress and speaking engagements throughout the country. He relished the agrarian life, claiming with pride that after several years' work the county's "hard and close-fisted farmers" had finally accepted him into their fellowship. "Nobody calls me 'professor,'" he bragged, "but plain Mr. Dodd and I am treated as an equal."[18]

Dodd's rural eccentricities amused his academic friends. "It is a dangerous business for a democrat like you getting land," teased one. "The next step will be the purchase of a cotton plantation, and then your up-country Calvinism and Jeffersonian democracy will be in a very bad way." But Dodd had other designs for the farm; he planned a multivolume history of the Old South, after which he would "be content to retire to the little farm near Washington and . . . to entertain . . . in a manner of a Virginian of the olden time, but without the profusion of the slave-holder or his successor, the industrial magnate."[19]

Dodd never permitted the farm to divert him from his profession; rather, it renewed his spirit, reminding him of his intense affinity for the South's masses. Steeped in yeoman traditions of labor and immersed in the mores of Baptist culture, he forsook what he saw as the frivolous pleasures of the sophisticated elites. He never smoked, rarely drank, and deemed wasteful and trivial such entertainments as cards, dancing, and golf. Strenuous cultivation of his Round Hill acres restored him both physically and emotionally. He sold milk to Washingtonians and enthusiastically shared an abundance of apples, grapes, and potatoes with his many friends. Then in January he would resolutely pack, board up the Round Hill house, and entrain for Chicago, his love for the South and its common folk reborn.[20]

But the midwinter chill of Chicago inevitably jolted Dodd's constitution. "I always feel like packing my trunk and going elsewhere," he would say. "But a week or two of sore throat and mild colds serve to acclimate me and I get reconciled." He then approached his seminars with renewed vigor, satisfied that "no other man in the country is doing my kind of work as a teacher of graduate students."[21]

Columbia University's William A. Dunning was Dodd's only serious competitor for youthful southern historians. But with the exception of

Ulrich B. Phillips, Dunning's disciples narrowed their focus to the Reconstruction epoch, largely ignoring the broader scope of southern history. Although Dodd shared Dunning's critical assessments of radical Republicans and carpetbag governments, he considered Dunning far too sympathetic to the South's ruling class. Dunning in turn had little patience with what he considered Dodd's negative views. "Perhaps . . . your peculiar contribution" will be "to throw light on the dark places of Southern history," he explained to his Chicago rival. "It will be useful service, beyond doubt, but I warn you . . . I am not going to coincide with all you say."[22]

Dodd trained many of the South's brightest young minds, opening to them the Old South's panorama by reflecting upon it, reminisced a former student, "in the familiar way that you or I might talk of the history of our own families—not so much that he knew everything about the South, as that he understood it and could guess how its people felt and acted." Dodd possessed that rare ability to enchant students, to compel them to touch the dynamics of the past. He "made American History as thrilling as any novel with a well laid plot," wrote Frank L. Owsley in 1917. "People . . . sit on the edge of their seats and almost forget to take notes. . . . Imagine a man who has been trampling on a brick walk for years being told suddenly that the bricks are . . . gold . . . then you have the way Dodd usually makes a class feel."[23]

These lectures reflected Dodd's plebeian values. He repeatedly indicted Old South aristocrats, condemned their oppression of fellow Southerners, and censured their subversion of Jeffersonian democracy. "From this native North Carolinian," wrote Herman C. Nixon, a disciple of similar origins, "I got my first appreciation of the difference and cleavage between the Southern Piedmont and the Southern lowlands. . . . This learning was good for my soul . . . and I no longer had an occasion to wish that my people might have been planters."[24]

By 1914 Dodd was cultivating a band of young historians, apostles who he hoped would spread his message of democratic liberalism across the patrician South, and he had weathered the difficulties of life in the city of Chicago by escaping to his peaceful haven in the mountains of Virginia. His diligent work, first at Randolph-Macon and later at the University of Chicago, coupled with perceptive and challenging publications, commanded respect from the best of his academic peers. He had paid his dues to the history discipline and seemed on the verge of receiving well-deserved honors and recognition from its chief professional organization, the American Historical Association. At that very moment, unfortunately, Dodd became a pawn in an internecine struggle for control of the society that not only challenged his democratic idealism but also forced upon him a crisis of loyalty to friends and colleagues who stood diametrically opposed.

Throughout his early career Dodd cherished his relationship with the AHA, and his progress within its inner circles became for him a barometer of his standing with the historical fraternity. Delighted by his first convention in 1900, he mingled with the association's intellectual giants and relished each honor bestowed by them. The invitation to read his Macon paper in 1901 and its subsequent publication in the *American Historical Review* had greatly enhanced his self-image, encouraging him to march boldly with his discipline's most noted practitioners. Dodd's fearless condemnation of the Confederate patriotic societies at the New Orleans convention of 1903 set him apart from those southern historians who slavishly parroted the prescribed historical dogmas and won him the respect of scholars who admired his intellectual integrity. The association's best men—Albert Bushnell Hart, Frederick Jackson Turner, J. Franklin Jameson, and Andrew C. McLaughlin—praised Dodd and bolstered his desire to improve his scholarship and advance to the summit of his profession.

Founded in 1884, the AHA reflected the growing professionalism of university specialists and their desire to establish codes of academic conduct while encouraging quality scholarship. Thirty years later the association could boast of its successes. Most of its three thousand members taught in institutions of higher learning or worked as archivists and librarians across the nation. Committed to high ethical and academic standards, they shared their research at their annual convention and in their journal, the *American Historical Review,* and debated not only the events of the past but also the philosophical approaches to their discipline.[25]

To be sure, only about two hundred fifty members attended the AHA's annual assemblies, and fewer still shaped its policy. The organization's governance was left, largely by default, to a coterie of fewer than a dozen individuals, eminent scholars from prominent northeastern and midwestern universities. Chief among these, Hart, Turner, Jameson, and McLaughlin considered themselves fair-minded arbiters of the historical profession; they encouraged promising young historians, recommended appointments to association committees, and nominated future officers.

When disgruntled outsiders challenged their prerogatives in 1914, they were shocked.[26]

Dodd counted himself fortunate to be among the promising young scholars recognized and advanced by the inner circle of the AHA. McLaughlin's influence proved advantageous, leading to Dodd's placement on sundry association committees, his invitation to deliver major papers at the conventions of 1910 and 1912, and his nomination to the *American Historical Review*'s prestigious editorial board in 1914. Blinded by ambition and success, Dodd seemed oblivious to his long-held notions of opposition to oligarchical rule, willingly playing his role in an organization in which a respected few determined the fate of the less distinguished many.

Dodd's presentations at the AHA conventions of 1910 and 1912 not only demonstrated his maturing scholarship but also marked him as a coming man in the profession. These papers clearly broke with his scientific training and placed him squarely within the Progressive school, which explained the course of human relations largely in terms of economic determinism and class conflict. Boldly interpretive, they moved Dodd toward his profession's front ranks, where prestige was rewarded with greater influence in the association.

When the AHA program committee for 1910 proposed a special session commemorating the fiftieth anniversary of Secession they considered Dodd a natural choice as one of the presenters. Taking advantage of research materials at the University of Chicago, he prepared his carefully reasoned paper "The Fight for the Northwest, 1860." Dodd postulated that as late as 1858 the northwestern states—Indiana, Illinois, and Iowa—were bound to the southern slaveocracy by geography, culture, and kinship. The "backbone" of the Democratic Party "was the South," he argued, "and the backbone of the South was slavery, the greatest single economic interest in the country." In their uncompromising quest to perpetuate the "peculiar institution," southern leaders depended upon their strong alliance with northwestern elites. The northwestern region was "peculiarly the child of the South. The local institutions . . . were Southern, . . . the prominent families as well as a majority of the people were of Southern origin, the rivers were their highways and the rivers ran southward."[27]

Even though the "Ordinance of 1787 forbade slavery in the Northwest," Dodd noted, "many hundreds, even thousands, of slaves were owned and worked in Indiana, Illinois, and Iowa." Prominent families and powerful institutions were allied with the South through human chattel. The region's most important politicians possessed this human property, most notably Illinois's Stephen Douglas, who "owned in his wife's name a hundred negroes in Mississippi." Churches, sensitive to their affluent patrons, gave religious sanction to slavery. Episcopalians and Catholics easily sided with the elites, and northwestern Methodists, Baptists, and Presbyterians broke with their northeastern brethren to staff their congregations with proslavery ministers. While Methodists softened harsh sanctions against slaveholders and Baptists hired preachers from the slave states Missouri and Kentucky, Presbyterians established in Chicago a prestigious seminary that looked with favor on slave interests. Virginia-born Cyrus Hall McCormick heavily endowed the school, gave it his cognomen, and insisted it hire a president and faculty dedicated to the belief that "slavery was not only not contrary to the Divine will but positively sanctioned by both the Old and New Testaments."[28]

Up to the very eve of the Civil War, Dodd reasoned, the Northwest's political establishment was bound firmly with the South. But the construction of the Illinois Central Railway opened vast, fertile acres in Indiana, Illinois, and Iowa to New England, German, and Scandinavian immigrants, individuals as fervently opposed to human chattel as they were devoted to the Declaration of Independence. Inspired by no more lofty motive than profit, the railroad sold them vast tracts, adding in Illinois alone more than four hundred thousand "to the population . . . between 1856 and 1860." These migrants fueled the Republican Party, shifting power to Abraham Lincoln and the antislavery forces. Thus, at the last moment the Northwest cast its fate with the Union, adding its considerable weight to the Confederacy's demise. Ironically, Dodd concluded, the contest "was won only on a narrow margin by the votes of foreigners . . . who knew the least of American history and institutions."[29]

Dodd's audience responded with enthusiasm. "I have never presented anything which cost me as much study," he wrote two days after the reading, "and I have never received half so many 'hearty endorsements' of a paper before." However much he savored this moment, his professional satisfaction increased even more after the work's publication in the *American Historical Review,* when Charles Beard announced himself one of Dodd's admirers. Revealing that he had read the essay "with genuine pleasure," Beard admitted that it "is the only article in that periodical that I have ever read twice or thought about afterwards." He praised Dodd for departing form "old fashioned American History" and demonstrating "how real history might be written."[30]

Although this paper constituted a milestone in Dodd's intellectual development, it was far from the convention's central focus, nor was it the most important presentation of the day. But for Dodd it represented a major step in his struggle to determine "how real history might be written," his quest to advance his scholarship from a simple recitation of past events to the development of academic discourses relevant to the present.

Just a few hours after Dodd's peers congratulated his work, he was himself enchanted by Columbia University's James Harvey Robinson's epochal essay "The New History." The time had come, Robinson professed at the convention's closing assembly, to depart from nineteenth-century scientific methodology, with its "scrupulous criticism of . . . sources, . . . detailed study of past events, . . . and elimination of the older supernatural, metaphysical, and anthropocentric interpretations." He urged his fellow scholars to embrace the Darwinian ethic of social struggle and to adopt the tools of social science: comparative religion, social psychology, and economics. From this would emerge a new approach to history that was more useful for the comprehension of human development.[31] Dodd agreed, and he began his own exploration of antebellum America, determined to define fresh fields for research. Two years later he would present his conclusions before the AHA meeting in Boston.

Dodd labored over this project, recognizing both its importance to his own intellectual development and its potential to advance his professional stature. He wrestled with ideas that had long been familiar to him—class conflict, economic dominance by antebellum southern and postbellum industrial elites, the masses' democratic aspirations, and established religion's subservience to dominant laity—determined to weave them all into a tapestry that would illumine the nineteenth century's titanic sectional disputes. "The purpose of my study and writing history is to strike a balance . . . between the North and the South, but not to offer any defense of anything," he explained to Theodore Roosevelt. "My greatest trouble as a student is to get the conservative South and the now reactionary East to recognize this sort of writing as historical." Dodd's Chicago colleagues, especially McLaughlin, carefully scrutinized his manuscript, pronounced

it "revolutionary," and bade him well in its presentation. Aware of the
paper's significance to his career, Dodd left for Boston full of trepi-
dation.[32]

In rituals peculiar to learned societies the AHA designated Dodd's paper "Profitable Fields of Investigation in American History, 1815–1860"
an event of note. The convention divided, with European scholars attending a similarly themed presentation while their American friends
gravitated to Harvard's Emerson Hall. There Frederick Jackson Turner
presided over Dodd's session, adding his prestige to the event.[33] Dodd
stood before his fellows no longer an apprentice haltingly sharing his narrow interests nor a journeyman working confidently through a complicated historical problem but a master craftsman charting paths for others
to follow. Dodd's able paper stirred controversy among the assembled historians and suggested fresh channels for research, though it perhaps fell
short of his usual standards of erudition.

In a long introduction, Dodd boldly embraced an economic interpretation of pre–Civil War America, blending this overriding causative factor
with lesser themes—nationalism, democratic and aristocratic ideologies,
and religion. "The group which in any country produces the largest annual surplus is apt to . . . determine policy," he opened. Enriched by slave-
produced profits, the southern planters were exporting $250 million
worth of goods by 1860, "almost twice" as much "as all other exporters
combined." Thus the planters set the agenda of government, subordinated
all other economic interests to their own, and dictated society's tone.
"The planter was the perfect gentleman of his time," Dodd reasoned,
"and the plantation the accepted economic and social model, not only
for the South, but for the remainder of the United States." Overpowering
all other interests, "the dominant Southern group" labored to win other,
less powerful Americans to their "view that all men are not equal." To
be sure, southern elites were nationalists, but only as long as the central
government protected their prosperity, which was based upon "the plantation system [and] negro slavery."[34]

By the early 1850s, Dodd argued, prosperous northeastern manufacturers were challenging the southern planters' economic supremacy. Focusing their attention upon the domestic market, they demanded high
protective tariffs and resented competition from slave labor. Throughout
the decade preceding the Civil War the industrialists and planters competed for the support of yet a third group, "the great majority of the

people, not less than two-thirds the total number, 'the peasant proprietors,' . . . [who] were not attached to either party." Rural, isolated, and
largely unconcerned with a market economy, these small farmers and
landless laborers remained ideologically faithful to the virtues proclaimed
in the Declaration of Independence. Given a choice between the developing feudalism of the South and the individualistic rhetoric of northern
manufacturers, the masses largely cast their lot with the opponents of
Calhoun and Hayne. Tragically, however, the people's quest for democracy was illusory. Following slavery's demise, northern industrialists
proved no more egalitarian than defeated southern aristocrats.[35]

After sketching his personal interpretation of the antebellum experience, Dodd turned "to the main purpose of the paper . . . to venture some
suggestions as to certain lines of study that may not have been followed
up by the writers of American history." At length he explored various
unchartered or little-explored areas, always suggesting social, class, and
economic themes. He called for detailed histories of cotton and tobacco
cultivation, advocated a thorough analysis of the transportation revolution and its political ramifications—praising Ulrich B. Phillips's *Transportation in the Eastern Cotton Belt* as a model study—and demanded critiques of the great churches' attitudes toward slavery. In every case, he
averred, economic self-interests dictated policy. "A poor church in 1800
was anti-slavery and very simple in its service," Dodd pointed out in his
overview of religion; in 1850 "the same church was composed of well-
to-do members . . . and it was naturally pro-slavery." To those scholars
drawn to regional studies he recommended a focus upon "western North
Carolina and eastern Tennessee," where impoverished citizens remained
faithful to democratic idealism, or an examination of the intense class
conflict of the northwestern states, where cultural struggles mirrored
events in the planter South. Ever the devoted disciple of Thomas Jefferson, Dodd urged further studies of "the faithful democrat of the 'little
mountain'" and encouraged biographical sketches of like-thinking Southerners, especially the Tennesseans William G. Brownlow and Andrew
Johnson. He contended that monographs devoted to these topics would
authenticate his assertion that the "history of the Civil War and the period immediately following" proved that Yankee industrialists "and not
idealistic reformers, had come to power as protagonists of nationalism"
after 1865, but theirs was "a nationalism which first of all 'took care' of
[its] economic interests."[36]

The speech sparked a lively discussion; some in the audience were genuinely impressed, others were intrigued, and still others were highly offended. As the designated respondent, Ulrich B. Phillips took exception to Dodd's economic determinism. Focusing upon his own area of expertise—labor in the old South—Phillips obliquely complimented "Prof. Dodd's paper, which all must agree is highly suggestive and admirable," and then launched into his own narrow review. "I must, however, take issue with the assertion that the slaves offered the most profitable investment for capital in the ante bellum South," he countered. In his view, the high cost of human property, coupled with cotton's low market value, yielded at best "a moderately good return only through the most efficient management and in the districts most favorable for the production of the plantation staples." Race, not economics, dictated southern policy. For too long, he editorialized, "the writing of American history" had been subservient "to the abolition tradition." Deeming social attitudes far more significant than monetary concerns, he suggested that Darwinian racism was prevalent in the North as well as in the South. "Whereas the [antebellum] North in general was considering only the institution of slavery," he reasoned, "the South was confronted with the problem of racial adjustments as its paramount consideration." In Phillips's view, the North could not fully appreciate the South's dilemma until it grappled with the problems of a multiracial society.[37]

Although other, less harsh public criticisms followed, and even Dodd's friend J. Franklin Jameson confidentially suggested that he had overstated the case for economic causation, Phillips's response particularly stung. Pleased with a positive review of the paper in the *Chicago Evening Post,* the always sensitive Dodd privately grumbled that "the attack by Phillips [was] somewhat needless, as it appeared to me."[38]

But the manly acceptance of academic judgments was the price Dodd and other ambitious scholars paid for professional recognition. The offices of the AHA "are considered honors," he wrote in 1914, and he craved them as an outsider might long "for the door-keeper's positions in the house of Lords."[39] But just at the moment when Dodd's growing aspirations seemed attainable, the association plunged into a profound internecine conflict. Bloodied by his role in the controversy, Dodd would draw back from his relentless pursuit of distinctions, reassess his career goals, and emerge on the leeward side of the events a more settled and mature scholar.

By 1913 the AHA leadership tottered on the edge of a serious internal crisis, largely unaware that their southern members chaffed at a closed election system favorable to a few northeastern and midwestern professors. In the name of efficiency the organization had evolved a highly undemocratic system of interrelated and self-perpetuating directorates: the executive council, a nominating committee, and the board of editors of the *American Historical Review*. The executive council, made up of the current president, all past presidents, and six elected members, appointed the nominating committee, which then made its recommendations from lists provided by the council; in turn, the *Review*'s board of editors depended upon the executive council to fill its vacancies from lists suggested by the board. This restrictive system was even more exclusive than it appears because a few officers dominated: J. Franklin Jameson exercised suzerainty over the *Review,* and Frederick Jackson Turner and Andrew C. McLaughlin had disproportionate influence within the executive council.[40] Cognizant of this, Dodd cultivated these men's patronage, fully aware of their potential to influence his career.

At the same time, Dodd had strong ties with two of the three principle insurgents. His close friend Frederic Bancroft led the dissidents, determined to pry Jameson from the *Review* and to wrestle control of the association from Turner and McLaughlin. Of Bancroft's chief allies, Dodd had only a passing acquaintance with John H. Latane, of The Johns Hopkins University, but he valued his association with Dunbar Rowland, who as the director of the Mississippi Department of Archives and History had shared rare materials for the Davis biography and had since remained a friend and frequent correspondent. As the battle was joined Dodd felt cornered, torn between much cherished old friends and powerful new intimates.

Dodd missed the AHA convention of 1913, tied to his farm while Department of Agriculture inspectors tested his newly purchased dairy herd. Just over a week after the convention he received his first hint of difficulty. "Take care of yourself and get back to the American Historical Association," urged a former student. "It needs you. Jameson is getting old [and] there is no one . . . his age, who can fill his place and . . . with his fall, the Association will totter."[41] Dodd soon learned that Bancroft and Rowland intended to precipitate Jameson's demise.

Initially Dodd was drawn to his southern friends, enticed by their call for greater democracy. Most association members "do not believe in self-government and in a learned society this is strange," mused Dodd in a letter to Rowland. "If you and I can be democrats in the South, how does it happen that the sons of the men who brought on the war for democracy in 1860–61 can not believe in it?" At the same time Dodd was disturbed by the tenor of articles written by Rowland and Latane in the *Nation*. Dodd contacted Jameson to ask for clarifications of the association's constitution, hinting at his support for reform but distancing himself from any personal vindictiveness. "The discussion of our History affairs seems to be taking an unfortunate turn," he lamented. "Nobody, so far as my acquaintance goes, has any feeling that anybody has been sequestering offices for himself and personal friends—and to make this a feature of the discussion seems to lead to ill-feeling and personal dislikes."[42] He quickly learned his error; the controversy was highly personal, a contest more for power than for justice.

Throughout 1914 the two factions—the insurgents and the establishment—jockeyed for position, and Dodd was trapped between conflicting loyalties. Newly elected to the powerful executive council, the iconoclastic Bancroft announced to Dodd that "I should like to experience the sensation of being a progressive and a reformer!" But if he expected his longtime friend to march in the crusade's van, Bancroft was disappointed. Dodd heard other and opposing voices, intonations by those who, if so inclined, could shorten his career. "My own preference would naturally be, to let things go along just as they have," wrote Jameson. "I am prone to think only of the question of efficiency in pursueing the Associations [*sic*] various lines of work." Nonetheless, he admitted that "insurgency is in the air" and that the council had for too long remained insensitive to the needs of the general membership. "I should not think of resisting a certain amount of change," he said, even though he believed that the immediate result would be "much less efficiency than at present."[43]

This somewhat flaccid concession won Dodd's neutrality. When pressed by Bancroft to make a "formal statement" at the December convention, Dodd temporized, arguing that it would only exacerbate the association's problems. "Perhaps," he sadly reflected, "it is not intended that historians should dwell together in unity and brotherly love."[44]

Pleading pressing obligations to publishers, Dodd absented himself from the 1914 convention, an assembly noted more for gamesmanship than scholarly display. The executive council, easily dominated by its former presidents, tried to appease its southern members by electing Eugene

C. Barker, of the University of Texas, and Ulrich B. Phillips, lately moved to the University of Michigan, to its number. The council then established a Committee of Nine, headed by McLaughlin and charged with suggesting reforms at the next convention. However much these concessions may have blunted the opposition, McLaughlin's nomination of Dodd to the *American Historical Review*'s editorial board proved disastrous. He had assumed that Dodd's friendship with Bancroft and his deep southern roots would placate the insurgents, but the rebels were irreconcilable, and Bancroft chose to interpret this to his advantage. This was yet another example of blatant croneyism, he railed; McLaughlin always reserved a spot on the board for the University of Chicago. Cowed by the opposition, McLaughlin retracted Dodd's name.[45]

Emboldened by the establishment's concessions and elated by their victory over McLaughlin, the insurgents spent the next year pressing for control of AHA. In a series of scurrilous pamphlets mailed to the association membership and in private correspondence with influential scholars, Bancroft, Latane, and Rowland exaggerated the power of the executive council, accused the council of misappropriating funds, and challenged the vague legal relationship between the association and its journal. They played upon discontent among southern and western historians and made inroads among the students of William Dunning, though the Columbia professor remained a vocal opponent of the insurgents.[46]

Dodd, although wounded by the rejection, clung desperately to his neutrality. In a letter to a North Carolina colleague he reaffirmed his support for democratic reform. "Democracy is the only thing worth fighting for," he declared, "but democracy is the last thing in the world that the leaders of the present fight desire." To "overthrow one group or oligarchy only to establish another is not according to my faith." This reticence to join either side earned Dodd the resentment of all. McLaughlin considered Dodd idealistic and naive and Turner resented his refusal to attack the insurgents, but Bancroft eventually became his harshest critic.[47]

In spite of his opposition to Dodd's appointment, Bancroft initially tried to avoid an open break with his old friend. Writing to Dunning and to Dunning's North Carolina protégé J. G. de Roulhac Hamilton, he condemned Jameson, Turner, and McLaughlin for nominating Dodd but assured his correspondents that the nominee "himself was perfectly innocent and takes no stock in their doings." But Bancroft needed Dodd's support, not his neutrality, and eventually lost patience. Frustrated, in

March 1915 he resorted to mild ridicule to move Dodd from his silence. Learning that Dodd had been granted extended leave to remain on his "Virginia farm, writing history and milking cows," Bancroft gently chided him for hiding from the controversy and once more entreated him to join the reformist campaign.[48]

Bancroft's sarcastic reference to the farm piqued Dodd, who felt the stress of avoiding friends on both sides. Dodd wrote, but did not mail, a long angry reply. "Now don't start fun-making about the farm," scribbled the offended scholar, who then lectured Bancroft that he had employed his time on serious history tasks, doing research in the Library of Congress, writing manuscripts, and proofing galleys. But during his self-imposed exile Dodd had paused for reflection, repented of his earlier lusting after status in the association, and critically assessed the character of the "large number of men [who] love office and the show of authority." Fed up with the conflict, Dodd proclaimed: "I would rather write poor books for you to 'score' in the *Nation* or Charles Francis Adams to patronize in the *Review* than to . . . correct the tendencies of the organization, especially as some of the men concerned are my very best personal friends." He wisely filed the indignant missive and days later mailed a less passionate but firm refusal to join the uprising.[49]

Scorned, Bancroft turned against Dodd. "You may be interested to learn that Bancroft and his friends . . . have given you up," Cornell University professor Carl Becker told Dodd. They claim "you were naturally peeved because Bancroft blocked your nomination to the Board of editors; and . . . that . . . with McLaughlin as head of your department [your position] is a delicate one." How they reconcile "this estimate of your mental and moral make up with Bancroft's former statement . . . that you were one of the most conscientious and independent men in the association, I can't conceive."[50]

It is likely that Bancroft's attacks on Dodd hurt the former's cause among southern historians. Charles H. Ambler, Dodd's successor at Randolph-Macon, initially sided with the insurgents even though he was a Turner student. "Clear [Dodd's] good name from all suspicion," he demanded of Bancroft. Personal attacks upon Turner were one thing, but they were "of minor importance as compared with the duty of clearing Dodd who" had not been with the establishment "at any time." Offended by Bancroft, Dodd cast his support with McLaughlin's Committee of Nine. Bancroft "has lost his balance," he complained to Dunbar Rowland; he "has ceased to be sane on the subject."[51] The crisis had cost Dodd one of his most cherished friends.

Disheartened by the controversy, Dodd remained quietly in the background at the December convention while Turner, McLaughlin, and Jameson easily defeated the insurgents. The Committee of Nine proposed modest changes: limiting former presidents to a three-year term on the executive council, increasing the number of elected council members from six to eight, increasing the jurisdiction of the AHA business meeting at the expense of the council, selecting the nominating committee at the business meeting rather than its being chosen by the council, and clarifying the relationship of the *American Historical Review* to the learned society. The convention readily adopted all of the proposals, depriving the insurgents of support from all but the most disgruntled members. In defeat, Bancroft resigned from the executive council and, along with Latane and Rowland, suffered the eclipse of his influence within the association.[52]

Dodd grieved for the association, lamenting the ill-will engendered by the controversy. As he left for the 1916 convention in Cincinnati, he anticipated a poor attendance. "For my part," he reflected, "I shall never attend again with the same sort of sincere interest and zest that I used to feel." Although he resolved to minimize his relationship with the association and to avoid its inner workings, by 1917 he again was playing a major role in its affairs. That December he, Turner, Jameson, and others served on an ad hoc committee to explore the historian's role in the war effort, and at the same meeting he was elevated to membership on the executive council.[53] Dodd had finally achieved a long-desired goal, to be placed in the highest councils of his profession. But like so much else in his life, it had come at a rending cost, the loss of a friend as well as the diminishing of his own innocence. Yet, in the final analysis, his honors in the association would now be less the result of his relentless campaigning and more a recognition of his intellectual maturation, an acknowledgment of his special expertise on the American South.

Throughout his early Chicago years Dodd had admired the work of Frederick Jackson Turner, applauding his sharp break with the scientific school. "I think I am not far from your own teaching," Dodd wrote to the Wisconsin historian in 1911. "Certainly your writings have influenced me more than those of any other scholar and I have always been grateful to you for the direction . . . you gave our historical studies." Nonetheless, Dodd gradually recognized the great man's one notable flaw. "Turner was in my opinion the first interpretive historian of his generation—[the] highest rank," he eulogized following his model's death in 1932, but "he did not write enough."[54] By contrast, Dodd wielded a fecund pen, rich in its production of books and articles.

In Dodd's view, history's chief value lay in its explanation of the present. This assumption seemed natural to a scholar reared in the post-Appomattox South, a region painfully conscious of its defeat and racked by the recriminations of blame-seeking Southerners. Although aristocrats created powerful paradigms to justify their actions, whereas nonelites privately condemned the planter class for the war's bitter harvest, both united to curse the damnyankees. Dodd concluded from this that "history and religion . . . and politics are so closely interwoven and . . . involve so many personal considerations that it is . . . a delicate thing to discuss with perfect freedom the story of the immediate past." This, he often lectured, was "conspicuously true of the South where so many people consider history a personal matter." Dodd held to his own interpretation of the South's past, which went against his Leipzig training. "I used to think of history as a science [as] possible, led to that idea by [Karl] Lamprecht," he admitted in 1917, "but I have long since got over that."[55]

At the end of his first decade at Chicago Dodd was fully conscious of his intellectual evolution. "I can write a fair book and I can make a fair lecture," he told a graduate student, "and as I grow older my method and spirit ceases to offend people trained in another school." He had come to test historical writings by their impact upon society, recognizing the historian's power to influence the present. Dodd often complained that the vast majority of "American historians are conservatives," with the result that the "great mass of inarticulate men who support government and maintain the social order have thus been led into a false position." Old-style historians hid vital facts from the public or molded information to sanctify the founding fathers and national institutions, but Dodd crusaded for a reformed America and believed that enlightened history would initiate a cry for justice. "If the real history of the United States should be taught in our schools," he quoted an unnamed but like-thinking scholar, then "a great crop of revolutionists would be the result."[56]

In large measure, Dodd's understanding of history's potential for societal impact derived from his conflict with the apologists for the South's antebellum planter class. Although he railed against their past perversions, seeing them as the defenders of a discredited aristocracy, he saw as their chief obliquity the prolonging of old and iniquitous values well into the twentieth century. Scoring authors of southern-biased textbooks, Dodd proclaimed: "I know of no other nation in which two distinct histories are taught in the schools. And it can not be a wholesome thing for us."[57]

Dodd despised the profusion of aristocratic accounts celebrating patrician heroes while clouding the issues leading to the Civil War. Reviewing the *Early Life and Letters of General Thomas J. Jackson, "Stonewall Jackson,"* Dodd cut through the laudatory passages to focus on the commander's early advocacy of slavery and his role in developing the Virginia Military Institute, a school whose only purpose was to prepare Southerners for a future war against the North. And in an otherwise positive account of William M. Meigs's *Life of John Caldwell Calhoun* Dodd censured the author for his slanted discussion of "the problem of slavery which [he] tends to defend." He considered loathsome the patrician authors of a biography of J. L. M. Curry, the Alabama secessionist and postbellum defender of the Confederacy. The authors took such "pains to argue that Curry did not fight for slavery, but simply for 'constitutional freedom' and the 'sovereignty of the individual state,'" Dodd wrote, that a discriminating reader would "suspect the accuracy and doubt the force of the claim." Any reasonable historian, he continued, would not only acknowledge Curry's defense of the slave-based culture but also recognize that his values were "being carried forward all over the South by his successors."[58]

Virginia's Attitude toward Slavery and Secession, by Beverley B. Munford, the scion of a Virginia first family, contained all that Dodd found contemptible in southern historiography. Born too late to participate in the Civil War, Munford had gained prominence among the Sons of the Confederate Veterans, and as a member of the state senate he had led the crusade against northern textbooks in 1898. "Our children shall be taught the history of this country from the pen of authors thoroughly informed" and in "sympathy for the cause to which the people of the South plighted their faith," he pledged.[59] Consumed with a passion to teach Virginia youth "correct history," Munford produced his own account of the past, an extended defense of slavery in antebellum Virginia.

Published in 1909, Munford's work was meant as "a contribution to the volume of information" from which future historians could "prepare an impartial . . . narrative of the American Civil War, or to speak more accurately—the American War of Secession." Written with the precision of an attorney's brief, the three-hundred-page book argued that Virginia had piloted the crusade to suppress the international slave trade, that such prominent Virginia leaders as George Washington, Thomas Jefferson, James Madison, James Monroe, John Marshall, and many more had spoken in opposition to slavery, and that Virginia and Virginians had been in the forefront of those colonizing Africa with manumitted slaves. In the end, however, the inability to compensate slave owners, the concern for the Africans' moral welfare in a free society, and the fear of anarchy engendered by the Santo Domingo's "carnival of blood" and the "horrors of the Nat Turner Insurrection" had frustrated emancipation. If "slavery was at war with the ideals upon which Virginians had founded their commonwealth," he reasoned, then the tyranny of an oppressive national government was even more repugnant. Thus, in 1861 Virginia had departed from the Union not out of any defense of slavery but out of solidarity with the South's crusade for state sovereignty. Firmly opposed to federal coercion, Munford argued, the people of Virginia "took a stand, predetermined by the beliefs and avowals of successive generations, and impelled by their supreme incentive . . . to maintain the integrity of principle."[60]

Called upon to critique Munford's book for the *American Historical Review*, Dodd was offended by the volume. "I could not find it in my heart to pronounce it valuable," he wrote a colleague, because the author "never once touched the core of the subject." To go to the "eve of the Civil War contending that nobody of influence and power in the Old Dominion favored slavery," read the review, "shows a lack of knowledge . . . disparaging to the author's claims. Yet this is just what Mr. Munford attempts to do." Unfairly selective in its presentation of the topic, the work was clearly deficient, with "many important facts and conditions . . . omitted entirely." Never once, for example, did Munford respond to the accusation that Virginia was a slave-breeding state, a charge supported by "Governor William B. Giles's published statement (in . . . 1829) that 6000 slaves were exported from Richmond and Norfork each year" and by the "effective propaganda of Thomas R. Dew . . . in defense of raising negroes for the Lower South." The book, Dodd summarized, "is too much of a defense to be final or convincing."[61]

Stung by the harsh denunciation, Munford wrote Dodd accusing him of overreacting, and he enclosed a circular with endorsements of the book by leading southern spokesmen. The work was indeed popular with the aristocratic establishment. Virginia's senate passed a resolution expressing its sincere thanks to "the Hon. Beverley B. Munford" for "fairly representing Virginia in the light of history," and the state board of education promptly mandated the book as required reading for high-school students. Tested over the material contained in the book, one enlightened youth proudly essayed: "I have been firmly convinced of the right of the Southern States . . . and feel that I can now break down the arguments of any Yankee on the subject of the American War of Secession."[62]

The use of history for aristocratic indoctrination infuriated Dodd, yet he intended to write his own account of the South as a rallying cry toward establishing a new social order, one congenial to his concept of common-man democracy. "No son of an abolitionist or a 'true Southerner' is entitled to do more in the writing of history than to protest," he explained to a potential publisher. But Dodd believed he could write the truth about the South, telling "the story as it will be told one thousand years hence." It would be a massive undertaking, chronicling the South's evolution from Jeffersonian democracy in 1800 to planter ascendancy in the 1830s and "finally to war on behalf of the vested interests."[63]

Envisioning a multivolume work, Dodd devoted considerable energy to research. He traveled often to southern archives and private collections in 1909, 1912, and 1913 and frequently sortied from his Virginia farm to the Library of Congress. Putting his discoveries to good use, he discussed them in his seminars, presented them in public lectures, and published them as preliminary findings.[64] His major writings included *Statesmen of the Old South; or from Radicalism to Conservative Revolt* (1911), *Expansion and Conflict* (1915), and *The Cotton Kingdom* (1919). These, along with specialized journal articles, were designed as precursors to a larger work scheduled for completion in the 1920s. Taken together, they mirrored his yeoman perception of class conflict, the vision of southern society as a constant struggle between the liberty-loving masses and the privileged few.

Dodd painted the antebellum epoch in broad strokes, a portrait of the poor, the small farmer, and the laborer yearning for democracy yet always frustrated by slave-rich aristocrats. For one felicitous moment Thomas Jefferson championed the common man's cause, but southern elites soon undermined his enlightened egalitarianism. Dodd affirmed sadly that by 1860 the "party of Jefferson had been transformed from an organization of small farmers and backwoods men, idealists in governmental theory, [and] believers in the Declaration of Independence" to a party "dominated by the 'interests,' . . . whose dealers enjoyed special privileges in the state and who could wield the whole weight of Southern public opinion and power in Washington without losing the support of the loyal masses at home."[65]

Dodd traced such themes in the period immediately prior to the Civil War. His Old South was marked by overbearing planters whose power rested upon wealth, education, and elitist ideology, by northern industrialists who shared the planters' goals, and by farmers and laborers who resided in the shadow of their affluent neighbors. Little wonder, Dodd reflected, that "successful men of all callings get to thinking the Declaration of Independence is only a glittering fallacy—that all men are not equal, and readily defend the appearance of cast in our life."[66]

In Dodd's view, the planters' self-assurance rested upon solid foundation. In the Old South a favored few savored society's greatest benefits, a "dangerous tendency" of concentration of wealth in aristocratic hands. He calculated that in 1860 the South's thousand wealthiest families possessed almost as much income as did all of its remaining white population. Looking at this gross maldistribution through the eyes of hard-toiling yeomen, Dodd condemned the planters' opulent lifestyle, disparaged their disinclination "to labor with one's own hands," and denounced the "younger members of the family [who] took pride in their immunity from the work that is the lot of most men." Freed from daily toil, the "favored class" grasped the reins of government, enacted laws harmonious with their goals, and educated their sons to follow that pattern. Dodd held that it "was plain that democracy could not exist in the presence of great fortunes in slaves and land, and the owners of these recognized the truth. . . . They only needed a great teacher or group of teachers to make the . . . faith of social articulation popular."[67]

The first professional historian to describe the intellectual rationale for a southern aristocracy, Dodd believed that as long as Jefferson lived no one possessed sufficient intellect or reputation to challenge his democratic philosophy. But almost immediately following Jefferson's death more pedestrian and patrician thinkers advanced new theories. The William and Mary professor Thomas R. Dew, the South Carolina jurist William

Harper, and the Virginia attorney and amateur sociologist George Fitzhugh had argued for a natural inequality of mankind, and their collective thoughts comforted the South's master class. Walter Scott's popular novels romanticizing Scotland's chivalrous age of knighthood complemented their essays. Dodd believed that the South's upper-class families easily identified with "Scott's gentle folk [who] talked and acted in lofty fashion, while his poorer and ill-placed people were rough and brutal, without refined feelings and half ready to accept as their just portion the kicks and cuffs of their betters." Scott's "incurable snobbery," Dodd reflected, "worked upon the southern psychology." Before the Civil War "the older Jeffersonian idea was totally abandoned, and the contrary idea of the inequality of man had been adopted."[68]

Dodd considered antebellum southern churches handmaidens of slavery and aristocracy, and he especially scored the "Presbyterians and Episcopalians [because they] had become so completely reconciled to the aristocratic life which slavery connoted." A planter made "a good Presbyterian," Dodd reasoned, "but a 'cracker' or a 'red neck' found the Princeton faith too drastic. . . . Presbyterianism, moreover, grew more aristocratic as its members became more wealthy and better educated." Although the more emotional Methodists and Baptists took on "the larger work of saving souls," they nonetheless mixed their concern for the common folk with a defense of slavery. In the end, Dodd explained, "even the masses of poorer people and church members became defenders of the existing regime."[69]

According to Dodd, nerved by wealth and intellectual arrogance, the southern planters set out to control the entire continent. Whereas a "democracy imbued with notions of equality, universal suffrage and free discussion" checked the ambitions of northern politicians, southern leaders almost always emerged from a "compact minority" of their wealthy peers and were largely unaccountable to the people's rule. Free to pursue the planters' narrow interests, southern "statesmen and diplomats" planned an "imperial republic" that would stretch slaveholders' power from Virginia to California and perhaps beyond.[70]

Dodd discerned in that quest a natural alliance between the southern patrician and a northern elite of wealthy bankers and textile magnates. The latter benefited from cotton manufacturing, maintained a lifestyle similar to that of the slave-rich aristocrats, and often intermarried with the southern dominant class. "Wealthy young men of the East went to

the homes of the planters for their wives, and ambitious young slave holders in the cotton belt married in Philadelphia, New York, and Boston. . . .
Every such union added to the power . . . of the cotton planters."[71]

The South's "inarticulate masses," on the other hand, "lived on the
poorer lands of the cotton belt, on the hills that border the lower reaches
of the Appalachian Mountains or on the sandy ridges of Louisiana and
Texas." These "plain, poor folk . . . made the bone and sinew of the lower
South" and "knew nothing of the gentle ways of Charleston or of the
French manners of New Orleans." Dodd praised the mountain yeomen,
isolated from the planters' culture. "To them the Declaration of Independence was a reality, and Thomas Jefferson the greatest man of all history
save one. . . . They did not like the great planters; and their leaders . . .
were often courageous opponents of the plantation system." Other small
farmers, he believed, lived adjacent to the planters and "were not all together contented; but were far from dangerous" to the aristocrats. These
yeomen sold their scant surpluses—"a bale of cotton, a little fresh beef
or pork, poultry, and eggs"—to the wealthy, agreed with slaveholders'
racial philosophy, and were often deceived by the aristocrats' democratic
pretensions. "The plantation owners were in full command," Dodd
charged, "and the older and small-farmer element [fell] into line behind
their pro-slavery leaders."[72]

Focused on the essential conflict between southern elite and nonelite
whites, Dodd hardly articulated his feelings toward black Southerners. To
be sure, he condemned slavery, seeing it as one element of the aristocracy's
callous exploitation of their fellow human beings even as he classed the
struggle of African Americans alongside that of the white underclass. But
while contemporary southern men of letters, most notably Thomas Nelson Page, Thomas Ryan Dixon, and John Trotwood Moore, engaged in
virulent anti-Negro rhetoric and historians trained in the Dunning school
openly based their writings upon the assumption of Negro rascality, Dodd
remained silent on the issue of contemporary race relations, never voicing
his opinions on the social and intellectual abilities of Americans of African descent. At best Dodd was ambivalent on the issue of race, unable to
adequately determine the place of African Americans in his intellectual
paradigm. When Dodd became chair of the University of Chicago history
department in 1927, he had to work closely with the Rockefeller family,
whose trusts not only financed the university but also took a special interest in Carter G. Woodson's Association for the Study of Negro Life and

History. Dodd reluctantly allowed himself to be named to the association's executive council, but he assiduously avoided council meetings and basically served the organization by using his influence with trust representatives and his prestige as a historian to secure Rockefeller funding.[73]

In Dodd's view, the white masses of the modern South remained as ignorant of their plight as their antebellum ancestors had been. He wished to collect his thoughts into a single enlightening work that would inform these people of their lost heritage of democracy and empower them to overthrow their aristocratic oppressors. Even as he plotted out his historical ideas and planned his magnum opus Dodd plunged directly into the arena of reform. Politics had always tempted him. He had never craved elective office, but he had dreamed of being the ultimate insider, the intellectual adviser to a great democratic leader. This thirst became his continual snare, diverting him from his purely academic pursuits.[74]

Neither the reflective life of the scholar nor the settled routine of a Virginia farmer soothed Dodd's restless spirit completely. The rage of a reformer suffused him with a crusading zeal to vanquish the masses' great oppressors. Encompassed by iniquitous congeries of southern aristocrats, Prussian Junkers, and Yankee industrialists, Dodd hungered for a modern messiah, a democratic chieftain worthy of an idealized Thomas Jefferson. "My Jefferson," he explained to one of his closest friends, "is a semi-populist back country leader who fights the oligarchy of the eastern counties of Virginia."[75]

Unaffectedly assessing his own limited abilities, Dodd longed to play a supporting role, to become both apostle and adviser. He could offer his wisdom as a scholar to guide his idol's path and employ his talents as a teacher to spread his leader's gospel. One of Dodd's colleagues recognized the "two forces at war in Dodd's personality. The one led him to scholarship; the other made him wish for an active part in public affairs." Dodd keenly felt this dichotomy that pulled him toward politics and away from "my real task in life which is history"; and yet, "what will history be worth if we lose our democratic and idealistic life!"[76]

Even after Dodd moved to Chicago in 1909 he intently followed Virginia politics, and nursed an abiding distaste for Thomas S. Martin's political machine, still bitterly resentful of its intrusion into his career at Randolph-Macon. Dodd looked upon his appointment at Chicago as an academic safe haven, immune to attacks from Martin's minions. From there he launched the occasional rhetorical raid to bolster Old Dominion reformers in their crusades to unseat the villainous senator.[77]

Dodd supported William Atkinson Jones's challenge to Martin in the Democratic primary of 1911. A congressman from Virginia's Northern Neck, the narrow region between the Potomac and Rappahannock Rivers, Jones had much in common with Dodd's friend Andrew Jackson Montague. Both were members of Virginia first families, both despised Martin's blatant corruption, and both advocated moderate progressive reforms, especially the primary system as a means of fighting the senator's political network. Montague nevertheless backed Jones's candidacy only lukewarmly. Although Montague remained bitter about his defeat by Martin six years earlier, he resented Jones as a rival for leadership of the state's independent Democrats. Following his pro forma endorsement of Jones, Montague pled work and family obligations and subsequently refused to play a major role in the campaign.[78]

Dodd could not condone Montague's inaction. Caught up in his idolization of Thomas Jefferson, Dodd had endowed both Montague and Jones with Jeffersonian attributes that they did not possess. He was gradually disillusioned. Shortly after an April visit to Richmond, Dodd confided to Montague that "I have often wondered in my heart whether your friends and the 'common man' in Virginia can ever get together." Democracy, "faith in the farmer and the mechanic and the clerk, the negro even," should undergird true reform, said Dodd, who lamented that the "trouble with the men who are fighting the machine is that they want office" more than they crave justice.[79]

Disappointed in Montague, Dodd offered his assistance to the Jones campaign. He proposed to speak on the candidate's behalf, suggesting a July or August address in the Hanover area. Desperate for supporters in an uneven contest with Martin and impressed with the dignity of a University of Chicago professor, Jones's campaign manager contracted for a Fourth of July speech in Atlee, a small community just south of Ashland.[80] This was but one mistake in a contest replete with blunders.

Jones never seriously threatened Martin, whose well-oiled machine mounted a phalanx of Virginia officeholders, massive financial support from out-of-state railway entrepreneurs, and the endorsement of every major newspaper in the state. The conservative senator easily branded his mildly reformist opponent as a radical and looked forward complacently to victory in the September election.[81] Ironically, far from upsetting the

Martin bandwagon, Dodd's ill-advised speech at Atlee played to the senator's strategy.

Dodd prepared a muckraking address in the well-ordered style of a university lecture. He posited the pandering of prominent southern politicians to corrupt Wall Street interests, deeming Martin chief among sinners. "Captains of Industry," he proclaimed, controlled "our national administration and our Federal courts" and "have made alliances with our party machines . . . to carry elections against decent citizenship. . . . Thus the decent and self-respecting citizens, the owners of small properties, the cultivator[s] of the soil, [have] no voice in taxation, no representation in legislatures, State or national." The South suffered under the burden of these sinister, self-seeking politicians, among them one North Carolina senator who was "the tool of the American Lumber Company." Virginia was particularly accursed. Senator Martin, Dodd charged, was little more than the lackey of "Thomas F. Ryan, one of the worst of the Wall Street gang," a New York millionaire with "more power in Virginia . . . than any Governor. . . . He intimidates your legislators, he subsidizes your party organization."[82]

Dodd's indictment of the alleged Martin-Ryan partnership reflected accusations made by Jones in his campaign of 1911 and by Montague in his race six years earlier. But as a historian accustomed to finding grand linkages in society, Dodd expanded his indictments to include the subversion of Virginia's newspapers by northern industrialists. Martin, Ryan, and a host of other millionaires had made a once "free and independent press" their personal propaganda agency. "When you read in your morning paper an editorial," Dodd warned, "don't deceive yourself into thinking it expresses the view of able, honest publicists who have your interest and the common good at heart. Far from it." The editors served the lumber barons of Chicago, "the tobacco brigands of New York, or [J. P.] Morgan," the banker who robbed the southern public in numerous railroad scandals. "I know good and able men in Virginia," he asserted, "who have been belittled and maligned by these conscienceless organs of Wall street; and I think Bismarck's term 'reptile press' fully applies to such papers." He particularly excoriated the state's largest journal, the *Richmond Times-Dispatch,* for becoming a shameless "advocate of the 'interests' as against the people." Its owners had financially tied themselves to Ryan's Equitable Life Insurance Company, and since that moment "the Times-Dispatch [had] not been a Democratic, but a plutocratic, organ." Ignore the biased press, rise above Martin and his suzerain Ryan, and support Jones, Dodd urged his listeners. Then you will "not only put out a bad man, but you will give the nation a good man and able leader for the trying times ahead of us."[83]

Livid, the *Times-Dispatch* led Virginia's newspapers in blasting Dodd for the "reptile press" slur. Pro-Martin politicians gleefully tied the Chicago professor to the Jones campaign; the president of Washington and Lee University spoke for the state's academic community in condemning Dodd's insult to Virginia's journalistic integrity; and the state press association passed a resolution damning Dodd as a slanderer. When the furor refused to die, Jones's campaign manager sent Dodd a tactful note agreeing with his assessments of both Martin and the state press but pleading with him to refrain from responding to his attackers. "While most of our friends agree that you are right in your facts and in your position, there are some who differ as to whether [your attacks] will be beneficial to our cause, and . . . others who think it would be unwise to wound the [Richmond] News Leader and cause it to close its columns to our propaganda." Dated 22 July, the letter was misplaced in the Jones headquarters and did not reach Dodd until late August. It hardly mattered. In the September balloting Martin walloped Jones, winning with 65,317 votes to Jones's 31,428.[84]

Chastised by his defeat but secure in his own congressional district, Jones returned quietly to Washington, where as chairman of the House Insular Affairs Committee he spoke out for Philippine independence but exercised little influence over Virginia matters; and in 1912 Montague also forsook statewide politics, as well as his posture as a reformer, to acquire a safe congressional seat.[85] For Dodd the campaign of 1911 was a shattering experience. Accustomed to the gentlemanly banter of his academic peers and the fond adulation of his graduate students, he was ill prepared for the unbridled calumny on the hustings. His friendship with Montague had also soured. The former governor could not countenance Dodd's support of Jones, nor could Dodd forgive Montague's failure to campaign for reform.

This estrangement ended the professor's hopes of influencing Virginia politics, and with no real connections to, or, for that matter, great interest in, Illinois affairs, he turned to his academic writings, the struggles within the AHA, and the development of his newly purchased farm. When Dodd's political aspirations flared anew five years later, his playing field would expand significantly, from the narrow boundaries of a single state or even the South as a whole to those of the nation and eventually the world.

The germ of this broader emphasis had surfaced in his ill-fated Fourth of July speech at Atlee, when he urged his listeners to consider the national ramification of Jones's campaign. Northern voters, he predicted, would combine with the solid South in 1912 to "put Woodrow Wilson in the White House"; if only the Virginia public would "send the right men to Washington," Wilson would lead them in a crusade to "make our country a place where all of us shall have equal chances to succeed in life."[86]

Dodd saw his prophecy fulfilled when Wilson was elected president in 1912. Ever the seeker, the plebeian scholar eagerly became a Wilson acolyte, shaping his icon in the image of Thomas Jefferson. Dodd viewed both as southern men of privilege converted to faith in common-man democracy. Even though he enthusiastically supported Wilson and in time became a confidant of the first southern-born chief executive since Reconstruction, during most of Wilson's first term the Chicago professor remained distant from the vortex of presidential power.

Wilson's birth and early years placed him in a social context far different from Dodd's and imbued him with personal characteristics fundamentally at variance with Dodd's perception of him. Born in Stanton, Virginia, in 1856, he inherited all the benefits of the South's patrician culture. His father, Joseph Ruggle Wilson, a Presbyterian minister ordained in Stubenville, Ohio, in 1849, adhered to a conservative theology tinged with a belief in the natural stratification of mankind. Such ideas made him a pleasing adornment to some of the South's finer pulpits. Shortly after Woodrow's birth, Joseph left Stanton for a prestigious calling in Augusta, Georgia, and later ministered to the spiritual needs of social elites in Columbia, South Carolina, and Wilmington, North Carolina. As Dodd later reflected, the Wilsons ingratiated themselves with the "best people" in the South's "sharply articulated" society. They mingled easily in a culture whose ruling "aristocracy, composed of planters of the countryside and the older merchants of the towns," held themselves "a class apart" from humble farmers and mechanics, while below all of these "the Negroes and poor whites quarrelled among themselves as to which group was entitled to precedence." The Wilsons readily adapted to the system and "became as good Southerners as if they had been to the manner born."[87]

Brilliant, studious, and devout, Woodrow Wilson matriculated at the finest schools. Graduating from Princeton in 1879, he earned a law degree from the University of Virginia two years later and briefly practiced in Atlanta, Georgia. Mundane litigation held little interest for him, however, and he soon entered The Johns Hopkins University intent on a career teaching history and political science. After receiving his doctoral degree in 1886, he taught briefly in Pennsylvania and Connecticut before receiving the offer of Princeton's chair of jurisprudence and political economy in 1890. As imperious as he was scholarly, Wilson held in contempt those wealthy students who cared nothing for academic achievement, trivializing their venerable school into an expensive and exclusive drinking club.[88]

Elevated to Princeton's presidency in 1902, he quickly gained national respect for his programs for enhancing the institution's academic integrity. His clash with its patrician eating clubs—Princeton's equivalent of fraternities—earned him an unmerited reputation as an egalitarian. Open exclusively to juniors and seniors, the clubs admitted about half of the upperclassmen into their luxurious accommodations through invitations extended on the basis of birth, wealth, and manners rather than intellectual acumen. Although the national media praised Wilson as a democrat crusading against aristocratic snobbery, his actual motives in opposing the clubs bore little relationship to social leveling. Wilson abhorred them for diverting students' focus away from the university and to activities that diminished learning in favor of social frivolity. He proposed their abolition and replacement with university-owned dinning halls, or "quadrangles," where faculty and all levels of students would commune as scholars and friends. Modeled on similar arrangements at England's Oxford and Cambridge, they would create a brotherhood of educated elites loyal to Princeton University.[89]

An autocrat by nature, Wilson consulted neither students, alumni, nor faculty before presenting his quadrangle proposal to Princeton's accommodating trustees. When he revealed the plan publicly as an accomplished fact in June 1907, he faced immediate rebellion from faculty who objected to his peremptory methods and from students and alumni who decried the loss of their exclusive institutions. Bowing to overwhelming constituent pressure, the trustees recanted in October and urged Wilson to find a face-saving compromise. But compromise proved alien to Wilson's constitution. Intransigent, he campaigned beyond the campus, seeking funds and support for his proposal. Although he assured the trustees that the controversy had little to do with democratic reformism, he soon found that the general public responded to his appeals best when he censured the undemocratic influences of wealth in higher education. Even though he lost the Princeton fight, Wilson gained a positive reputation that extended well beyond academic circles. He was perceived as an idealistic and progressive reformer who remained faithful to principle even in defeat.[90]

Wilson's public image overshadowed the fact that by 1910 he had ceased to be effective as Princeton's chief administrator. Impressed by his reputation, officials of New Jersey's Democratic Party saw his political potential and cultivated him as a fresh spirit for their otherwise moribund organization. That spring they inaugurated a movement to elevate him to the White House, and they furthered that goal by engineering his successful run for New Jersey's governorship. Bolstered by his reputation as an academic innovator, his prestige as New Jersey's chief executive, and his support for progressive reform, Wilson won the Democratic presidential nomination in 1912 and commenced his campaign against a profoundly divided Republican Party.[91]

Even though Dodd enthusiastically embraced Wilson's cause, he played only a minor role in the campaign of 1912. In 1904, when he was a little-known professor at Randolph-Macon, Dodd had briefly met the esteemed president of Princeton University, but he had no inkling of the future importance Wilson would have in his own career. Dodd's favorable impression of Wilson evolved largely through the influence of mutual acquaintances. When Frederick Jackson Turner invited Dodd to his home in 1908, the Wisconsin professor reminisced about his graduate student days with Wilson at Johns Hopkins and predicted great things from him; and when Dodd later visited his friend Josephus Daniels in Raleigh, he learned that the North Carolina editor not only had endorsed Wilson for New Jersey governor but also meant to support him for president in 1912. Dodd soon counted himself a Wilson stalwart. He "is the only wise choice," Dodd wrote in early 1911. "His radicalism just suits me," as does "his learning, though I do not count him a real historian."[92]

Wilson's public crusade against the Princeton eating clubs appealed to Dodd, who did not like the elitist privileges so evident in American higher education. "The college which does not keep in touch with the masses in a democracy," Dodd wrote privately in 1908, "can not hope to lead." Shortly thereafter he moved to Chicago, where he was chagrined to find

that the university faculty was overwhelmingly conservative by his standards and that its president, Harry P. Judson, seemed hopelessly reactionary. In a missive to the *Nation* magazine he charged that in the United
States "the great teachers, [and] the scientist, will generally be found on
the side of reaction, of restraint, [and] of privilege." Little else could be
expected from an educational system in which the "wealthy and the privileged classes identify themselves with the university life—not as professors, but as trustees or benefactors, both of State and privately endowed
institutions—and . . . assume the position of authority which in mon-
archies of the older kind is occupied by the court or its hangers on." In
Germany, Dodd explained, "the university asserts its position as against
both court and aristocracy; in Italy, it is the seed plot of Socialism," but
in the United States and England "the universities have always been hostile to reforms and nearly always friendly to the court." Dodd urged
higher education to cease its opposition to democracy and respond positively to the "aspirations of the masses, who, in the final analysis pay
the bills."[93]

Aware of Dodd's views, Wilson courted the professor's support in his
struggles at Princeton. "It is delightful to find how much sympathy exists
for my somewhat lonely fight here," wrote the beleaguered Princeton
president. "It is a hard fight, a long fight, and a doubtful fight, but I think
I shall at least have done the good of precipitating a serious consideration
of matters . . . fundamental to the whole life and success of our colleges."
Dodd cherished this letter, seeing in Wilson two attributes that he much
admired: a commitment to academic excellence and a disinclination to
waste it upon the unappreciative wealthy. Looking back upon Wilson's
eating-club controversy a decade later, Dodd reflected that it was "not
surprising that Princeton resisted the reforms which President Wilson
pressed upon her nor that other universities viewed askance the plan of
democratizing college life. The sons of rich men have almost always resisted the persuasions of their teachers to enter upon the toilsome road
that leads to learning."[94]

Because of the superficial similarities between Wilson's views on higher
education and his own and because of the trust in Wilson expressed by
Dodd's friends, the idealistic Chicago professor overlooked Wilson's affinity for the English university system, with its aristocratic features, and
cherished thoughts of playing a significant role in the crusade of 1912.
Dodd had envisioned his activities in the Jones campaign as preliminary

to more important participation in Wilson's presidential bid. But the debacle following his Atlee address, Jones's overwhelming defeat, and his estrangement from Montague had combined to sour Dodd on politics, leaving little emotional energy left for the events of 1912. He delivered a single address before the University of Chicago's Wilson club, for which he received a letter of appreciation from the candidate, and he may have engaged in a few other similar activities, but on the whole he watched the campaign from university cloisters.[95]

Shortly after Wilson's election political realities clashed with Dodd's view of social responsibility, further diminishing his confidence in the president-elect. Chicago newspapers spread the rumor that the Virginia nabob Thomas Nelson Page would soon become ambassador to Great Britain. Appalled, Dodd complained to Josephus Daniels, imploring his old associate to block the nomination. Page's appointment, he lectured, "would please every son of Virginia and the old South," the patrician elite that had long fought democracy in the state. An enemy of reform, Dodd explained, Page was also "a strong 'onhanger' of Thomas S. Martin." Dodd predicted that if the president-elect made this move in an effort to win "popularity with certain old families," he would be putting a "real enemy" of his cause "in [an] official station." The rumors proved only partially correct. North Carolinian Walter Hines Page received the posting to London, and Thomas Nelson Page presented his credentials in Italy.[96] Even so, Dodd interpreted these and similar events as political concessions to the enemy.

Unable to cope with pragmatic politics, Dodd initially made little effort to cultivate influence within the Wilson administration. When his friend Daniels entered the cabinet as secretary of the navy, he refrained from asking any governmental favors, save advice about which Washington hotels might purchase milk from farmer Dodd. "Woodrow Wilson represents my almost perfect public leader, but his trying time is just beginning," he commented in December 1912.[97] For the moment at least, Dodd chose to step back from the new administration, reserving judgment on its fidelity to democratic reforms, and concentrate on more personal concerns.

In August 1914 German armies bludgeoned neutral Belgium and fought the French and British forces to a stalemate, initiating a conflagration that would eventually draw the United States into its vortex. However ambiguous the causes of the conflict, Dodd immediately blamed Germany. He recalled with distaste the Teutonic chauvinism of his Leipzig teachers, their beer-table predictions of an invasion through neutral countries, and the martial pomp of peacetime Berlin. "Germany is the enemy of mankind in this war," he raged in a letter to Mattie. "I am almost ashamed that I have my doctorate from such a people."[98]

In Dodd's mind, German aggression reflected the will of Germany's aristocratic class, the Prussian Junkers. "The German people are deluded," he reasoned. They follow their leaders into a war that was but "another blow to the poor everywhere and a means of fixing the yoke of helplessness upon the necks of mankind." Dodd discerned a pattern, freely associating the Junkers with antebellum southern planters and imperialistic business elites in his own era. Admitting that the southern aristocrats were marginally less warlike than their Prussian counterparts, Dodd nonetheless held that in the 1850s "the South came to adopt a social philosophy wonderfully like that of Germany."[99]

Dodd looked on with horror as the swirl of European war excited the American public. He feared that American business elites might seize the moment to shape a permanent military caste dedicated to their imperialistic policies. In early January 1915 such apprehensions stirred Dodd to lecture his friend the secretary of the navy. He urged Daniels to stand against the rush to build greater armadas. The United States must adhere to its "legacy of . . . idealism" and remain faithful to the founding fathers' distrust of a permanent military. With the exceptions of "sins against the Philippines and Mexico," the American people had "stood for a hundred years for peace . . . claiming that if we do not menace other peoples [then] other peoples will not go to war with us." If the United States steered clear of the paths of the "militaristic nations," Dodd predicted, "at the end of the holocaust of murder our influence will count in just proportion to our faithfulness of American ideals."[100]

Dodd soon shared with Wilson's former secretary of state, William Jennings Bryan, his fears concerning the developing alliance between American business elites and the military establishment. Confessing his long admiration for the "Great Commoner," Dodd noted his deep regret that Bryan had been defeated in 1896 because a Democratic Party victory in that crucial campaign would have saved the country "from the clutches of powerful interests which seek to destroy all that is worth while in our national life." Nonetheless, as secretary of state Bryan had maintained the hopes of peace within the Wilson administration. For that reason, Dodd explained, "I was doubly distressed when you found it necessary to leave Mr. Wilson's cabinet. . . . Wilson's mistake consists of yielding to the militaristic forces of our time."[101]

These missives of concern mirrored Dodd's agitation in his personal crusade to counter Major General Leonard Wood's preparedness campaign. In December 1915 Wood, long recognized as one of the army's more militant expansionists, angered Dodd by his visit to the University of Chicago, in which he advocated the creation of a military department that would enroll the university's best students in a professional officers' corps. With the European war adding urgency to these efforts, President Judson endorsed Wood's program and outlined it before the May faculty assembly, only to meet fierce opposition from his professors. Angered, Judson tabled the proposal but thereafter singled out the opponents of the plan, among them Dodd, for special scorn.[102]

Dodd's stand for principle was augmented by his intense disdain for Wood. In his view, the general "personifie[d] the spirit of Prussianism"; his goals went far beyond the crisis of the moment: he aimed to create "the beginnings of a system which [would] give our great commercial and industrial leaders an instrument, a weapon, for future use." Born into comfortable New England stock with *Mayflower* roots, Wood boasted of his Anglo-Saxon purity. By tradition his male grandsires had gravitated to careers in medicine or the military, and Wood combined both by first graduating from the Harvard Medical School in 1885 and then joining the United States Army in 1886. Early recognized for his administrative genius, he rose rapidly in rank, and at the conclusion of the Spanish-American War was made military governor of Cuba. There, in the words of an admiring biographer, he "became, in fact, if not in name, a monarch." He "built . . . and repaired all the civil institutions of the island . . . the courts, the customs and postal system, [and] the electoral system." In 1903 he transferred to the Philippines, where he ruthlessly imposed American rule over the Moro tribesmen. When he visited the University of Chicago Wood was posturing in hopes of a presidential bid in 1920.[103] Dodd feared that he and Judson and their allies in the business community would eventually wear down opposition to the military department. The professor sought an audience with President Wilson, hoping the Commander in Chief would rein in his autocratic general.

Dodd's White House visit on 23 August 1916 profoundly altered his

life. Frankly disappointed "with President Wilson's policy in war and military matters," he requested a ten-minute appointment to present the University of Chicago faculty's protest against Wood and the military department. The audience lasted well beyond the time scheduled, and charmed
by Wilson, Dodd succumbed to the spell of the Oval Office. To be sure,
he had met Theodore Roosevelt in the same room nine years before, but
he found Wilson's style far more alluring. Roosevelt, Dodd remembered,
had garishly decorated the walls with a huge portrait of Abraham Lincoln
and "the antlers of a great deer," monuments to his Republican heritage
and his overweening virility. Wilson kept his walls bare. Similarly frugal
in his own habits, Dodd pronounced his pleasure at the president's "Presbyterian austerity" and judged this arrangement much more fitting for a
great leader, who must put his supplicants at ease.[104]

Wilson assured Dodd that he too distrusted Wood, that he had taken
steps to limit his influence, and that at the first opportunity he would
force his resignation. "From this conversation which was frank and sincere," Dodd recorded in his diary, "I was confirmed in my former view
that Wilson is really the chief of pacifists seeking to work out pacifist ends
with the men and materials at his commands—He is a politician and
statesman combined—as were his masters Jefferson and Lincoln." Dodd
had found his idol, a national leader molded in the Jeffersonian image.
"I have no doubt of his democracy," he rejoiced, "an aristocratic democrat
if that be possible."[105]

In the months following Dodd's August visit to the White House he
supported Wilson's reelection with much greater fervor than he had manifested four years earlier. "I believe Mr. Wilson far and away the greatest
of all our present day leaders," he wrote to the editor of the *New York
Evening Post*; "ten years from now I expect he will be called great." On
Monday, 6 November, Dodd privately reflected that "tomorrow we shall
see whether the people have the judgment to decide their own interests."
The Republican nominee, Charles Evans Hughes, "stands for reactionary
and tory ideals in politics and society, Wilson for progress and democracy." Hours later he and Mattie breakfasted and then strolled two blocks
to the polling booth. Having voted for the Wilson-Marshall ticket, they
spent a long, tense day that ended at midnight with the Dodds' being
depressed by the thought of Wilson's defeat. But the morning newspapers
held a glimmer of hope: the contest remained in the balance; and the
afternoon journals broadcast a Wilson victory in California, his second

term assured. Released from his anxiety, Dodd took comfort in Mattie's conclusion that "the prayers of the righteous Democrats had brought their answer overnight."[106]

After 1916 Woodrow Wilson overmastered Dodd's life. The historian cultivated Wilson's friendship, sought to influence his policies, authored a eulogistic biography, and following the president's death became an apostle of the Wilsonian message preaching, its doctrines across the United States. Through it all, this son of a North Carolina yeoman who had been trained in the careful methods of a scientific historian lost his objectivity. Just two years before he had criticized Leipzig scholar Enrich Marcks for allowing his Teutonic chauvinism to overwhelm his historical judgments: "A noble man is Marcks, only passionate . . . and a passionate man *sometimes* fails to be a historian and attains the rank of a pamphleteer."[107] Caught up in the Wilson mystique, Dodd did the same. In the years ahead he would dedicate his skills to advancing liberal Democratic causes.

CHAPTER FOUR

A *Wilsonian Scholar*
in the Republican Interlude

William Edward Dodd talked with his dying friend Woodrow Wilson for the last time in late 1923. Both Wilson and Dodd were southern-bred intellectuals who had spent their academic careers in the North, both were vocal advocates of American democracy, and both were deeply bitter about the failure of Wilson's international initiatives. Dodd recalled that when Wilson spoke of the 1919 Versailles conference the former president became agitated, salting his discourse with "some very unChristian damns and God damns, [and] some terrible word lashings of both men and women high in French life." Former British Prime Minister David Lloyd George had recently called on him, Wilson told Dodd with an oath. "Well, I told him: 'I hope the Germans will get them a good leader and beat hell out of the French.'"[1] Neither Wilson nor Dodd could have imagined the upshot of this malediction, but exactly ten years later United States Ambassador Dodd presented his credentials to that hoped-for chieftain, Adolf Hitler.

The president's passing on 3 February 1924 profoundly distressed Dodd. "Wilson's death nearly killed him," wrote a graduate student who was then courting young Martha. "He went to bed ill and it was all the family could do to keep him from having a complete breakdown." In the seven years following their initial White House meeting the professor and the president had drawn close. Dodd venerated Wilson and longed to perpetuate his goals as well as his memory. Although he had played only a small role in the great scheme of the Wilson administration, Dodd had been a frequent and welcome visitor to the executive mansion, had ingratiated himself with the Wilson family, and, benefiting from his insider's knowledge, had written a best-selling but controversial biography of the president. Stung by contemporary negative assessments of Wilson and infuriated by unfavorable reviews of his book, Dodd lashed out, taking to the lecture circuit to defend the Wilson record. "Never before in my life have I felt compelled to read such lectures," Dodd boasted to a friend in 1920, and to another he revealed his frustration at being unable "to accept half the invitations" to expound upon the themes of the biography.[2]

During the decade of Republican ascendancy Dodd became thoroughly identified with the Wilsonian legacy. He was encouraged by a small circle of friends who shared with him both a reverence for Wilson and a southern orientation. The professor formed a friendship with Colonel Edward M. House and also found common cause with his North Carolina friend Josephus Daniels as well as with the South Carolina–born attorney and political activist Daniel C. Roper and the Indiana journalist and popular historian Claude Bowers, whose books strongly sympathized with the South's interpretation of its own past. This circle shared the goal of electing a chief executive worthy of their hero. "The next Democratic president," Dodd reflected in 1923, "must connect with Wilson groups everywhere; . . . he must rely upon ideas, as Wilson did; and he must have united party support."[3] Eventually they found their champion in Franklin Delano Roosevelt, and all participated in the conduct of his international affairs.

Dodd's path to Berlin began when he became fascinated with Colonel House, months prior to his first interview with President Wilson on 23 August 1916. The chief executive's intimate friend and political adviser, House was the scion of a wealthy Texas banking and plantation family and used inherited wealth to indulge his passion for politics. Although he was a powerful behind-the-scenes figure in the administrations of four Texas governors, he suffered from the oppressive heat and humidity of his native Houston and for relief established a seasonal residence in New York City, which eventually became his principal home. In 1904 and 1908 presidential candidates Alton B. Parker and William Jennings Bryan invited House to participate in national politics, but he refused, sensing the futility of their campaigns. Governor Woodrow Wilson courted this influential figure in 1911, convinced him of his commitment to reform and his potential for victory, and established a political friendship unique in the American chronicle. Following Wilson's election House declined several government appointments, preferring instead the role of informal adviser. Wilson sought and honored his views on key appointments, and with world war imminent, he employed the Texan on sensitive but unofficial international missions. By 1916 this quiet, self-effacing counselor to Texas governors and an American president had become a somewhat mysterious figure, recognized as a major player in the Wilson administration.[4]

House was the man Dodd longed to be, the consummate insider largely removed from public view but dedicated to guiding the chief executive toward democratic reform. After reading journalist Herbert H. Childers's article "A Friend's View of Colonel House," Dodd immediately wrote the author that House's "ideas . . . and practices all appeal to me as an exceedingly good thing to do. . . . If we could have a few more men of his calibre and will to serve the public, our country might yet become the home of democracy." Dodd craved to be counted among such men, and to that end he cultivated House's acquaintance. He wrote to House inviting him to visit either his Chicago home or his country retreat in the Virginia foothills. House in turn encouraged the scholar to dine with him at his New York apartment or to join him in a Washington meal when the two were next in the nation's capital.[5] Although they would not actually meet until the following year, this was the genesis of a firm alliance cemented by their mutual admiration of Woodrow Wilson.

The cataclysmic European events that brought House before the public eye also shaped Dodd's relationship with Wilson. Although Dodd lacked House's economic independence and leisure to devote his full time to politics, he possessed considerable prestige as a historian and University of Chicago professor, attributes Wilson hoped to employ in his quest to be honored in time's annals. Taking little comfort from Wilson's promise to him that he would resist militarism, Dodd watched uneasily as the United States coursed toward conflict.[6]

The American government moved steadily toward war in the early months of 1917, and Dodd was torn between his desire for the defeat of the Prussian ruling class and his fears that war would devastate democracy at home. "Germany was the one ruthless autocracy in Europe in 1914," he wrote in his diary. "She is autocratic still. . . . If she loses she must become democratic." But at the same time a warring and victorious United States would risk its own cherished liberties. "A war party in this

country is always anti-democratic," he reasoned. "To go into war to maintain democracy or a measure of it in Europe and risk its loss in this country is a hard choice—but there is no other."[7]

On 2 April 1917 Wilson urged intervention in Europe, and Congress
concurred four days later. In the interim Dodd shared with Secretary of
the Navy Daniels his complete "accord with the position of the Administration. From the beginning I have thought Germany the enemy of the
whole world and we should certainly have to contend with her some day
if she emerged victorious." Nonetheless, he warned that if America was
to succeed, Wilson and the forces of democracy would have to ally with
antidemocratic industrial elites and their minions in the Republican Party.
"Do not mistake the support of Republicans," he lectured. "They are patriotic, but they are constitutionally Junkers. . . . Death is the only cure
for their disease."[8]

As Dodd had feared, the war effort severely restricted free speech and
other democratic activities, but it was the Wilson administration, and not
Dodd's much-feared industrial elites, that assaulted First Amendment values. Confronted with clamoring antiwar elements—socialist unions, pacifists, German Americans loyal to the Fatherland, and Irish Americans
hostile to the English—Wilson turned to the Committee for Public Information, headed by George Creel, for a justification of belligerency. The
Creel Committee joined with state and local patriotic associations to promote the war effort, whip up national spirit, and sell war bonds; it also
suppressed dissent. Threatened by government-prompted violence and
discrimination, German Americans Anglicized their names, gave their
communities new, less ethnic names, and canceled cultural events. Antiwar labor unions were suppressed, and both secular and religious pacifist
publications were silenced. At war "to make the world safe for democracy," the nation quenched freedom at home.[9]

Dodd defended the Creel Committee, declaring that its objective was
"not so much to censor and issue orders to public speakers and writers
as to persuade and lead them to publish only such information as would
assist the government in its efforts to bring Germany to her knees." To be
sure, some "men were imprisoned for speaking too freely, and for giving
aid to the enemy, . . . and some periodicals were temporarily suppressed."
Such abuses, Dodd asserted, were not the fault of Wilson or Creel but the
overzealous actions of the Senate Judiciary Committee in response to a
perceived Bolshevik threat. "When the history of the war is finally writ-

ten," he believed, "the work of the Creel bureau will have a curious if honorable place in the record."[10]

Caught up in the Wilsonian rhetoric of democracy and the Creel Committee's bellicose chauvinism, Dodd showed no sympathy for dissenters, not even his University of Chicago colleague Karl Piestch. In December 1917 Piestch's son raged at his draft board for denying his exemption based on the premise that his relatives were fighting in the German army. The distraught youth lashed out, shouting that he would "stick a knife into the President if" he got the chance. For this sophomoric outburst he was arrested, his father was detained by the police, and his family was placed under surveillance. "Piestch is one of the greatest authorities on medieval Spain," Dodd reflected complacently in his diary, "but he is also a rabid German. . . . He has never made himself a part of our life and, I judge, he has never intended to be anything but . . . a sort of emigre saying his prayers facing the Fatherland. . . . Nothing helps a German quite so much as . . . the heavy arm of the law."[11]

Although Dodd strongly wished to serve the war effort and especially to shape the postwar order, he played at best a minor role in the formal structure of the Wilson administration. At House's urging, Dodd was invited to join the American Preparatory Commission, or Inquiry, whose task was to develop position papers for use in the anticipated peace negotiations. Assigned the topics of "the problem with American trade, the open door policy in the Far East, and the Monroe Doctrine," he stole moments from his autumn classes to write the Monroe Doctrine analysis and then secured a leave of absence from the university to pursue the other topics.[12]

Dodd's flaccid thirteen-page discussion of the Monroe Doctrine reflected on the one hand his democratic faith and on the other his myopic interpretation of Wilson's foreign policy. He hypothesized that in 1823 President James Monroe had issued his famous edict in order to protect South America's feeble republics from Europe's Holy Alliance of Russia, Prussia, Austria, and France, powers committed to the suppression of democracy in both Europe and America. Whatever Monroe's original intent, later American presidents employed the doctrine to reserve for the United States alone the right of imperial expansion in the hemisphere. The violent annexation of half of Mexico into the American Union and the occupation of various Western Hemisphere lands by Presidents McKinley, Roosevelt, and Taft made a mockery of American ideals. Ignoring the fact that Wilson had carried out more armed interventions in Latin America than had his three predecessors, Dodd proclaimed that his regime represented a sharp break from the past. "Certain arrangements were made with Nicaragua which made . . . that country a sort of protectorate of the United States," Dodd admitted, and "the refusal to recognize the usurpation [of power] of [Victoriano] Huerta led to a sort of intervention in Mexico; but Wilson managed in all these difficult matters to proceed . . . as to hold the good will of the Greater South American states." Supporting Wilson's affirmation that the principles of the Monroe Doctrine ought to apply to Europe, Dodd argued that all nations should formulate "a rule of conduct which shall become a law on both sides of the Atlantic, a rule of democracy whereby no nation shall encroach upon the rights and territory of another and whereby no annexation shall be made anywhere except upon a free vote of all the people concerned." [13]

Anxious to pursue his other assignments—Asian affairs and America's trading policies—Dodd left for Washington at the earliest possible moment, abandoning Mattie, his son William, and his daughter Martha to a lonely Christmas in Chicago. By early February he had discerned patterns in the United States' Far Eastern activities consistent with his canted view of American capitalism. "It is railroads, banks, mining concessions and utility corporations every where," he lectured House. "When one studies any phase of this great struggle, one always finds at the end of the job great economic interest, exploitation of some sort." [14]

At first committed to the Inquiry, Dodd gradually tired of this work; deeming his talents wasted on minor position papers, he left unfinished his essays on Asia and trade concessions. Unable to breach the formal structure of the president's administration, he employed his well-honed skills in a more informal way. He set out to write his hero's biography with the expressed prayer that "some misinformed people will come to a saner view of Woodrow Wilson and a more historical interest in the development of our country along liberal lines." [15] In the process, Dodd wandered across the boundary separating the scholar from the polemicist.

"Good biographers," Dodd had written in 1914, "should be hero worshippers." [16] True to this dictum, he canonized Wilson in a biography that not only marked him as one of the president's most fervent disciples but also altered his career, moving him into circles well beyond cloistered academia. Although Dodd clung desperately to his commitment to writing

southern history and to his quest to reconstruct the region's values, events
and opportunities awakened by the biography diverted his attention, placing him first on a national and then on an international stage. Through
it all, however, Dodd's perception of the class-ridden South colored his
approach to the broader world beyond his native land.

Dodd began his Wilson biography in the summer of 1917. For House
he laid out his plan not "to eulogize or criticize, but to analyze and understand" the president. Nonetheless, the professor also revealed his personal bias: "It is not empty praise to say that I regard Mr. Wilson as the
greatest man who has ever held the office of President. To understand and
evaluate him is to understand our time, a most critical time in world-
history." In his mind, he was writing "current history," articulating for his
own age the interpretations that "the historian must write later." [17]

Dodd was motivated not only by his admiration for Wilson and his
ideas but also by the North's negative assessment of the southern-born
president. "Never in my life," he lamented to a friend in 1919, "have I
seen so much sectional bitterness as I have seen in Chicago since Wilson
entered office." He complained to Frederick Jackson Turner that "New
England hates Wilson with a consuming hatred" and to a Chicago colleague that the "North is hostile to all our larger international duties, not
because its leaders are ignorant but because they hate and fear the South
and the best leaders it can give the country." Dodd earnestly hoped that
the "South would not resist, certainly would not pray for the President's
death as Republicans and Episcopalians do every night." [18]

The northern press—the *Philadelphia Ledger, Nation* magazine, and
the Macmillan publishing house—further enraged Dodd by rejecting his
Wilson manuscripts, judging them too favorable to their subject. The editor of the *Nation*, Oswald Garrison Villard, grandson of the abolitionist
William Lloyd Garrison, especially disappointed him. Long willing to
print Dodd's critical assessments of the South's aristocratic establishment,
Villard could not countenance his positive interpretation of Wilson. "I
fear," reflected the disappointed professor, that Villard, "who is a great
champion of free speech, . . . has allowed his feet to slip into . . . common clay." [19]

Even as Dodd stumbled in his quest to publish Wilson articles, he
wrote accounts of two contemporary political figures for the magazine
Public that both demonstrated his partisanship and hinted at the bias
of the forthcoming biography. Choosing Josephus Daniels and Theodore

Roosevelt as subjects, he judged each man by the standards of his class paradigm. No one "in the [Wilson] Administration has rendered the country better service than Daniels," he informed the journal's audience in June 1918. "A democrat of the Jefferson school," the secretary of the navy despised class divisions and lived by the dictum that "caste works injury." With this commitment Daniels launched his work in 1913 by attacking the navy's entrenched aristocrats, "who opposed democracy on principle." He then created a new agenda, one designed to give "all men a chance" according to their abilities. He established apprentice schools for common sailors, elevated hundreds of meritorious seamen to officer status, and altered the Naval Academy's admission policies to ensure that the "common herd" of Americans as well as the sons of the wealthy and influential could taste its offerings. "No future Secretary of the Navy will go back to the old rigid caste system," wrote a satisfied Dodd. With Daniels stoking the "spirit of the Wilson Administration," the American people could rest assured that the European crusade "would make both this country and Europe safe for democracy."[20]

In sharp contrast to his eulogistic essay about Daniels was Dodd's assessment of his former friend Theodore Roosevelt. Writing scant months after the ex-president's death, he found much to admire but in the end judged that he should not be called great. "There was something delightfully human about Roosevelt," Dodd began. "He loved his family; he preached devotion . . . to wife and children; he . . . loved to talk of the power of America; he wished everyone to hate a weakling, even when it was no fault of the weakling; he talked about the urgent need of fighting for the right and dying for the country." Roosevelt "was a sort of renaissance man, in love with the world and all that was in it." But Dodd questioned whether he "loved men, common men, dirty, ignorant, and prejudiced as common men are want to be?"[21]

In life Roosevelt was too much the overbearing patrician for Dodd's taste. At the popular president's death the praise heaped upon him by the elites in business, education, and journalism rankled the plebeian scholar. "When Jefferson went out of office," Dodd mused, "there was one loud chorus of attack and jeering from articulate men; when Jackson retired, Clay and Webster and Calhoun and John Quincy Adams breathed a sigh of relief," and while Lincoln suffered through the last year of the Civil War he endured Thaddeus Stevens's sarcasms. Through it all, however, these reviled presidents demonstrated a trust, even love, of the common man, and in return they were loved and adored by the masses. Driving home his lesson, Dodd editorialized that the "people who now shout in honor of Roosevelt are the men whose names appear in 'Who's Who' and who have credit in the bank," whereas the average American seemed little moved. If the working classes did not revere Roosevelt, "it will not be because writers have not shed ink enough, nor because orators have not shed tears enough. It will be because Roosevelt did not love common men." Little aware of how deeply his own partisanship was influencing his writing, Dodd did not resist a cutting interjection. Woodrow Wilson, he informed the readers of the *Public*, "represents what common men say."[22]

On leave from his academic duties for the winter quarter of 1918, Dodd returned to Chicago in March of that year, taught his spring classes, and then packed his family for a summer and fall residence on his Virginia farm. From there he frequently explored Washington archives, searched through the books in the Library of Congress, and interviewed senators, congressmen, and administration functionaries. Each visit stoked his anger, stinging him with the virulence of Wilson's enemies and steeling him even more to his self-assumed task of presenting the Wilson mission in its most favorable light.

At midmorning on 19 June the Dodds arrived at the Washington train station, ate a hasty breakfast, and then marched to the House of Representatives. Anxious to sample the legislators' opinions of Wilson, Dodd sought out his friend Virginia congressman Andrew Jackson Montague. He "did not talk to me two minutes," recorded the shocked professor, "before he commenced to attack President Wilson: The president was ambitious, he must rule everything, he wants a third term, he insists on retaining a weak cabinet and he gives nobody his confidence." Those moments chilled whatever warmth had once existed between the two men. Months later, considering such disappointing interviews, Dodd complained that senators and congressmen alike "hate the President, Democrats quite as cordially as Republicans." Montague "is of the same general attitude, . . . he is bitterly opposed to the President as any Republican."[23]

By late summer Dodd's research had progressed to the point where he thought it was time to seek an interview with the war-burdened Wilson. The president's personal secretary quickly responded: Wilson not only wished to share a luncheon but had set aside the entire afternoon of 13 September for the meeting. With his senses heightened by the generous time allotment, Dodd entered the same room where a decade earlier he had banqueted with Theodore Roosevelt and a few months before he had met Wilson and fallen under his spell. In 1907 Dodd had been an anxious neophyte warmed by the recognition of the nation's chief executive and the company of his eminent guests; by 1918 he was a mature scholar, comfortable in the presence of great men but unnerved by the magnitude of his purpose. As he waited for the president Dodd reflected once again on how the room had changed since Roosevelt's occupancy of the White House. Once cluttered with the dynamic Republican's ostentatious trophies, it now reflected the simple, more refined taste of the dignified Wilson. The alterations suited Dodd.[24]

The meal was an intimate affair, with only Mrs. Wilson and a close female friend joining the president and the professor. Wilson led them in polite conversation, establishing a relaxed and informal tone for the more significant exchange to follow. At the appropriate moment he suggested that he and Dodd retire to his private study, where a "remarkable conversation followed; the most remarkable series of earnest statements I ever expect to hear from a responsible leader of a great democracy."[25]

Wilson, appreciative of Dodd's ability to define his place in the historical firmament, skillfully guided his would-be biographer. In response, Dodd, long the champion of the common man's culture, slipped further into his worship of this august figure. Wilson "is a very great man," he wrote in his diary that evening. "His manner is aristocratic beyond comparison; the tone of this voice is beautiful above any that I have heard. If he were a demagogue, how could he stir men's souls—he can do it—only he stirs the souls of thoughtful men."[26]

Setting the agenda for the interview, Wilson stressed ideas and themes congenial to Dodd's historical paradigm. As the professor eagerly scribbled notes, the president cast himself as the champion of a Christian and democratic society threatened by demons both foreign and domestic. "I have given up trying to understand the Germans," he began. "The fact is they are not Christian to any great extent. . . . If they had been Christian they would be more democratic." In fact, Wilson affirmed, "I believe that Christianity and democracy with the little d . . . are the same. Men cannot be real Christians without being democratic." The United States, he continued, was filled with un-Christian, undemocratic elements every bit as dangerous as the Germans. The nation's "newspapers are not free," he told Dodd; they have "sold out to Morgan" and other northeastern industrial barons. Such was the bitter lesson he had learned as Princeton's chief executive. He said that when he was a student it was a "simple wholesome and democratic" school. But when he returned first as a professor and then as president, it had evolved into the abode of "rich men's sons," a college that allowed the wealthy families of New York and Chicago to "direct its trustees in their policies." Recalling a seminal incident, Wilson told how a wealthy widow had contributed from her abundance and then exclaimed, "How fine and aristocratic [are] these buildings and the tone of this institution." Such experiences had awakened him to the greatest dangers facing American society. "It was Princeton, the presidency there, that showed me how to direct things here at the head of the Nation. I see and know the way the great enemies of our democracy think and work."[27]

Ever the student of American government, Wilson closed the interview with a discourse on the current state of political affairs. He believed that as president he represented the democratically expressed will of the people but that on the whole the American "constitution and system of government was the worst we could possibly get on with." Looking back on this element of the conversation a year later, Dodd remembered that Wilson complained of his inability to work with the senators, men who retained their autocratic style even after the Seventeenth Amendment mandated popular elections to the upper house. "Nothing short of a change of powers . . . between the senate and the executive will make the country democratic," Wilson had stated, and Dodd agreed. "Personally, I think the senate must go," he wrote a Virginia friend. "Then I would make the house responsible for co-operation with the Administration. . . . Wilson thinks he has prepared the way for such a change."[28]

Dodd had so identified with Wilson that he seemed to have merged his own personality with that of the president's and lost all but the pretense of objectivity. With the Wilson biography moving toward completion in the spring of 1919, he found that the president's activities during the opening sessions of the Versailles conference necessitated another interview, and Wilson's staff budgeted a brief audience with the returned president on Saturday, 1 March. Flushed with the success of his negotiations with Europe's pugnacious leaders, Wilson glowed as he recounted his triumphs in getting them to agree to his League of Nations Covenant and to accept in principle the other ideas expressed in his Fourteen Points.

But although things had gone well in France, he felt undermined by the United States Senate, where a recently elected Republican majority had savaged his crusade for world peace.[29]

The interview lasted a brief thirty minutes, and afterward Dodd learned that Wilson had created the time by canceling an appointment with a delegation of distinguished Irishmen, who had been "extremely angry" that they had had no chance to promote Ireland's quest for independence from England.[30] Perhaps this was a harbinger of what lay ahead for Wilson upon his return to Versailles. Planning to refine the broad achievements of the first European sessions, he discovered to his horror that the fervid chauvinism of the Continent had undermined his idealistic extranational goals. With more of the autocrat's rigidity than the politician's flexibility, Wilson painfully endured one compromise after another, each a devastating personal defeat. These defeats and the rejections that followed at home would destroy both his spirit and his health.

Dodd felt Wilson's bitterness and laid the president's troubles at the feet of American business interests, German sympathizers, and Irish fanatics. "President Wilson . . . will have a democratic peace or think the war has been lost," he confided to a friend in June 1918. "But the old Republican Party, as represented by . . . the larger industrial interests" demands the "exploitation of foreign markets even at the expense of our allies; and they . . . hate Wilson who represents the farmers and inarticulate . . . men of the cities." Dodd was convinced that American business elites intended to subvert the president's free-trade proposals at Versailles and found common cause with German Americans, who still "admired the great aristocratic and efficient German machine" and who were "angry at France, jealous of the power of Great Britain, and peeved at President Wilson." At the same time, Dodd believed there was yet "another angle to the story." Irish Americans, loyal to their ancestral land, meant to oppose the League of Nations unless it guaranteed a sovereign Ireland. Catholic prelates, with their "violent demands for Irish independence" and their political influence over the masses of Irish parishioners, particularly angered Dodd.[31]

As Dodd raged at the millions of misguided Americans who were unappreciative of Wilson, he saw in the powerful newspaper baron William Randolph Hearst a symbol of all that he found threatening to the promised millennium. Considering the controversial publisher pro-Republican, probusiness, pro-German, and above all pro-Irish, Dodd warned Wilson's friend Edward M. House that "the Hearst newspapers are doing all they can to defeat you."[32]

Dodd worked feverishly through the spring and summer of 1919. As fall approached, he decided that he needed one last conference with Wilson to clarify certain points and to question the president about the epochal events that had followed their March encounter: the signing of the Treaty of Versailles, the titanic struggle with the Senate for approval of the treaty, and Wilson's desperate nationwide tour to obtain public support to override the Senate's intransigence. He asked for an October appointment, but before it was arranged tragedy struck.[33] Physically and mentally exhausted, Wilson collapsed in Pueblo, Colorado, and within the week the White House announced that he had suffered a complete paralysis. For months afterward the stricken president lay comatose as a constitutional crisis paralyzed the government. Even after his partial recovery Wilson's mental capacity and political judgments remained severely diminished.

Dodd considered Wilson's stroke both a personal and a professional disaster. With the president lingering near death, Dodd's publisher, Doubleday, Page and Company, anticipated heightened interest in the biography and pressed him to rush its completion. Consumed by his own grief and little worried about financial considerations but deeply concerned with Wilson's place in history, Dodd agreed to accelerate the project. "The President was planning his work for the rest of his life," he anguished in mid-October. "Now he seems doomed never to do very much work. What a long way forward he has helped us in these eight years, or nearly that! We shall not see his kind again in the White House."[34]

During October and November Dodd urgently drew his research to a close, corresponding with Wilson associates, especially Edward M. House, and culling information from newspapers, magazines, and public documents. Wrapped in his admiration for Wilson and pressed by the publication deadline, his scholarly objectivity slipped badly. Appealing to House for insight into the Versailles negotiations, Dodd pled that he wanted "to make the first and the most accurate historical narrative of the conference, for as you know first accounts of events always have much, too much, influence upon later writers."[35]

During these hectic weeks Dodd focused so narrowly that he offended

Frederick Jackson Turner, one of his oldest and more important allies in the historical profession. Turner had praised Wilson in his first conversations with Dodd in 1908, but he had since altered his view. "After long experience and friendship with Mr. Wilson," he wrote in 1916, "I have completely lost faith in the man. I do not think that he has a principle for which he will stand or any fixed belief that he will not sacrifice for political reasons or personal gain."[36] With this mind-set, Turner was unprepared for Dodd's tactless letter of 3 October 1919 suggesting that Wilson deserved equal credit for ideas Turner had expressed in his famous essay "The Significance of the Frontier in American History."

Having read "all Wilson's writings," Dodd began, "I came to the conclusion that he advanced the idea of the importance of the West in shaping American ideas . . . contemporaneously with you." Dodd referred to Wilson's little-noticed article "Mr. Goldwin Smith's 'Views' on Our Political History," which had appeared in the December 1893 issue of *Forum* magazine. He courteously pointed out that Wilson had modestly disclaimed all originality for the frontier thesis for American democracy and credited Turner with the first thoughts. Would Turner agree, Dodd asked rather clumsily, that given this "attitude and the other highly complimentary things he said about you," this obvious humility undermined Wilson's enemies, who daily charged him "with all the selfishness and ambition that man could be guilty of?"[37]

Turner most certainly did not agree. In a sharply worded response he declared that although Wilson's article closely paralleled his own career-making AHA paper, Dodd clearly did not appreciate the chronology of events. To be sure, the *Forum* article had appeared in December, and normally the American Historical Association met during that same month. But in 1893 the organization had met in conjunction with the Chicago World's Fair. "My paper was read in July 1893," Turner stressed, months "before his Forum article."[38]

Embarrassed, Dodd promptly apologized for even intimating that Wilson deserved partial credit for Turner's frontier thesis. "I am sure you could not have felt that I, in the least, even in my mind, discounted the originality or importance of your famous paper." Still Dodd felt compelled to reaffirm his admiration for the stricken chief executive, who "will rank as one of our great presidents. He narrowly missed being the greatest of all in my opinion."[39]

Woodrow Wilson and His Work, published in March 1920, was an extended morality play in which a heroic Wilson was cast as a crusader for national justice and international democracy struggling against a multitude of adversaries bearing close resemblance to Dodd's personal villains: southern patricians, northern industrialists, self-centered politicians, and unpatriotic Americans of foreign ancestry. Far from an objective assessment, it largely reflected both the tone and structure suggested by Wilson in the interviews of September 1918 and March 1919 and became a panegyric celebrating the president's growth, from the aristocratic hauteur of his southern birth to his enlightened support for common-man democracy. Dodd rejoiced that by the time Wilson emerged from academic obscurity to become a respected national figure he had repented of his youthful conservatism and embraced the more egalitarian ideas "of Abraham Lincoln."[40]

Dodd's Wilson entered the political arena a champion of the common man's struggle against entrepreneurial plutocracy. Casting Wilson's modern dilemma with that of Lincoln, he argued that the "concentration of wealth" in the early twentieth century had shaped a national crisis as grave as that fired by the coalescing of "social and political power in the hands of a few thousand masters of slaves." "Wilson entered the White House against the utmost protest of nearly all the wealthy people of the country," Dodd declared, and he detailed the immense power of those arrayed against his hero. Benefiting from the defeat of the South's master class, northern capitalists seized control of the national government and enacted tariff and banking legislation suited to their needs. "Fortunes piled upon fortunes," their accumulations built upon the ruins of a broken South and the poverty of the laboring masses. The newly opulent business elites developed extravagant tastes. "Men traveled in special [railroad] cars, luxuriously fitted out, then in special trains with private diners, parlour cars, smokers, and liveried servants"; they "built yachts that only monarchs like William II could rival"; and they constructed "palaces [which] occupied blocks and double blocks in the great cities."

The election of Wilson, who opposed the power created by such excessive wealth, represented a victory for the "masses of men of the older American ideas and agrarian interests." In dramatic fashion the newly elected president pushed through Congress the innovative Underwood Tariff, favored the farmer over the industrial tycoon, secured the Federal Reserve Act to curtail bank abuses, created the Federal Trade Commission and gained passage of the Clayton Anti-Trust Act to tame corporate monopolies, and instituted the federal income tax to place the burden of government finances on those best able to pay.

Stunned by Wilson's initial thrusts, his enemies soon recovered, and by 1914 senators and congressmen backed by business interests—notably the Thomas S. Martin machine in Virginia and "the former Republican and Progressive party chieftains" of the industrial North—had rallied in opposition. They found allies among the judges of the Supreme Court, "the popes and cardinals of the American system," whose decisions favored business over every democratic impulse. Behind all of them, of course, stood the great capitalists, "so powerful in all the Northeastern states, connected with the old diplomacy of Europe, in full control of the metropolitan press, putting out billions' worth of goods" into the world economy. In August 1914 the European war forced Wilson away from his home crusade and thrust him into the grand scheme of international diplomacy. If he reluctantly "abandoned his domestic policy," he then moved "to advance to meet industrialism on a world stage. It was only a shifting . . . from a reform of industrial abuses at home to a prevention of greater . . . tyrannies of industrial men on a world scale."

Victorious in his war to "make the world safe for democracy," Wilson led the American delegation to the Versailles peace conference determined to create a new world order, one free from the power struggles of international elites. He bravely confronted the entrenched forces of European aristocracy, nationalistic power, and excessive wealth. Dodd was convinced that however potent Wilson's adversaries, the American and European masses supported his crusade. In December 1918 the "common man of the United States, in spite of the groanings of the conservative press, was content to have Wilson go to Paris." And if "the inarticulate folk of the United States looked upon Wilson as a great democrat set out on a momentous mission, the mass of European peasantry, shopkeepers, and day labourors looked forward to his arrival in Europe as men looked in medieval times to the second coming of Christ."

Wilson returned from Europe armed with the Treaty of Versailles and with a precious commitment to the League of Nations. Tragically, this enlightened leader immediately confronted bitter opposition from a host of malignant forces. German Americans, who could not openly support the war efforts of the Fatherland, did express their distaste for Germany's treaty humiliations; Irish Americans demanded that any compact must decree Ireland's independence from England; and business Americans, who scorned Wilson for his domestic liberalism and his international free tradism, pledged their opposition as well. The Senate's Republican majority listened intently to these dissidents and then took actions subversive to the president. Dodd scored the anachronous senators, particularly Idaho's William Borah, who "declared that, if the Republican Party accepted the League of Nations, he would form a new party and make certain the defeat of the Republicans in the next campaign." This, said Dodd, "was not the conduct of men of balanced judgment. It was hysteria."

Against these implacable foes Wilson launched one last campaign for world peace, marching into the American heartland to "Kansas City, Des Moines, and Minneapolis," where he addressed "great audiences, audiences that spoke the English language without accent." In this last dramatic appeal to the masses Wilson almost won his point, but fate decreed a massive stroke, leaving him broken and ineffectual. As Dodd penned these last thoughts the Treaty and the League lay in abeyance, their fate and world peace dependent upon the fragile wisdom of the United States Senate.

When Dodd finished *Woodrow Wilson and His Work* he was overwhelmed by the futility of the president's crusade and fearful of the book's reception by a critical public. "If I were a literary artist I would write the story in the form of a tragedy," he mourned, adding that one of his Chicago colleagues had warned that the biography "will damn me with all parties and all groups, unless the historians be excepted." But a pessimistic Dodd lamented that "historians are not historians when they read or talk of Wilson. So, there is no hope for me."[41] It was a prophecy that would largely be fulfilled.

The biography sold well. Its first edition vanished within three weeks, a second proved equally popular, and by June 1920 Dodd anticipated a third printing. All this in spite of his complaint that "Doubleday, Page and Company . . . regard my study of Wilson as certain as old Southerners regarded their bastard offspring. They disliked to sell it and they are embarrassed with its presence." The *New York Times* review hinted at why its publisher might be plagued with schizophrenia: "It is too much to expect that an entirely impartial survey of any public man should be made in his lifetime." Those "who bitterly dislike [Wilson] and his policies will consider the book too much too sympathetic in its point of view, while his uncritical admirers will consider it not sufficiently laudatory."[42]

Even as eager readers purchased the book its obvious partisanship di-

minished Dodd's professional reputation. Turner railed at Dodd for over-
estimating Wilson's scholarly virtues and for suggesting that the White
House's "master egoist's" stature as a historian was equal to Turner's.
William Dunning revealed that one of his fellow professors had castigated
Wilson and his biographer "at a public meeting" and proclaimed that
Dodd "ought not be permitted to teach in an American college," and
Dodd also learned that the respected historian Edward Channing held
"the same opinion" concerning him and "a worse opinion of Wilson."
But Dodd scoffed at these criticisms, deeming them the prejudiced pronouncements of petulant Yankees. These same men, he reflected, had
praised his Davis biography and his *Cotton Kingdom* when he bared the
foibles of the antebellum planter class. But now that he was boldly praising the first southern-born president since Reconstruction, they damned
him with the simple epithet, "Southern prejudice."[43]

Suffering from the taunts of previous admirers, Dodd interpreted their
barbs as a rejection of both his hero and himself. Anger compounded by
disappointment led to frustration and a petulance that almost destroyed
his friendship with the Cornell University historian Carl Becker. Their
mutual admiration had begun shortly after Dodd's appointment to the
University of Chicago in 1908. After Becker sent him a copy of his dissertation on the class struggle in colonial New York, Dodd had come to
admire both the work and its author; over the next decade he had greatly
assisted Becker's advancement in the historical profession. They complimented each other's scholarship and cherished their rare opportunities for
personal conversation and intellectual stimulation. In June 1920 they met
by chance in Cleveland, but a congenial breakfast turned acrimonious
when Becker mildly criticized Dodd's *Wilson*.[44]

Still raging days later, Dodd wrote an intemperate missive defending
himself, the president, and the biography. "I need not tell you that I have
long counted you as second to no historian in this country in penetration
and in the power to arrive at just conclusions," he told his estranged
friend. If in turn Becker respected him, how could he accuse Dodd of
partisanship and, more importantly, join with those who denounced Wilson as a man of impure motives and egocentric opinions? Dodd affirmed
Wilson's greatness, measuring him by the standard of Abraham Lincoln.
"We shall never know really . . . either Lincoln's or Wilson's inward soul
till we have their private writings," he argued. "But the conversations I
have had with [Wilson] do not suggest any egotistical or cruel traits. I do

not believe his most private correspondence will show it—as I do not believe Lincoln's will."[45]

Sensing that their friendship was in jeopardy, Becker responded with a palliative letter spiced with humor. "My dear man, you take me too seriously," he soothed. "I do not think your book a bad one. . . . You are one of the two or three most honest and straight thinking men I know." Besides, he suggested, the conversation "was nine o'clock in the morning, and I had not yet had my coffee." Becker only hoped that Dodd would acknowledge that Wilson's enemies were "honest men" who were doing what they thought was best for the country, however misguided their goals. Calmed, Dodd sought reconciliation. "I flatter myself that our minds are quite akin," he responded in apology. For that reason, he had simply been shocked that Becker might have a less than admiring opinion of Wilson. Their friendship reaffirmed, Dodd confided that he was suffering from a larger feeling of rejection. "The South has never regarded me as her own; the North now condemns my Wilson with united voice." At least, he mused, these "facts cause me to think I am not far on the way of sectional bias."[46]

Dodd hardened himself to his critics, accepting that he would be "damned by all the articulate folk" but warmed by the biography's steady sales. Yet even his publishers quarreled over the book, some of them arguing against its reissuances. The supportive faction prevailed, and revised editions appeared following the election of 1920 and Wilson's death in 1923; the volume remained in print as late as 1927.[47]

Whatever the biography's financial success, Dodd hungered for a positive assessment in the *American Historical Review,* the chief measuring rod of historical professionalism. The managing editor, J. Franklin Jameson, delayed assigning a reviewer, hoping that a revised edition might soften some of the book's more strident passages, but at last assigned Edwin S. Corwin the task of assessing *Woodrow Wilson and His Work.* Corwin found in it little virtue. To be sure, he praised Dodd as an unexcelled student of American history whose writing style demonstrated an "aptitude for the irony of bald, unvarnished statement . . . worthy of a Tacitus." Other than that, the volume was singularly "unhappy." Dodd fashioned "certain abstractions, like 'militarism' and 'industrialism,' . . . into veritable" scapegoats; he never credited Wilson's opponents "with a worthy purpose or a moral conviction; and though he commended his hero for refusing to indict the German people, Mr. Dodd himself [did] not hesitate to indict sooner or later the great portion of his country men." Such should be expected from a biographer who was a "friend and correspondent of the former president," who hailed "from the same section," and who exhibited "much the same political and religious traditions." Having written his share of caustic reviews, Dodd tried to remain stoic. Are "you not enjoying the skinning I got in the *Review*," he joked with North Carolina historian J. G. de Roulhac Hamilton, seeing it as just another example of prejudiced northern scholarship, which held that if "Southerners were to come to rule this country and other Southerners to write its history," then there would be "hell . . . to pay."[48]

By early 1922 such negative reviews could have little impact on Dodd's career path. He was satisfied that his biography had served the purposes of forwarding Wilson's message and of warning that fragile democracy suffered in times of grave national crisis. Moreover, the biography had confirmed Dodd's status as a proponent of Wilsonian ideas and provided new ways for him to spread his gospel. "I have had to speak very frequently . . . on Wilson or some part of his work," he revealed in the summer of 1920, and throughout the coming decade he toured the country promoting the cause.[49] If Dodd had once failed to become part of the inner circle of the Wilson administration, his book, lectures, and forthcoming articles earned him a place among the faithful guardians of Wilson's memory during the decade of Republican ascendancy.

For a dozen years Dodd proclaimed the Wilsonian message with prophetic zeal, spreading the word from Boston to Los Angeles, from Iowa to Alabama. Amherst, Rutgers, Cornell, Vanderbilt, Rice, and the Universities of Illinois, Pennsylvania, Kentucky, Virginia, and Georgia were only the major markers among the host of colleges who opened their pulpits to his gospel. He was a welcome guest before state legislatures, Wilson Clubs, veterans organizations, chambers of commerce, and sundry civic, learned, and patriotic societies.[50]

From his bases in Chicago and Round Hill, Virginia, Dodd planned speaking tours with military precision. He disciplined himself according to railroad schedules, riding the night train to his destination, refreshing each morning at a local hotel, giving afternoon and evening lectures—often interspersed with receptions and brief talks—and darting for the next train to repeat the procedure. At first he charged fifty dollars for each lecture, and then he raised his fee to one hundred dollars, always with expenses paid. Dodd's calendar for November 1923 provides a typical example. In early November 1923 Dodd departed Round Hill to speak before the Emory University student body and the Atlanta Chamber of Commerce. From there he filled appointments in Birmingham and Tuscaloosa, Alabama, before turning eastward to Greensboro, North Carolina, and a last-minute address in Richmond, Virginia. After resting briefly on his farm, he headed north to Smith College in New England, lectured there on 26 and 27 November, and finally returned to his family in Chicago after a last speech in Cleveland, Ohio. In just over a month during the spring of 1928 he gave talks before the Citizens Forum in Washington D.C. and like groups in South Carolina. Then he spoke to the Virginia legislature and the Brookings Institute before charting a circle that included the University of Cincinnati, Ohio State University, a small New York public college, and the Naval Academy. He finished his trip with repeat performances in Cincinnati and before the Brookings Institute. He had given twenty-five "addresses and asides at teas or luncheons." "Rather a fair performance so far as amount goes," he boasted.[51]

Dodd's repertoire reached well beyond a narrow concentration on the Wilson administration. He offered discourses on the civilization of the Old South, the Civil War and postbellum society, the character and importance of prominent American statesmen, as well as his various Wilson themes. Even so, his speeches generally formed a complete unit, with each element complimenting the others and leading ultimately to his hero's central place in the American epoch. Possessed of a rich knowledge of American history as well as the gift of tailoring his lessons to the level of his audience, Dodd easily adapted his efforts to an eight-week symposium before the Brookings Institute or a three-hour series repeated to endless clubs and associations. Rushed to fill his many engagements, he almost always spoke from hastily scribbled notes, and in spite of repeated requests for written manuscripts, he rarely detailed his thoughts on paper. As he explained to Edward M. House in 1930, "I [lecture] before general or University audiences on strategic men at critical moments in American History, the Revolution, the Civil War and the Great War and the story of your friendship with Wilson and your and his efforts to bring a mad world to peaceful solutions." But, he lamented, "I have never written the lectures," and thus he had few documents to share.[52]

The thoughts Dodd expressed before hundreds of assemblies were a compilation of ideas evidenced throughout his writings, from the Nathaniel Macon biography to that of Woodrow Wilson. He entertained his audiences with the dynamic American story, which he portrayed as an epic conflict between the laboring masses and the privileged few. The American Revolution had been a grand victory of democracy over colonial aristocracy, only to be subverted by the reactionary forces that framed the Constitution. Thomas Jefferson had emerged as the common man's champion, had promoted democratic principles, and with his ally James Madison had fought "against the first United States bank" in order to prevent "privilege" from creeping "into the American system." But they had been defeated by John Marshall's Supreme Court, an institution that nurtured the least democratic elements of American society. Jefferson's own South, made rich by slave labor, had repudiated him and followed after the dictum of Robert Toombs: "Common men are born to obey; men of property to rule." The "makers of the old South worked their constitutional privilege of holding slaves into a great social and political system closely analogous to . . . ancient feudalism," Dodd explained, but ultimately had been defeated in Lincoln's magnificent crusade for democracy. Yet the Great Emancipator, in order to subdue the South, had been "compelled to grant concessions and privileges quite as dangerous as slavery." His Republican Party had been subordinated to northern business, which through it had secured protective tariffs, railroad land grants, and favorable banking regulations, making them an aristocracy more powerful and more malignant than the vanquished planters. By the beginning of the twentieth century these "masterful men" were "only a little less ruthless than those of the business-military clique which had surrounded the Kaiser in 1914." With such rhetoric Dodd prepared his listeners for the advent of Woodrow Wilson.[53]

Dodd praised his idol with a pulpiteer's passion. The president had a mission to "make a world, sadly out of repair, safe for democracy, a world in which the plain man might have the best chance possible, where the great might not domineer." Wilson "represented for the world in 1918 what Jefferson and Lincoln represented for their own country. The Fourteen Points were nothing more nor less than a new American declaration of independence; no standing armies, no great navies, a freer, if not free trade among nations, self determinations of peoples and equality of nations, great and small." Based upon traditional American values of fair play, Wilson's message was a "gospel of political generosity and anti-imperialism. . . . It was a rebaptism in the ancient American spirit." Confronted with a blighted world of hostility, "the spirit of Wilson" was "too fair to be unjust even to the German people; too generous to ask aught for the country; too democratic and too Christian to indulge in the language of hate." Yet, others despised Wilson. America's business elites, fearful of his democratic fervor, fanned the flames of resentment nursed by Americans of German and Irish descent, and together they played "the ancient game of American politics, politics at its worst." These were the people who persecuted the "simple, gentle, yet austere, embodiment of democracy [who had come] to rule over" the United States. Dodd would close his homily with a benediction worthy of American civil religion. "Who was the man whose words moved men's hearts to the noble ideals set forth 2,000 years before in Galilee? It was a student of our life, a devotee of those older American ideals which Thomas Jefferson wrote into our great declaration, which Abraham Lincoln worked into the fabric of national life. . . . It was Woodrow Wilson, the schoolmaster of New Jersey and the old south."[54]

Throughout the decade of Republican ascendancy Dodd's stature as a Wilson scholar increased. Whenever newspaper or magazine editors were faced with writing the occasional memorial article, Dodd was their natural choice to reflect upon Wilson's death and the various anniversaries of his administration's major achievements.[55] Dodd's unfettered lectures and only slightly restrained articles won him the affection of the Wilson family, noted for its jealous guardianship of the president's reputation. Although they were difficult to work with, they generally appreciated Dodd's efforts, accepted his admonition to deposit Wilson's private papers in the Library of Congress, and allowed him to co-edit with Ray Standard Baker *The Public Papers of Woodrow Wilson.*[56]

Whereas many of Dodd's peers in history were unenthusiastic about his Wilson infatuation, other men, as much interested in making history as in studying it, welcomed him into their fellowship. Dodd shared with Josephus Daniels, Claude Bowers, Daniel C. Roper, and, most important of all, Edward M. House a crusader's quest for another hero worthy of Wilson. In turn these seasoned politicians valued Dodd's friendship, seeing in him a respected intellectual capable of perpetuating the Wilson image before a forgetful public. They encouraged him with their prodigious correspondence, invited him into their homes and councils, and arranged many of his lecture appointments. "Your book is the most tremendous political document we could have for the next campaign," Bowers wrote Dodd in early 1923. "Just now, with the public convinced as to the mediocrity and stupidity of the [Harding administration], it is of the greatest importance that we recall as vividly as possible the constructive work of Wilson."[57]

During the presidential campaign of 1920 the Democratic National Committee had asked Dodd to deliver some of his earliest Wilson lectures. Having spoken to assemblies in Lansing, Michigan, St. Louis, Missouri, Frankford, Indiana, and Cleveland, Ohio, and to many gatherings "in and about Chicago," he had proudly recorded in his diary that there "were large audiences in most places—at some . . . the meetings proved earnest almost religious in their character." He deemed Secretary of the Treasury William G. McAdoo, who was also the president's son-in-law, the "single national figure who symbolized the Wilson ideals" and hoped for his nomination, but he reluctantly supported the race of Ohio Governor James M. Cox. Although Dodd considered Cox "indifferent to Wilson" and his goals, he worked for a Democratic victory, hopeful that the party's success would signal popular support for the League of Nations.[58]

Warren G. Harding's resounding triumph devastated Dodd. He detested the Republican's oft-repeated theme:

> Stabilize America first,
> Prosper America first,
> Think of America first,
> Exalt America first.

This oath, wrote an angry Dodd, "is the same thing as 'Deutschland über Alles' as all know who have lived a considerable time in that country. That was the slogan which [took] the place of the more famous declaration: 'Make the world safe for Democracy.'"[59]

This rejection of Wilson's internationalism led Dodd to redouble his efforts, to preach with greater fervency his hero's message. "It is now my idea to assist some people to a revision of their thinking about foreign matters," he informed Bowers in 1922. "When we as a people learn to examine with open minds our national conduct, we shall begin to enter the road that leads to international good will." Wilson may have been the once-rejected prophet of world peace, but Dodd had every intention of converting a skeptical people to his cause. He explained to the ailing former chief executive that "many times I have had occasion to observe the depth of popular feeling on the subject of your worth to the world." When enlightened by the truth of the past, entire audiences had repented of their hatred toward Wilson and embraced his vision. "Even very wealthy men, [whose] minds [were] poisoned by their wealth or by the false estimates of their wealth, [had] been deeply moved."[60]

Dodd looked eagerly to the 1924 presidential race, confident that McAdoo would successfully carry forth Wilson's promise. In the spring of 1923 he returned from a family trip to the West Coast, financed in large measure by lectures given along the route, and rejoiced at the outpouring of support for McAdoo. Because his hosts in New Mexico, California, Wyoming, Colorado, and Nebraska had spoken positively of a McAdoo-led ticket, an encouraged Dodd prophesied "that in another two years the country may be ready to face the front." Of course Dodd feared that the same malignant forces that had defeated Wilson also opposed his new champion. "All the outstanding economic powers are now, exactly as in 1912, organizing to defeat one man," he warned in December, "and that man is McAdoo."[61]

Fortunately, the Harding scandals, and especially the Teapot Dome scheming of Harry M. Sinclair and Edward H. Dohney, had tainted both the Republican Party and the sitting president. Harding's death in August 1923 had temporarily improved the "Republican outlook," Dodd judged, but the party's future was blighted because eastern businessmen ruled "it just as slaveholders ruled the Democratic Party from 1852–1860." Dodd predicted that if the Democrats united behind McAdoo, the progressive and disillusioned elements in the Republican Party would join his camp, ensuring victory. Dodd the political idealist and Wilsonian liberal was not emotionally prepared for the looming disaster.[62]

For Dodd the month of February 1924 proved doubly tragic. The death of Woodrow Wilson was compounded by the disgrace of Wilson's heir apparent, McAdoo. Receiving word that Wilson's demise was imminent, Dodd rushed to Washington, where he joined Daniel C. Roper and other devoted followers in a long last watch. Even as they performed this mournful duty, an even greater calamity was unfolding. Called to testify before the Senate Public Lands Committee on 1 February, Dohney had revealed that while Wilson was residing in the White House his son-in-law McAdoo had represented Dohney in delicate Mexican oil negotiations. Although the petroleum millionaire revealed no hint of impropriety, McAdoo's close association with this infamous representative of Ameri-

can business tarnished his image. Dodd found solace only in the knowledge that the unconscious Wilson would never learn of the disgrace.[63]

Within hours after Wilson's passing on 3 February Dodd and several
others gathered at Roper's Washington residence to share their grief, but
the conversation soon turned to pressing issues of the living. They agreed
to confer with McAdoo and urge him to make a public apology for his
association with Dohney; if he failed to agree, they would suggest that he
withdraw from the presidential race. Representing this informal cabal,
Dodd drafted a letter to McAdoo setting forth the group's desires. On
the evening of Wilson's funeral Dodd, Roper, and other political friends
confronted McAdoo at Washington's Hamilton Hotel. Dumbfounded by
their proposals, the presidential contender begged for time to consider
them.[64]

Pressing the issue, Dodd wrote McAdoo a letter on 8 February that
was little more than a short history lesson replete with examples of politicians who had successfully weathered crises through their public honesty
and others who had been destroyed by their stubborn refusal to admit
frailties. If McAdoo would only publicly state his error, Dodd suggested,
the voters would soon forget the incident. "Men do not blame a great
leader for making a mistake, they blame him for refusing to acknowledge
it." Bowers soon endorsed Roper and Dodd's position, and House sent
McAdoo a telegram adding his name to those who were pushing for dis-
closure.[65]

McAdoo demanded a meeting with Dodd and Roper in Chicago.
There on 18 February the professor and the South Carolina attorney renewed their plea for a public apology. But the candidate had brought with
him supporters Cato Sellers of Texas and, in Dodd's words, "an Iowa
man who . . . made a fortune there [and was] in close connection with, if
not a leader of the Ku Klux forces." The latter two argued for a continued
campaign. "Sellers," Dodd complained, "describe[d] the way it would be
done. He had never a thought or a scruple about the moral quality of
anything." Thus encouraged, McAdoo announced that he had every intention of continuing his quest for the presidency and no intention of
issuing an apology for work legally and honorably done.[66]

Dodd, who saw nothing honorable in an association with the worst
elements of American capitalism, lost faith in Wilson's would-be successor. From February to early May he raged, unable to reconcile himself to

the candidate's betrayal. "McAdoo made me sick," Dodd wrote in his disappointment. "Democracy as we work it breeds so few leaders worthy of the name." To Bowers he confided his belief that a "Democrat must be beyond all suspicion. . . . Privilege is a part of the Republican party. That is what makes it so terrible for Wilson's son-in-law to be found in that company. Wilson would have starved before he would have done that thing." From the sidelines Dodd watched as McAdoo continued his quest. "He has lost," Dodd affirmed in late April. "I can not guess who will be nominated."[67]

To Dodd's horror, New York Governor Alfred E. Smith emerged as the leading candidate. Catholic, antiprohibition, and the product of New York City's Tammany machine, Smith represented forces anathema to the North Carolina–born scholar. Dodd possessed a profound distaste for the Catholic Church's active participation in American politics, derived in part from his Southern Baptist youth but in larger measure from his resentment of the clergy's pro-Irish, anti-Wilson preachments in 1919.[68] Dodd, who rarely consumed alcoholic beverages, approved of the grand experiment in temperance, a view hardly shared by Smith. When one associate argued that alcohol consumption should be a matter of personal choice, Dodd retorted: "All the talk about personal liberty is rot. The amount of suffering and misery that men and women and children have been spared by prohibition repays a hundred fold the little distress that some few people may think they suffer." In his view, the liquor interests were but another evil holding down the working man, and when labor groups also demanded that the Eighteenth Amendment be repealed, he pontificated: "I think ere another ten years pass these will recognize the blessings of prohibition."[69] For Tammany Hall Dodd had nothing but contempt. The New York political bosses, along with their corrupt brethren in other northern cities, willingly sold the birthrights of Jefferson and Wilson for the pittance in graft grabbed from American business.[70]

Fearful of a Smith victory, Dodd put aside his distaste for the Dohney indiscretion, rejoined the McAdoo campaign, and composed lengthy pro-McAdoo letters to key convention delegates. Looking back on the frantic weeks of May and June, he acknowledged that he "favored McAdoo because of his enemies as well as because I thought he had learned his lesson." By early June Dodd had slipped into a campaign euphoria. "The Republicans in the country are most apt to be defeated," he enthused in a letter to his cousin Charles Horne. "I have felt that McAdoo was as good as defeated by his connection with Dohney. Now it appears he will get the nomination; and if he gets the nomination, he is apt to be elected." [71]

Dodd badly misread the portents. A bellicose convention assembled in July, rejected both McAdoo and Smith, and on the one hundred third ballot nominated John W. Davis, a conservative attorney from West Virginia. Roper urged Dodd to support Davis, and although the professor agreed, he soon found a convenient excuse to avoid active campaigning. "All this summer I have been very busy working upon the *Wilson Papers*, he informed his friend. "This has compelled me to leave many things unconsidered. One of which is the proper attitude for one to take this year in national politics." [72]

On the eve of Davis's defeat Dodd reflected morosely upon what might have been in this once hopeful year and contemplated his party's bleak future. Harding's death had "saved the Republican Party because it removed the personal representative of [a] crooked and corrupt regime"; and McAdoo had further exacerbated affairs by not apologizing for his Mexican oil dealings. "For the son of the Prophet, so close to him, not to have *felt* the issue an event of international significance," amazed Dodd, who lamented that "it simply broke the back of the Democratic Party." Even worse, the campaign of 1924 contained omens for a bitter 1928. Smith's candidacy "casts its shadow athwart the path of democracy," he reflected, because it made the Catholic Church an instrument of national politics. Dodd warned that if Smith won reelection as governor of New York and Davis lost his presidential bid, then "we shall be started on the way toward the next and sharper conflict." And so it happened. In the wake of the Calvin Coolidge landslide Dodd could only grouse, "I am in a bad humor; . . . I think anybody ought to be, that is anybody who knows history and gives a damn what happens to his country." [73]

Dodd, who never slacked in his lectures and articles on Wilson, sorrowfully watched his party slide into the hands of Alfred E. Smith. In early 1925 the scholar sought Daniels's advice, desperately concerned about his party's direction. To nominate Catholic Smith would "alienate the South," and a Tammany candidate would "permit the big business element . . . to play their economic imperialism . . . and make us enemies all over the world." McAdoo offered himself as an alternative and invited Dodd to join in another campaign, but the professor had completely lost confidence in his one-time champion. McAdoo "was the legatee of Wilson till Dohney was exposed," he mourned in 1927. "A Democratic candidate can not have even the remotest connection with the great crooks; [but] it does not hurt a Republican." They are "elected to work with the great thieves."[74]

When Smith—Catholic, wet, and Tammany—seized the Democratic banner in 1928, Dodd assured his friends Roper, Daniels, and Bowers that he could not and would not support the candidate. Asked to join the College League for Alfred E. Smith, he replied tersely: "There is no place this year for men who knew and believed in Woodrow Wilson." As if to emphasize this point, Dodd and his family sailed in September for an extended European sojourn. The apostle of the Wilson message and advocate of American democracy refused to vote in the fall elections.[75]

Dodd needed a respite not only from political disappointments but also from burdens imposed upon him by his profession. "I for once intend to go without books in my bag and to stay without consulting a library," he promised but then reneged. He sought opportunities to spread Wilsonian ideas in England and gratefully accepted invitations to speak at London University, the University of Durham, and Oxford. However disgruntled he may have been with current American affairs, he still longed for a reborn Wilson. Four years hence Franklin Roosevelt would fulfill his criteria, but for the moment Dodd drifted, despondent at the nadir of his political hopes.[76]

Dodd's infatuation with Wilson occurred just as his scholarly career reached its maturity. By 1920 he was counted along with Ulrich B. Phillips and William A. Dunning as one of the three outstanding pioneers in southern studies. At Chicago he attracted scores of the finest budding intellectuals, among them Henry Steele Commager, Walter Prescott Webb, and Frank L. Owsley; he mentored his department's junior members, especially Avery O. Craven and J. Fred Rippy; and, by the end of the decade he had taken on the thankless burdens of a department chair. Under these circumstances Dodd struggled to maintain his own writing goals. Although his little volume *The Cotton Kingdom* was widely praised, he saw it as a simple precursor to a more complex multivolume history of the Old South, a massive work that would illuminate the region's heroic class struggle, and he diligently gathered materials for its completion. In 1933 friends in the American Historical Association who appreciated his dedication to the discipline and applauded his concern for students and colleagues alike elevated him to the organization's highest office.

Throughout these hectic years Dodd considered himself a lonely sojourner at odds with his cultural environment. He had fled the oppressive world of pretentious southern aristocrats only to confront a northern society sympathetic to his antagonists. "From the passing of Lincoln the people of the North grew into a social philosophy like that of the South," he wrote in 1919. "I hear . . . in the so-called best circles, most frequent approval of negro slavery and constant apologies for the North's ruthless breaking down of a social system that ought to have been left alone." Eight years later he excused himself from a dinner party with former Indiana Senator Albert Beveridge and other representatives of "the old and wealthy families" of the upper Midwest because "for more than a half hour, perhaps an hour," the conversation had "turned on the folly" of emancipation. "I have come more and more to the view that the well-to-do North is now more pro-slavery than any part of the South," he reflected. "A great many, if not most of the prominent people in this part of the country are disposed to apologize both for the war that was made on the South and for the abolition of slavery." Dodd's willingness to associate northern elites with the evils of the Old South plutocracy intensified with the collapse of Wall Street. "The slave holders had worked their wills upon the old South and the country and were on the verge of economic disaster when their more radical leaders precipitated secession," he propounded in the summer of 1932. "Our organizers of corporations and issuers of securities . . . have [had] their own course till ruin is upon them, and us."[77]

The class-conscious Dodd gleaned from his interpretation of the past a message for the present. As he focused upon his projected magnum opus Dodd determined that his portrayal of the antebellum South would be an extended parable for modern contemplation.[78] After all, he reasoned, history as taught by the South's upper classes perpetuated antique values harmful to democracy. "I was brought up to think of Lincoln as the worst a man could have to study," he confided to Carl Becker in 1920. "His picture in Barnes' History of the United States was offensive to me." But as a mature scholar Dodd embraced Lincoln as a hero; he condemned the South's elite establishment not only for perverting his image but also for subverting his democratic crusade and determined to expose its stranglehold upon southern society. "I am working on a book in three volumes," he had revealed a year earlier, "treating in some detail the old South. . . . if I can resist the temptations of publishers, always begging for a book I can 'do' in a short time, I shall get this work out in the next ten years or less."[79] But for the next decade and more Dodd was continually beset by temptations, deflecting him from his consummate goal.

Dodd entered the project confident that a lifetime of scholarship had laid the foundation for his work yet keenly aware that much research remained to be done. Even though lengthy summer and autumn vacations on his Virginia farm enabled him to delve into the Library of Congress treasures and to make occasional forays into Richmond and other eastern archives, he bemoaned his long months in Chicago isolated from primary sources. Desperate for ready access to a rich collection of southern materials, he sought an opportunity to combine his classroom responsibilities with research opportunities. After considerable negotiations, the University of Chicago trustees approved Dodd's exchange of teaching duties with University of Texas historian Charles W. Ramsdell for the winter quarter of 1923.[80]

In a spirit of friendship the two professors not only traded classrooms but also moved into each other's homes. On 3 January the Dodd family settled into Ramsdell's comfortable Austin house and the Chicago professor looked forward to profitable weeks of scholarly endeavor, but for once he also indulged in some of the refined recreations associated with academic life. He and Mattie enjoyed "the pleasures of Austin," delighted in its "charming social life," and luxuriated in its warm winter climate. Dodd even gave in to the enticements of Ramsdell's "golf sticks," confessing to a close friend that "you would be surprised to see me trying to hit a golf ball in a hole or heading it toward the center of the green!"[81]

Whatever distractions lured Dodd in Austin, he remained focused on his principal objective, doing research in the University of Texas's vast collection of southern materials. Long a severe opponent of the Confederate patriotic societies and of their blatant manipulation of historical ideas, Dodd seemed unaware of the irony that his mining of rich sources had been made possible by those very entities. A decade earlier Eugene C. Barker, the chair of the University of Texas history department, had negotiated with Austin banker and Confederate veteran George W. Littlefield and other "prominent Confederates and Daughters of the Confederacy" to endow a library fund dedicated to southern newspapers and manuscripts. By 1920 Littlefield and his estate had donated over

$125,000 to the project. The beneficence had come, however, at the cost of academic integrity. In 1911 and again in 1913 Barker had bowed to Littlefield's demands to remove from the university's classrooms textbooks condemned by the local John Bell Hood Camp of the United Confederate Veterans.[82]

Dodd found the university's archives ideally suited to his needs. "I am making all the use of the historical material in your library that I can," he wrote Ramsdell on 3 February, "but I shall not get half through." A month later the quarter came to a close, and Dodd deemed his stay "a delightful experience. . . . The work has been interesting and . . . the library always enticing."[83] Satisfied with the progress of his research, he commenced writing, anxious to flesh out his themes, confident that they would fill several volumes, and frustrated by the many diversions that hindered his efforts.

However difficult Dodd found the execution of his work, he easily articulated its promised thesis, writing in a rushed, almost stream-of-consciousness style. He explained to a friend in 1926 that the "book on the old South is intended as a first rate tragedy, democracy in a long struggle, before and after the Revolution, at the point of victory in 1830, [but then] meeting its first great catastrophe in this country." It would continue with the epic story of "the southern victors over democracy meeting their Waterloo in 1865, only to find themselves humbled in the dust, under a minority in the North who were making an end of democracy there in the same ways the slaveholders had beaten democracy in the South prior to 1860."[84] The haste with which Dodd scribbled his themes reflects his life's dilemma after 1923. It took far more time to expand these phrases into paragraphs, chapters, and books than a much harassed Dodd possessed.

Even though Dodd faithfully pledged to focus on his Old South work to the exclusion of other projects, he was easily diverted. While he was doing research at the University of Texas, his friend J. Franklin Jameson urged him to submit his preliminary findings to the *American Historical Review*, but Dodd refused. "You will think we are all pretty poor workers not to find plenty of short by-products of scholarship," he wrote in apology. "I simply have not found such as yet, fit to publish in the *Review*."[85] Sincere in his determination to avoid "short-by products of scholarship," Dodd nonetheless gave into the many opportunities presented to him to write essays for mass-circulation journals, especially when his historical expertise could also further his political and ideological goals. "I am preparing a brief popular study of the presidency," he told Edward M. House in November 1923. If it were published in a national magazine, he said, it would "help us to clear up peoples [*sic*] minds for the next [presidential] campaign, a campaign in which some very vital matters ought to be settled."[86]

Even this project met delays. Dodd's commitments to lecture on Wilson and related topics, his grief over Wilson's death and McAdoo's disgrace, and his editing of Wilson's public papers diverted his energies until early 1924, when H. L. Mencken, the irrepressible and irreverent editor of the *American Mercury,* offered Dodd a public forum and more. Unaware of Dodd's views on alcohol, the libationary Mencken boasted of his and Dodd's mutual friendship with Charles A. Beard, who often slaked his thirst with offerings from Mencken's well-stocked cellar. The distinguished historian was undergoing "treatment for deafness," Mencken informed Dodd, "but I noted with great joy that he was still able to hear a cork coming out of a bottle." Mencken then invited Dodd to his Baltimore home because, in his words, "I crave the honor of introducing you to some very friendly jugs." Whatever Dodd thought of Mencken's flaunting of the Volstead Act, he relished the invitation to write articles critical of some of the nation's most revered and conservative icons for Mencken's journal. Although Dodd tentatively committed to four manuscripts, in the end he wrote only two, the first exposing George Washington's aristocratic temperament and the second demonstrating how Supreme Court Justice John Marshall had undermined Thomas Jefferson's egalitarian idealism.[87]

Appearing in the *American Mercury*'s March and July 1925 issues, the two articles evidenced Dodd's lifelong condemnation of aristocracy's subversion of democracy, themes he intended to develop more richly in his scholarly study of the Old South. In Dodd's view, Washington became a reactionary conservative, a confirmed patrician who cooperated with Alexander Hamilton, "the bankers of Philadelphia," and other leaders hostile to democracy in order to subvert "the Fourteen Points of the Revolution." Along with other high-born leaders from Maryland, Virginia, and the Carolinas, Washington joined the patriot cause, voicing the rhetoric of democracy but in reality subverting its execution. Faced with radical state assemblies elected by the newly enfranchised common folk, Washington and others of his ilk created new constitutions that rendered the legislatures "subject to judicial revision and rebuke." Washington presided over the Constitutional Convention of 1787, an assembly that clearly repudiated the cause of pure democracy, and then as president of the United States he initiated policies to protect his class from the peoples' expressed will. Having accomplished his purposes, Washington retired to the orderly splendor of Mt. Vernon, with its "oak forests to screen a man from the gaze of the vulgar, and a hundred slaves to doff their hats to master." [88]

Dodd was generous to his long-worshiped Jefferson, choosing instead to concentrate upon the villainy of John Marshall. Jefferson had risen above his status as a Virginia aristocrat, embraced the common man's cause, and championed democracy, but he had been defeated by the national judicial system originally created by Washington. The powerful Supreme Court, dominated by Marshall, proved itself a fearful "menace to democracy." Dodd excoriated Marshall's decision in *Marbury* v. *Madison,* which asserted the court's absolute right to review the acts and policies of Congress and thus severely restricted the "bounds of the President and his advisors." As a result of this action fragile democracy could not long survive Jefferson's presidency, especially when Chief Justice Marshall, appointed for life, made decisions that carried the power of a "papal decree." [89]

Mencken and Dodd had contracted for two additional articles, but the scholar in Dodd soon doubted the propriety of his association with the *American Mercury,* a magazine that consistently challenged the bounds of good taste. Mencken followed an editorial policy of "damning to all eternity to such an extent that I thought he was overreaching himself," Dodd informed Beard in 1927. Thus, when Mencken suggested that Dodd's third article was a third too long, Dodd "thought it a good time to stop." [90] Having repented of his association with the *American Mercury,* Dodd soon found other, more sedate outlets for his thoughts.

From 1925 to 1932 Dodd repeatedly took time away from his Old South project to write about Andrew Jackson and Abraham Lincoln for *Century Magazine,* to produce topical essays for the same journal, and to compose feature articles on historical and contemporary subjects for the *New York Times.* [91] Impressed by the popularity of Dodd's articles on Lincoln, the Century Company reprinted them in the little volume *Lincoln or Lee.* "My thesis," Dodd explained to one admirer, was that "when the war was over the South had won" because there had come to power sympathetic elements in the North, a "minority of well-to-do and wealthy industrialists and commercial magnates [who] remained in power until this day, barring a short period under Wilson. I look upon the whole Civil War as one huge tragedy in which everybody lost."[92]

In these and other essays, Dodd echoed his familiar themes of class conflict. Contributing to the *Virginia Quarterly Review*'s inaugural volume, he assured its readers that the masses in 1776 desired "radical democracy," but he said that with the exception of Thomas Jefferson and Patrick Henry, Virginia's leaders were committed to the philosophy "that the majority ought not to govern."[93]

Throughout the latter 1920s Dodd faced a personal conundrum. He desperately wanted to make headway on his Old South manuscript, but personal and professional obligations continually interfered. Dodd's grief over Wilson's death and his intermittent participation in the McAdoo presidential campaign initially frustrated his efforts. In the years that followed he grew in professional stature but at the same time agonized over his failure to advance his chief work. His relationship with the American Historical Association illustrated Dodd's constant torment. From his first convention in 1900 he had longed to be counted among its most honored members, yet his increasing prestige within the organization brought him little joy. In 1925 Dodd chaired the important program committee; instead of being pleased, he regretted that it took him away from his Old South endeavor. Two years later he attended the organization's Washington convention, where he found himself constantly put upon by "so many [who] seem to be my friends, literally hundreds—half of whose names I can't call for my life." All the while, he confided to his beloved Mattie, "I felt rather lonesome" until he found "Becker and two or three others from whom I keep no secrets, mature men growing old." When the AHA assembled for its convention in 1930, it appointed Dodd second vice-president for 1931, a posting that assured his advancement to president in 1933. But he confessed that he was not "very much elated." His inability to finish his Old South work made him feel unworthy.[94]

The rancorous politics of the University of Chicago history department added to Dodd's burdens. When McLaughlin stepped down from his post as department chair in 1927, Dodd reluctantly took his place. Supervising a department of fifteen contentious professors, two hundred graduate students, and a thousand undergraduates severely taxed his abilities. "It is not the sort of position I ought to hold," he confided to Josephus Daniels.

"You need to pray for me."[95] Overwhelmed by this task and agonizing over the lack of progress on his book, Dodd seriously considered openings at Cornell, the University of Virginia, and Johns Hopkins in 1928, but in the end he could not break with the University of Chicago, which had nurtured his career for two decades.[96]

The politics of the Democratic Party, the history department, and the AHA took their toll on Dodd, diminishing his ability to work on the Old South volumes. "There are chapters in existence, [and] other chapters, once thought to be finished, that must be recast," he acknowledged in 1926, yet he added with optimism, "I do not think I shall die with this work unfinished." But Dodd's heavy responsibilities as department chair hindered his long-term scholarship. In late 1927 he complained that he had invested "twenty years on a history of the Old South" but the projected work remained in an "inchoate state," with various chapters only partially completed. "I am fifty-eight years old," he lamented, "every year adding to my burdens."[97]

Having to construct class schedules, determine faculty increments, satisfy the dean's demands for bureaucratic minutia, and much more, Dodd had little time to indulge his creative urges, and even when he was free for short periods he found concentration difficult. On 12 February 1931 he recorded in his diary that he had spent "as much of the day as possible" in the library "but wrote only four pages." Looking back on his efforts after five years, Dodd expressed profound dissatisfaction with the impact his post as department chair had had on his scholarship. His work load since 1927 had been "so pressing" that he had written "only about 300 pages of real critical work; and time flies." Perhaps, he thought, a separation from academia was his best course. Reflecting upon Franklin D. Roosevelt's recent election as president and his own loyal service to the Democratic Party, he asked his friend Daniel Roper to help him obtain a political sinecure. Could there be, he inquired, "a minor diplomatic post . . . available—where I could finish the history of the South before it is too late?"[98]

Long a proponent of Wilsonian internationalism, Dodd believed that he had earned consideration for a diplomatic posting. Aware of Edward M. House's influence over President-elect Roosevelt's foreign appointments, he watched with approval as Roper became secretary of commerce, Daniels, ambassador to Mexico, and Bowers, ambassador to Spain.[99] In time

Dodd would also receive an appointment, but it would be far from the quiet benefice he envisioned.

Following Herbert Hoover's resounding victory in 1928 Dodd's interest in political affairs had quickly rekindled. He despised the Republican Party's close association with American business elites, repeating his mantra that northern industrialists were the natural successors to the oppressive slavocracy of the Old South; and although he took no pleasure in the human suffering generated by the collapse of the stock market in 1929, he rejoiced that it portended a revival of the moribund Democratic Party.[100]

Nonetheless, when Roosevelt emerged as the leading contender for the Democratic presidential nomination Dodd was initially skeptical. "Roosevelt may be the best candidate," he wrote to Daniels in November 1930. "I doubt it. The Easterners had it last time; the Westerners do not exactly trust the New Yorkers." Dodd retained his intense dislike of Alfred E. Smith, and he viewed Roosevelt as a Smith protégé, another son of Tammany. "Roosevelt stands to lose the nomination," Dodd predicted in May 1931. His refusal to repudiate Tammany had convinced "the great independent public of the country" that he could not "deal with the problems of corruption as they deserve."[101]

But Dodd gradually warmed to the New York governor. In August 1931 he shared with Roosevelt several of his recent newspaper and magazine articles castigating the alliance between the Republicans and the business elites. The "policy so long followed by the party of Lincoln has now brought us face to face with the worst economic situation ever known," he wrote in his cover letter. "Like slavery in the old South, the policy has run its full course and its beneficiaries are fast hanging themselves both figuratively and actually." Roosevelt thanked Dodd, said that he agreed with his basic themes, and encouraged him to continue to write to him.[102]

Flattered by this attention, Dodd seriously considered joining the governor's presidential crusade until he was jolted by Roosevelt's repudiation of the League of Nations on 2 February 1932. Having served as Wilson's assistant secretary of the navy and campaigned for the League in 1919–20, presidential candidate Roosevelt found himself challenged by the powerful and conservative newspaper magnate William Randolph Hearst. A proponent of isolationism, Hearst published an open letter on 31 January demanding that Roosevelt make clear his views on internationalism and the League. Well aware of Hearst's power to derail his candidacy, Roosevelt responded two days later in an address before the New York State Grange. He acknowledge without apology his support for the League in 1920. "If today I believed that the same or even similar factors entered into the argument, I would still favor America's entry into the League," but "the League of Nations today is not the League conceived by Woodrow Wilson." It had degenerated into little more than a forum for the "discussion of strictly European political national difficulties. In these the United States should have no part." With such artful words Roosevelt bought Hearst's silence and perhaps won the votes of a few Republican isolationists, but he also frightened and infuriated legions of Wilsonian Democrats, among them Dodd. Troubled, the Chicago professor asked Roosevelt to clarify his statement. "I yield to no one in my desire to further the cause of international amity and peace," Roosevelt wrote in his smooth response. "I have lived through one World War, seeing it from both sides of the Atlantic, and have no desire to repeat the experience."[103] These words won Dodd's loyalty.

By late spring Dodd perceived Roosevelt as a recasting of Woodrow Wilson and himself as a solid supporter of the candidate. With that in mind he offered the Democratic National Committee twenty-five copies of his just republished Wilson biography. He hoped that it would make prominent participants in the forthcoming convention more willing to nominate a man of Wilson's caliber. At the end of May he wrote Edward M. House of his enchantment with Roosevelt. "It is clear that [Roosevelt's] line of thought is much the same as yours and mine all these decades," wrote an encouraged Dodd, who said that Roosevelt inspired all men who longed for "a co-operative social order as Franklin and Jefferson and Wilson hoped to see."[104]

Pleased with the letter and intent upon calling Roosevelt's attention to Dodd, House shared Dodd's missive with the governor and described Dodd's stature as a historian and his close association with Wilson. Moved by Dodd's commitment and impressed with his academic credentials, Roosevelt penned an effusive response. "I wish much that I could have a talk with you," he told Dodd. "I know well your contribution to the administration of President Wilson and of your very clear understanding and thinking." Perhaps Dodd "could run up and spend the night . . . at the [governor's] Mansion. Do please do it if you can." Although he was unable to arrange such a visit during the last weeks of the heated campaign, Roosevelt graciously scheduled a brief meeting with Dodd at the Democratic National Convention in Chicago.[105]

Dodd hoped to play a major roll in Roosevelt's subsequent campaign, but he found few ways to do so. His closest political friends had long appreciated and encouraged his partisan lectures on Wilson and the League, but now they feared that Dodd's enthusiasm for the late president might embarrass Roosevelt. In late August Dodd informed Roper that the *Chicago Tribune* had solicited an article speculating on Roosevelt's foreign-policy views. "I received and carefully read your . . . letter," Roper responded. "It struck me as so important that I took the liberty of forwarding it to Franklin D. Roosevelt." Louis Howe, the candidate's secretary, immediately asked Roper to intercede tactfully with Dodd. Could the professor write the letter without referring to Roosevelt's attitude toward the League of Nations? Reluctantly, Dodd agreed, pledging to focus on tariff issues and the problems of reciprocal armament agreements and to avoid mention of the League.[106]

Immediately following Roosevelt's resounding victory in November Dodd made little effort to secure an administrative posting. Although he had long desired a position of power in a Democratic administration and his friends House and Roper exercised considerable influence within the Roosevelt circle, Dodd hardly knew the president-elect and certainly had not contributed significantly to his election. Moreover, Dodd had to focus on the serious internal problems of his history department and the significant budget cuts brought on by the Depression; in addition, he was agonizing over his lack of progress on his Old South history. By mid-December, however, Dodd was intrigued by Roosevelt's selection of advisers from among elites in higher education. He voiced his approval of this trend to both House and Roper and was gratified to find them in agreement and even hinting that he should be included in that number. House responded encouragingly on 27 February 1933: "I, too, have wanted a university man closely connected with the administration. I have had you in mind as my choice for such a place."[107]

In spite of his earlier musing concerning a "minor diplomatic post," Dodd had not seriously contemplated dedicated service to the Roosevelt administration. Taken aback, he immediately informed both House and Roper that with one exception there "is no position that would justify my abandoning my work on the Old South." For "thirty-two years I have taught American History," he explained, "having put more than fifty doctors of philosophy into universities. . . . This has kept me from the major work of my life. . . . Any appointment in Washington would carry obligations too serious to allow the finishing of my prior task." Yet Dodd retained one important ambition. He envied House's intimate relationship with Wilson and dreamed of having the same exalted relationship with the new president. "I can think of only one possibility and that would be in violation of precedent . . . a position without portfolio, as the British often have, if a certain type of person is worthy of it." [108]

Apparently both House and Roper had in mind the less grandiose but perhaps more important ambassadorship to Berlin. Skilled political maneuverers, they agreed to explore Dodd's goals and arranged for an intense schedule of appointments in Washington. At Roper's invitation, on 15 March Dodd spoke before fifty government insiders at a luncheon held at Washington's University Club, after which Dodd was rushed to meet important functionaries at the State Department. For the next two weeks Roper shuttled him from one office to another in a campaign to win administrative support for Dodd and to convince Dodd to enter government service. [109]

Wearied by the constant politicking, Dodd became discouraged. "There is no place suitable [to] my kind of mentality," he confessed to Mattie. "There has never been a cabinet member without portfolio in this country," and clearly House and Roper did not have sufficient influence to create one. But there had been some discussion of an appointment to "high diplomacy (London, Paris, Berlin)." Dodd shrugged, "I am not the sly, two faced type so necessary to 'lie abroad for the country.' If I were I might go to Berlin and bend the knee to Hitler." Caught in a moment of self-pity, he lamented to his spouse: "it must be distressing to . . . have so inept a husband at [a] critical moment in history which he has so long foreseen, one who can not fit him-self to high position and thus reap some of the return of a life of toilsome study." But Dodd quickly pushed such thoughts aside, and before leaving for Chicago he gave in to Roper's suggestions concerning Berlin and sent the State Department a letter requesting the assignment. In his capacity as secretary of commerce, Roper added a letter of endorsement, but Secretary of State Cordell Hull seemed little impressed. In curt words of bureaucratic indifference Hull responded to Roper: "I shall . . . have your letter, as well as Dr. Dodd's letter in which he applies for appointment as American Ambassador to Germany, placed on file for consideration at the appropriate time."[110]

As late as 18 May Dodd was not among the leading candidates for the Berlin post. But Roper and House continued to promote his cause; Roper even spoke directly to the president. Dodd, he argued, would serve as an excellent symbol of American democratic virtue in a Germany soon to be dominated by Hitler's totalitarianism. Dodd represented Wilsonian idealism at its best, spoke fluent German, and possessed a doctoral degree from one of Germany's most prestigious institutions. Roosevelt agreed. He reached his decision on 3 June and requested that Dodd meet with him at the White House five days later. Unable to make travel arrangements on such short notice, Dodd was still in his Chicago office when at exactly noon on 8 June his telephone rang. "This is Franklin Roosevelt," sounded the disembodied voice. "I want to know if you will render the government a distinctive service. I want you to go to Germany as Ambassador."[111]

CHAPTER FIVE

An American Scholar in Hitler's Court

When Franklin D. Roosevelt announced William E. Dodd's appointment to Berlin, friends, former students, and admirers quickly forwarded congratulations. Jane Addams of Hull House, long an acquaintance, thrilled at his designation. "The situation there is so difficult," she wrote, "that I can think of no other American so well equipped as you are, with both historic perspective and human understanding, to deal with its problems. It is one of the president's most brilliant strokes." Carl Sandburg, a frequent guest in the Dodd household, dashed off a short celebratory poem, and Carl Becker jocularly offered to sacrifice his writings to future Nazi book burnings. The often flippant H. L. Mencken wrote seriously that "the news of your appointment . . . has naturally filled me with pleasant sentiments. The president has honored himself by appointing you." Hundreds of missives echoed a similar theme: the right-minded American scholar was going forth to properly instruct a Europe marching toward cultural disaster. Perhaps one of his former students best articulated the meaning of the momentous event: "A joy mingled with sadness due to the loss to the historical field [is] compensated only by the historical justice of one of understanding being at Hitler's Court."[1]

Considering himself an apostle of Wilsonian idealism, Dodd arrived in Berlin determined to be something more than a dispassionate foreign representative. He intended not only to preach international cooperation and American democracy to fascist Germany but also to impose upon his own embassy, perhaps even the State Department, his distinctive concepts of social egalitarianism. And as an astute observer of European events he would provide Roosevelt with critical insights; unfortunately, Dodd's dogmatic personality and unbending values were better suited to the professor's podium than to the diplomat's table. For four and a half stormy years he irritated the German government, frustrated his largely unsympathetic staff, and perplexed American political figures both within and outside of the State Department. He returned to the United States in 1938, his vision of a Wilsonian millennium shattered.

A man of deep convictions, Dodd worked from a powerful intellectual model that was rooted in the class assumptions of his impoverished southern youth and had flourished during his turbulent career as a historian and a political activist. His intense class consciousness guided his diplomatic behavior, for the democratic pronouncements of this respected intellectual masked a profound bitterness toward those elite groups whose interests conflicted with the rights of the masses. In 1933 he described his mission to Roosevelt: "My purpose [is] to put forward the best possible American ideas as you, *Wilson,* Lincoln and Jefferson interpret them. . . . Europe, especially eastern Europe, needs to have American principle put before their people as clearly as possible."[2]

Dodd's appointment perplexed State Department professionals. Few knew him personally, and fewer still fathomed his unique perspective on international relations. Early in Dodd's tenure Jay Pierrepont Moffat, the State Department's chief of division of western European affairs, confessed to the acting chargé d'affaires in Berlin: "Your chief, Mr. Dodd . . . is a curious individual whom I find it impossible to diagnose." He could not have know that Dodd, as the son of an impoverished North Carolina farmer, viewed with suspicion the people who were traditionally drawn into the foreign service. "Our State Department is filled with men of independent fortunes," he had observed in the early 1920s, "with undemocratic men who do not know they are undemocratic."[3]

Moffat and his fellow professionals in the American foreign service labored in a patrician preserve. Although the ambassador was the nominal head of the embassy, in reality his staff constituted the permanent bureaucracy, dedicated to smoothing the intercourse between the U.S. government and that of the host country. The president generally chose his ambassadors from among his largest campaign contributors, on occasion from among favored party stalwarts, and in the case of the rare sensitive assignment from among the best of the long-term foreign-service officials. Usually little more than figureheads, ambassadors were expected to be men of sufficient wealth and sophistication to entertain well beyond their illiberal salaries of $17,500 per year and to follow carefully orchestrated protocols outlined by their staffs. A cozy fraternity largely recruited from Ivy League universities, especially Harvard, Yale, and Princeton, foreign-service professionals focused their attention on daily administrative duties. Of the reams of information they gathered on their host country—on economic conditions, political trends, military developments—most was forwarded to State Department officials in Washington, who summarized conditions worldwide and set administrative policies.[4]

Dodd had neither the predilection passively to follow his staff's prescriptions nor the inclination to be daunted by prestigious diplomas or family pedigrees. He had long held the view that the more prominent northeastern colleges were little more than finishing schools for the indolent wealthy. "Let undergraduate loafers go anywhere" other than the University of Chicago, he advised a former colleague in 1934. They would be especially welcome at "Yale and Harvard where swaggery manners and curious accents can be learned easily."[5] Dodd wanted a hardworking staff of thinking professionals and chaffed at the personal habits of those whom he considered the mission's aristocratic personnel.

Although he was an enigma at the State Department, Dodd possessed attributes that made him well suited to the task of taking American democracy to Berlin: he held a degree from a German university, he spoke German fluently, he was well respected by German intellectuals, and he had an intense appreciation of much in the German culture and an admiration for its common people. "It is my opinion," he wrote shortly after his arrival in Europe, "that I can render the greatest service here by seeking to understand and interpret the German people rather than its government."[6]

Dodd had not been Roosevelt's first choice for ambassador to Berlin. Rumors persisted that former presidential candidate James Cox and New York judge and socialite Frederic Kernochan had rejected the posting. If these rumors were true, Roosevelt was forced to reflect upon the nature of this assignment and to define his goals more carefully since ominous developments suggested that Germany required more than a party loyalist or a wealthy dilettante. On 20 January the octogenarian German President Paul von Hindenburg appointed Adolf Hitler as Reich chancellor; on 28 February Hitler issued decrees suppressing Germans' freedoms of speech, press, and assembly; and on 23 March the Reichstag endowed Hitler with extraordinary powers, making him in effect the country's dictator.

Roosevelt needed to have a representative in Germany who was skilled in analysis and reporting, someone familiar with the German psyche and capable of placing current events in their historical context. Prodded by House and Roper, he came to see Dodd as the person best suited to the task. The Chicago professor had the additional benefits of being a loyal member of the Democratic Party, a noted Wilsonian internationalist, and an intellectual known for his admiration of Jeffersonian democracy.[7] That Dodd lacked the diplomatic temperament so necessary to his new craft was a failing that only time would reveal.

When Dodd received Roosevelt's telephone call on 8 June he could hardly hide his surprise. He demurred, pleading for a suitable period of contemplation. "Two hours," responded the exuberant President. "Can you decide in that time?" Shaken, Dodd agreed to the schedule but wondered aloud whether German authorities might find his Wilson biography an irritant. "I am sure they would not," Roosevelt enthused. "That book, your work as a liberal and as a scholar, and your study at a German university are the main reasons for my wishing to appoint you. It is a difficult post and I want an American liberal in Germany as a standing example."[8]

Dodd immediately called Mattie, sharing with her the honor proffered by the president. Cradling his telephone a second time, he rushed to the office of University President Robert M. Hutchins only to discover that he was out of town. He then hurried to meet with Dean Frederic C. Woodward, who urged him to the task and promised to make the necessary arrangements with Hutchins. Following an intense luncheon discussion with his spouse, Dodd called the president's secretary at exactly 2:30 P.M. Roosevelt, in session with his cabinet, received word of the positive response and promptly interrupted the moment's discussion to announce the appointment. Pleased, Secretary of Commerce Roper later informed Dodd of the cabinet's universal approval, with Secretary of the Interior Harold Ickes of Chicago and Secretary of the Navy Claude Swanson of Virginia expressing their deepest confidence in the ambassador-designate.[9]

The following day, Dodd telegraphed Washington confirming his acceptance and adding a proviso that might have amused Roosevelt but certainly appalled State Department regulars. Noting his government salary, the plebeian Dodd affirmed: "It would need to be understood that I cannot spend more than the allowance." Elevated to an exalted position as his nation's principal representative to one of Europe's chief capitals, he had declared war on diplomatic expectations. He would be a Jeffersonian radical in a world attuned to Louis XIV traditions.[10]

Three days later events began to carry Dodd inevitably toward Berlin. Roosevelt requested an immediate meeting with Dodd, and on 16 June the ambassador-to-be had a private hour-long luncheon with the president. They had a crowded agenda, conversing first about the threatened German moratorium on repaying private American debts, then turning to Nazi persecutions of Jews, and finally discussing Dodd's provocative pledge to conduct a frugal social schedule in Berlin. Roosevelt agreed with Dodd's contention that American bankers had taken advantage of German penury in the 1920s but insisted that loans, however usurious, must be repaid lest American economic recovery be retarded. Condemning the German administration's shameful Jewish policies, he regretfully insisted that according to international custom it must be considered a German domestic problem, beyond the legitimate diplomatic concerns of the American government. At a time when Jewish groups in the United States were pressuring Roosevelt to retaliate against Germany, he stressed to Dodd that "this is . . . not a governmental affair. We can do nothing except for American citizens who happen to be made victims." Nonetheless, he admonished his ambassador to do whatever he could "to moderate the general persecution by unofficial and personal influence." As for Dodd's startling proposal to live on a strict economy, Roosevelt happily endorsed the experiment, saying that Dodd need give only "two or three general dinners" a year as well as the occasional reception for "Americans in Berlin and . . . Germans interested in American relations." The meal closed with the two men touching briefly upon their mutual support for tariff reduction, admiration for Edward M. House, and desire for arms limitations. Roosevelt urged Dodd to resolve his American interests quickly; he wanted his newest diplomat to be in Berlin by mid-July.[11]

That evening Ambassador-elect and Mrs. Dodd attended a formal gathering given in their honor at the Germany embassy. It was a foretaste of the European protocol that would stir Dodd's disdain. "Almost twenty people sat down to an elaborate dinner," he recorded in his diary. "There was no good talk though we stayed until 12 o'clock."[12]

If Dodd found his first exposure to diplomatic pomp distasteful, he was even more distressed the following day, when he had his initial meeting with the economist Raymond Moley, one of Roosevelt's closest advisers. When the respected Columbia University professor acknowledged an absolute ignorance of American tariff policy prior to 1900, the historian in Dodd was devastated. Dodd decided that for all their reputed intellectual achievements, Roosevelt's "brain trusters" had little interest in gleaning lessons from the past. Months later he shared his concerns with Bessie Louis Pierce, a junior member of Chicago's history department. "Few people now rendering final decisions know any history or enough of it to see its relation to all social and political behavior." Moley in particular lacked "any real knowledge of human nature or even of economic history."[13]

Little wonder that State Department regulars found Dodd a mystery. He was not a wealthy political appointee who acquiesced to polite suggestions from his professional staff, nor did he rank among those who had risen from within the service to command an embassy considered too sensitive for a mere amateur. He was an intellectual, a scholar, and a professor who had left his confining Chicago classroom to teach on a world stage, to instruct presidents, dictators, senators, and foreign-service officials. He was a Jeffersonian Democrat determined to cut through the diplomatic obfuscation that he believed hindered efficient relations between nations. And he was a southern-born yeoman suspicious of all aristocratic affectations, seeing in them the arrogant oppression of the common man. Confident in his own ideas, he boldly stepped into a new world that was far more dangerous than he had ever imagined.

This sudden career transformation prompted rituals both public and private. On short notice Dodd's Illinois friends prepared a farewell banquet worthy of one with his long service to the American intellectual community and his new status as an important international personage. On 23 June some two hundred representatives of Chicago's "cultural, business, civic and official life" toasted the new ambassador. Quickly thereafter, he acquitted himself of his university responsibilities, turning his position as department chair over to his successor, Bernadette Schmitt; rented his house, storing in its leaking attic thirty-five years of personal correspondence; and entrained south, going first to a State Department orientation and then to North Carolina to pay respect to relatives living and dead.[14]

On Saturday, 1 July, Dodd spent an emotion-filled day performing filial duties. Having arrived in Raleigh the previous night, he left for an early morning drive to the nearby community of Fuquay Springs and the home of his eighty-six-year-old father, an unlettered rustic whose recent newspaper interviews must have caused his distinguished son discomfort. William, the old man bragged, owned his own farm in Virginia, where he "goes to work . . . just like a Nigger." However much the younger Dodd enjoyed his rural respite, this statement lacked the dignity associated with his ambassadorial appointment and further deteriorated a relationship strained since his mother's death in 1909. In the late morning Dodd formally called upon Governor J. C. B. Ehringhaus, an official for whom he had little respect, and then as rapidly as decorum and newspaper reporters allowed he left to visit his maternal relations in Clayton. He lingered over his mother's grave, saddened by the neglected state of the Horne family cemetery, symbolic of their decline in fortunes after Ashley's death. With the day's shadows lengthening, Dodd strolled across the hilltop where he had been born, his father's crude house having long since disappeared. Almost four decades earlier he had forsaken Clayton as an innocent youth questing for a German education and a career of importance; now Dodd once again was leaving his native community for Germany, a somber man of importance sent on a perilous quest. It had been a "rather sorrowful day," he reflected, "though our kinfolk did all they could to give us a pleasant sojourn." [15]

Forty-eight hours later Dodd, Mattie, and their two children, now young adults, arrived in New York City. He met with prominent Jewish leaders, who, though disappointed by Roosevelt's official position on German persecutions, judged Dodd a liberal and humane scholar who could be trusted to seek justice within the restraints placed upon him. The next day Dodd celebrated the Fourth of July with Colonel House, paying his respects to the man who deeply appreciated his efforts "to tie the Wilson influence to" President Roosevelt. Dodd's American rituals completed, on 5 July he and his family boarded ship; Berlin awaited them. [16]

Even as Dodd was concluding his rites the State Department was negotiating with the German Foreign Office to obtain him his official diplomatic accreditation. Largely unaware of the debate over his forthcoming Berlin reception, Dodd would have found the careful and restrained haggling a disagreeable and superfluous exercise. As a scholar comfortable within the world of broad intellectual theory and academic debate, he

was ill prepared for the reality that the simplest act, in this case the accreditation of a new chief of mission, required hours of painstaking conversations and consultations.[17]

Far from the cause of any ill will between the United States and Germany, Dodd's investiture was simply a delicate matter of timing and logis-
tics. On 12 June Under Secretary of State William Phillips telegraphed
George A. Gordon, the chargé d'affaires in Berlin, that Dodd anticipated
sailing for Europe on 5 July. Having informed the appropriate officials
in the German Foreign Office, Gordon learned that the ailing President
Hindenburg had left for his summer retreat at Neudeck and was unlikely
to return to Berlin until late August or early September. Given that Dodd
could not present his letter of credence to the absent head of state, Gordon strongly urged Washington to delay Dodd's departure. But Roosevelt
insisted that Dodd "enter upon his duties as quickly as possible." Tasked
with solving this problem, Phillips worked through Gordon to recommended politely to his German opposites that they consider the American
expedient when faced with similar difficulties. Whenever the president of
the United States was away from the nation's capital, new ambassadors
were received by him at his temporary residence or the new envoy was
designated an "appointed ambassador," with all of the appropriate em-
powerments, until he could be formally received at the White House.[18]

After appropriate deliberation, the German Foreign Office courteously
rejected the first proposal—Neudeck lacked proper facilities for a formal
reception—but accepted in principle the second American suggestion.
This necessitated more tedious negotiations to define precisely the meaning and legal status of an "appointed ambassador." On 15 July Dodd
assumed command of the American legation, and six weeks later, on 30
August, President von Hindenburg officially received the new ambassador
in Berlin.[19]

In his first weeks Dodd focused on simple problems: finding appropriate lodging, becoming acquainted with his perplexed staff, and,
equally important, allowing his mystified associates to adjust to him. The
Jeffersonian Dodd had stepped into a Federalist citadel where precedence,
appearance, and decorum counted much in determining the status of men
and nations. A clash was inevitable, not with the German civilization,
with which Dodd was well acquainted, but with his own diplomatic family, whose customs were alien to him. No sooner had embassy employees
learned, to their horror, that Dodd had chosen a proletarian Chevrolet

for his official automobile than he telegraphed for them to reserve for his family "modest quarters in a modest hotel." The legation's senior officials met in emergency session, fearing that Dodd's requested lodging would diminish American prestige and despairing of a solution. In the end, Counsel General George S. Messersmith volunteered to resolve the dilemma personally.[20]

Unlike his patrician-born peers, Messersmith had plebeian roots and understood the ambassador's mind-set. "Dodd was a man of very exaggerated ideas about the way an Ambassador should live," he reflected years later. "He felt that he should live most inconspicuously and modestly. While I understood this and how he felt about it, I knew that the German officials and German people would not." The consul general immediately made an appointment with the manager of the Esplanade Hotel, which ranked third among Berlin's top three establishments. Would the manager accept the honor of hosting the newly designated American ambassador? Of course, the official agreed, because the distinguished envoy's residence would measurably increase his hotel's prestige. Messersmith then smoothly outlined Dodd's personal circumstances: his lack of wealth, his determination to live within his modest compensation, and much more. In the end, the manager weighed his hotel's increased distinction against a trifling monetary loss and agreed to furnish a first-class suite at one-third of the usual rate.[21]

Messersmith and his wife met the Dodds at the railway station and guided them to their temporary home. Shocked by the sight of "six embarrassingly elegant rooms with beautiful furniture," Dodd insisted on moving to cheaper accommodations. But when Messersmith told him the cost, without revealing the circumstances, Dodd gave in, noting simply that "one could not complain." He never discovered the deception. Several times over the next two weeks he told Messersmith that "the Esplanade was too elaborate." But in Messersmith's more sophisticated thinking, "it was anything but too elaborate, . . . [it] was simply a good Berlin hotel-apartment."[22]

Ironically, Nazi anti-Semitism expedited Dodd's quest for housing suitable both to himself and to his condescending associates. Messersmith easily located a Jewish family threatened with the loss of their opulent mansion. Since leasing it to the American ambassador circumvented newly promulgated regulations limiting Jewish property rights, the family gladly made arrangements, renting it at a fraction of its market value.

Incredibly, the usually discerning Dodd was slow to appreciate this special situation. Two years later, when the owner sensed that persecution was declining and requested that the contract be renegotiated to arrive at a more equitable compensation, Dodd reacted with furor, deeming him a "cantankerous landlord who wishes to exploit us, since he knows we like the place." This crisis necessitated the intervention of Raymond Geist, Messersmith's successor, who employed all his considerable skills to soothe Dodd and placate the owner. Writing to his Washington superiors, Geist reported his success but warned that it "almost resulted in a scandal in Berlin."[23]

Because of the reduced rates at the Esplanade Hotel and the favorable rent for his permanent residence Dodd had a skewed perception of what it cost to live in Berlin. Since he was able to live comfortably on his government compensation, he could not understand why the members of his staff could not maintain their luxurious lifestyles on their earned salaries alone. Long suspicious of unearned wealth, Dodd believed that their financial independence not only lessened their loyalty to government service but also diminished their professionalism.[24] A lifetime of discontent with class divisions underscored reforms he soon instituted at his embassy.

Changes occurred immediately. Within thirty days Dodd's shocked staff realized that he was no ordinary political appointee and that nothing in their previous experiences had prepared them for his management style. He insisted that the ambassador was the actual, not the nominal, head of the legation. If his predecessors had been weak because they knew neither the language nor the customs of their host country, Dodd saw himself as the prototype of the new ambassador, an expert comfortable with the German tongue and the nation's heritage. "I would rather resign . . . than simply to remain a protocol and social figurehead," he explained to Assistant Secretary of State R. Walton Moore. "Too much of my life has been devoted to historical work for me to be content with a score of expensive men around me who can not function in a highly efficient way."[25]

Dodd had every intention of turning what he considered the embassy's lackadaisical and wasteful operation into a professional, efficient one. He mandated budget cuts, limiting secretarial support, restricting telegram submissions to the United States, and initiating Draconian staff reductions. Dodd argued that the army and navy attachés could be replaced

with a single military expert, that the "commerce men might all be retired" and their duties redistributed among the consular men, and that
the agricultural analyst's position should be reevaluated. More than anything else, he demanded that his subordinates forswear their obsessions
with "past etiquette and behavior, the punctilios of Louis XIV and Queen
Victoria times," and become instead "informed men" useful to government service. Such officials, Dodd averred, would not be "golf loafers"
or partygoers who drifted into their offices at midmorning only to leave
in the early afternoon for appointments on the putting greens. Insensitive
to the argument that such social engagements directly related to foreign-
service work, he ordered his staff to arrive at their offices no later than
9:30 A.M. and leave no earlier than 6:00 P.M.[26]

Chargé d'affaires Gordon was the first casualty in the ensuing war. An
internecine rivalry already existed between him and Messersmith, with
the latter better appreciating and more easily adjusting to Dodd. But as
the ranking career officer, Gordon ran the embassy in the ambassador's
absence and under normal circumstances was the real power behind the
figurehead appointee. Already frustrated because the State Department
had ignored his recommendation that a career diplomat be assigned to
the sensitive posting, Gordon, who possessed significant wealth and considerable hauteur, found Dodd's designation galling and his insistence
upon personal frugality incomprehensible. Palsied during the crisis over
Dodd's living arrangements, he had allowed Messersmith to make the first
and better impression.[27]

Although Dodd immediately recognized the factions polarized around
the two antagonists—he had dealt with factions in his post as department
chair—he lacked the expertise to mediate between these two highly
skilled opponents. Fortunately, Gordon, a victim of his own intransigence
and Messersmith's shrewd maneuvering, made the resolution easy. The
critical battle occurred on 24 July, when Messersmith asked Dodd to
come to his office for a brief consultation with Gordon and one other
official. The Jeffersonian-minded Dodd saw nothing amiss, walked to
Messersmith's domain, and was piqued when an indignant Gordon refused to join. Hours later the raging chargé d'affaires lectured Dodd on
proper embassy etiquette: an ambassador never entered a subordinate's
office; he always commanded an audience in his official suite. Nothing
could have offended Dodd more. Gordon "is an industrious career man,"
he snorted in his diary, but he has "punctilio developed to the nth degree."

Dodd soon demanded and got Gordon's recall; he later used his influence with Edward M. House and President Roosevelt to have Messersmith appointed ambassador to Austria.[28]

If these initial conflicts established the tone of Dodd's embassy management, events early in his tenure also set the pattern for his relationship with Germany's Nazi overlords. Dodd's boycott of the massive Nürnberg rallies constituted his first and strongest challenge to the new German order. On 18 August Reich Chancellor Hitler requested that the American ambassador and other accredited chiefs of mission be "his guests in Nuremberg on September 2nd and 3rd on the occasion of the caucus of his party." Since Dodd considered this merely a gathering of the Nazi Party rather than an official government function, he at once cabled the State Department for guidance. The State Department's response was noncommittal, leaving the final decision to Dodd. Dodd decided not to attend, arguing that it would endorse "the present regime and accept the theory that the Nazi party is synonymous with the German Government and nation." Other democratic ambassadors followed Dodd's lead. Nazi functionaries never forgave this refusal to honor their party and retaliated following each subsequent boycott, making routine embassy business more difficult.[29]

Although Dodd's boycott worried German officials, it was a passive response. However, his first public speech made clear his unfriendly view toward the Nazi regime. When he was invited to address the American Chamber of Commerce on 12 October, Dodd prepared his talk with care, employing the sophisticated stratagems of an accomplished historian. On the surface his was a simple lecture, an outline of past events from ancient Rome to nineteenth-century America, and no reference was made to Germany or to the Nazi Party. If his listeners arrived at thoughts applicable to their contemporary world, it was because of their own intellectual acumen. His chargé d'affaires clearly missed the parables. Gordon looked the speech over for offensive utterances, deemed it an innocuous discourse on the past, and approved its delivery. He was oblivious to its oblique critique of the host government.[30]

On the appointed evening Dodd stood before an audience of two hundred American businessmen and their German guests. Having announced that his topic was economic nationalism, he pointed out that whenever society departed from the entrepreneurial freedoms of democracy and relied instead upon dictatorship and planned economy, the result was social

collapse. Step by step, he led his listeners through the parallel lessons illustrated by the manipulations of Julius Caesar, the failures of Spain's New
World policies, the mercantile mistakes of England's Charles II, and the
monetary follies of Jean Baptiste Colbert in France and Henry Clay
in America. In Dodd's interpretation each effort to structure economies
benefited a privileged few, created hardship and discontent among the
masses, and led to either war or famine. "One may safely say," he concluded,

> that it would be well if statesmen learned enough of history to realize that
> no system which implies the control of society by privilege seekers has
> ever ended any other way than in collapse. . . . The statesmen of today
> [must have] sufficient knowledge of the blunders of the past to realize that
> if Western civilization is to survive they must find a way to avoid the crime
> and terrific disasters of war; they must learn to develop in a friendly spirit
> the resources of the undeveloped regions of the world; they must lower,
> not raise, barriers against the migration of surplus populations and they
> must facilitate and not defeat the interchange of surplus goods.

The audience burst into thunderous applause; but some who studied the
discourse for its more subtle meanings found less in it to please them.[31]

Dodd was aware of the potential impact of his speech. "It was because
I had seen so much of injustice and domineering little groups," he wrote
a Chicago friend days later, "that I ventured as far as my position would
allow . . . and by historical analogy warned men as solemnly as possible
against half educated leaders." Hitler, chief among those leaders, boiled at
the implied critique and instantly ordered his minister of foreign affairs,
Konstantin von Neurath, to deliberately slight the American envoy. Dodd
had scheduled an appointment with the foreign minister for the morning
of 13 October; it was twice postponed, reportedly due to urgent cabinet
business. Messersmith detected the significance of the postponements. Although Dodd "waited patiently all day, it was not until 8 o'clock that he
saw Neurath," Messersmith told the State Department. "In the meantime
Neurath had had time to lunch with the Chilean Ambassador [visiting]
from London."[32]

Versed in the intricate gamesmanship of international relations, American foreign-service professionals fully appreciated the calculated insult.
Washington officials were livid with Dodd, but to their consternation
Roosevelt was amused. Edward M. House, who was spending several
days at the executive mansion at the time, enjoyed the dichotomous re-

sponse. "It was delightful to hear the President say he was pleased beyond measure with the work you are doing in Berlin," he informed his friend. "I spent some time at the State Department. In strictest confidence, they did not speak of you with the same enthusiasm as the President."[33]

Under Secretary of State Phillips allowed several weeks to pass before he composed a carefully worded rebuke. "It is good to respond to invitations to speak on really important occasions," he explained to Dodd. "Certainly, the State Department could not lay down any rules and regulations" on public utterances, but Dodd should remember "that an Ambassador, who is a privileged guest of the country to which he is accredited, should be careful not to give public expression to anything in the nature of criticism of his adopted country, because, in doing so, he [will lose] the confidence of those very public officials whose good-will is so important to him in the success of his mission." Words were the crux of the matter. To Phillips, Gordon, Messersmith, and Neurath they were the tools of international harmony. Used judicially, they soothed feelings, obscured differences, and made possible the smooth intercourse of nations. To Dodd the academician, words were the expression of ideas that stirred men's passions for good or ill and the convenient mechanism by which a skilled observer conveyed information critical to human understanding. Frustrated by State Department regulars, Dodd eventually confided to his Chicago colleague Bernadette Schmitt, "I am more of a historian than a diplomat."[34] But it was his skills as an acute observer of men and nations, skills honed during his career as a historian, that proved his greatest worth. Roosevelt needed such a man in Berlin.

Little in history prepared twentieth-century man for the Hitler phenomenon. Who could have predicted that an obscure political demagogue would quickly and securely capture cultured Germany, construct for himself an unrivaled personality cult, resurrect the nation's defeated army and employ it to conquer most of Europe, and in the process murder millions of Jews and other "undesirables"? Such malignancy was beyond the imagination of liberal men educated in the faith of human perfection. Dodd shared that liberal perspective, believing that if only the United States and other nations would follow the scriptures of Woodrow Wilson, international harmony would pacify a world too long blighted by war. But Dodd met the villain, rapidly assessed his intent and his potential, and quickly thereafter shed his innocence. He warned officials in his own government, broadcasting a message none wished to hear and perhaps only Roosevelt fully appreciated. Dodd's reports were consistently gloomy, but as the president explained to Breckinridge Long, his equally negative ambassador to Rome: "You and Dodd have been far more accurate in your pessimism . . . than any other of my friends in Europe." [35]

Dodd's personal acquaintance with Hitler inspired his pessimism. Early in his tenure he twice interviewed the dictator—experiences that were intensely painful to him—and thereafter limited his meetings to requisite diplomatic appointments. "I decided," he affirmed at the end of his first year's service, that "I would never again . . . seek an interview for myself except upon official grounds. I have a sense of horror when I look at the man." But as the accredited American minister to Germany it fell to him not only to entreat with the Nazi leader but also to report his observations. Hitler's volatile personality, his subversion of the fate of the German people to his powerful will, and his iron determination to dominate Europe, if not the world, soon impressed Dodd. After his first audience with the Reich chancellor, Dodd recorded simply: "My final observation was of his belligerence and self-confidence." [36]

Earlier Dodd had held quite a different opinion of Hitler. Arriving in Berlin in mid-1933, Dodd had shared with other educated men a healthy skepticism toward those Hitler critics who warned of his malevolence. In particular, he considered Messersmith's negative judgments far too extreme. [37] But after lengthy talks with the Führer on 17 October 1933 and 7 March 1934, Dodd reversed his view, endorsed Messersmith's assessments, and became one of the more strident prophets of a Hitler-inspired catastrophe.

Dodd's much delayed appointment with Neurath on 13 October had been a preliminary to a formal session with Hitler four days later. Satisfied with the American ambassador's chastisement, the German chief of government received his petitioner with sufficient pomp to demonstrate the Führer's exalted status and just enough humility to show his businesslike intent. Dodd recorded that the meeting took place in the same "palace where Bismarck once lived and worked." He entered the opulent structure, climbed "broad stairways guarded at every turn by Nazi soldiers with hands raised in the Caesar style," and, following a diplomatically correct delay of five minutes, was ushered into the chancellor's cavernous office. Hitler's "simple work-a-day suit" contrasted with his surroundings, and he looked "somewhat better than the pictures which appear in the papers." [38]

The forty-five-minute conversation remained correct, even congenial, as long as Dodd moved through the two topics of their prearranged agenda—the persecution of American citizens who refused to give the "Hitler salute" and German debts to American bondholders—but when the Wilsonian Dodd touched upon the unscheduled subject of Hitler's just announced withdrawal from the League of Nations, his host became vehement, revealing a dark nature. Hitler placated the U.S. ambassador by promising to exempt Americans and other foreign nationals from the obligation to honor Nazi symbols and to punish party zealots who disobeyed the decree, and he patiently explained to Dodd Germany's difficulties with American bankers. Contrary to his instructions, Dodd sympathized with the latter position, having no love for what he considered avaricious American capitalists. When Dodd unexpectedly pressed Hitler on the League issue, the German nationalist suddenly raged. The Treaty of Versailles was unfair, the United States and other powers had reneged on promised disarmaments, and Germany suffered the indignity of being "in a defenseless status." Nonplussed by this sudden change in demeanor, Dodd limply replied that all losers in war suffer injustice; "witness the treatment of our southern states after the Civil War." It was hardly an adequate response. [39]

The following February Secretary of State Hull ordered Dodd to protest German anti-American activities in the United States, and so Dodd again entered the Reich chancellor's office. Following each point made by the ambassador, Hitler responded with the same simple, emphatic, and chilling answer. When Dodd complained about the distribution of a brochure issued by a Nazi Party publishing house that appealed to Germans "in other countries to think themselves always as Germans . . . owing moral, if not political, allegiance to the fatherland," Hitler exploded, "That is all Jewish lies. If I can find out who does that I will put him out of the country at once." Warming to his theme with great emotion, he claimed that Jews "were responsible for substantially all the ill feeling in the United States toward Germany." Dodd, sensing an opening to discuss the potential emigration of German Jews, strayed from his intended purpose and implored Hitler's support for the League of Nations Commission on Refugees and its project to expatriate German Jews. Hitler dismissed it, claiming "that nothing could come of such a movement, no matter how much money [was] put into it; . . . the Jews in Germany and outside would use the organization to attack Germany and to make endless trouble." Frequently using the expression "damn the Jews," he lectured that Dodd failed to appreciate the worldwide Zionist conspiracy. Fifty-nine percent of all offices in Russia were held by Jews, he claimed. They had ruined that country, and they intended to ruin Germany. "If they continue their activity, we shall make a complete end to all of them in this country." Desperate to alter the course of the conversation, Dodd warned Hitler that the American people feared his government's warmaking potential and urged him to join in a multinational disarmament conference. But Hitler would not be turned from his theme. Dodd reported that he continued "attacking the Jews as being responsible for the feeling that Germany wants to go to war."[40]

That evening, still shaken by Hitler's virulent belligerency, Dodd pondered a long time over his diary, speculating on the Führer's nature and the essential characteristics of his two principal lieutenants, Joseph Goebbels and Hermann Goering. "The Hitler regime" was "composed of three inexperienced and very dogmatic persons" who had "been more or less connected with murderous undertakings in the last eight or ten years." They represented different groups that together facilitated their iron grip upon German society. Hitler, "romantic-minded and half informed about great historical events and men," had risen to power as the champion of the masses disillusioned by unemployment and national defeat. Having grasped the importance of symbolism as a tool to move millions, he had brilliantly modeled his personal style upon Mussolini's, appropriated the martial emblems of ancient Rome, and organized colossal patriotic displays. However much Dodd wished to believe that Hitler was sincere in his pacifist professions, he knew that the dictator demanded peace only on his terms, that he would be a tough negotiator with the French, and that in "the back of his mind [he held] the old German idea of dominating Europe through warfare."[41]

Goebbels and Goering perfectly complemented their political master. Having earned a doctoral degree in philosophy, Goebbels was a master propagandist who despised foreigners in general and the French in particular and continually declared "that the German people, once united, would dominate the world." In complete control of "all newspapers, radio, publications and art activities," he stimulated an intense xenophobia.

The sophisticated Hermann Goering represented "more clearly aristocratic and Prussian Germanism." Capitalizing on his reputation as a war hero, he had "mobilized the old Prussian extremists" in supporting Nazi rule. "Animated by intense class and foreign hatreds," these three willingly resorted "to the most ruthless methods." Dodd doubted that "there has ever been in modern history such a unique" triumvirate. But, he mused, "there was such a group in ancient Rome." As the months passed, he found dealing with the Nazi leadership increasingly difficult. "They are the governors of Germany," he wrote in late 1935, but "it is so humiliating to me to shake hands with known and confessed murders."[42]

In contrast to his patrician staff, who associated only with people at the highest levels of German society, Dodd's affinity for the nation's common folk led him to seek opportunities to move among them. On days stolen from his official duties he traveled incognito, motoring to villages and provincial cities, riding in second- and third-class passenger coaches, and conversing with laborers in small cafes. Initially encouraged, he reported to House in December 1933 that although Hitler's militaristic following might become dangerous, for the moment "public opinion is democratic, not autocratic." Within the year, however, this optimism faded to despair as Hitler's volatile rhetoric and aggressive nationalism increasingly beguiled the masses. During a brief drive across Germany he saw everywhere rallies of Hitler Youth and "of SS and SA men in uniform." One time their "marching and singing kept me awake nearly all night." As Messersmith later recalled, Dodd "knew Germany before the Nazi regime," and he "was always speaking of how incredible it was that" such activities "were happening . . . in the Germany he had known."[43]

During a leisurely tour though southern Germany with William Jr. Dodd finally grasped Hitler's intent. On Sunday, 28 October 1934, father and son lunched at a pleasant outdoor cafe in the small city of Hechingen. A contingent of Hitler Youth marched past, two thousand adolescent voices antheming victory over the despised "Frankreich." As fascinated as he was disturbed, Dodd drank in every detail of the occasion. He spied in the cafe window a large placard recruiting would-be pilots for "Goering's Air Ministry." He was struck by the fact that it was also "a color map of Germany." Fully appreciating the symbolic importance of perceived national boundaries, he was chilled by its "sharp colors [outlining] the parts of the Baltic region, Poland, Denmark and France that should be annexed." Dodd asked the proprietor if he could have the poster, and he collected additional placards as well. On his return to Berlin he immediately forwarded one to Roosevelt, citing it as clear evidence of "what lies behind the [Nazis'] intensive military preparations." The cafe owner had boasted that his community was already home to twenty expert flyers and that much larger Stuttgart had registered two thousand more.[44]

Considering the Goering map damning evidence, Dodd gathered additional information to construct a convincing paradigm that pointed to only one conclusion: Adolf Hitler intended to expand Germany's borders by war. On the same trip to southern Germany Dodd had passed through Bitterfeld, "a town with a huge munitions development, aglow with industrial activity, every smokestack busy," and shortly thereafter he visited Wittenburg, sacred to Martin Luther's memory, where he found the "great poison gas manufacturing plant" fully employed. From late 1934 onward Dodd's official and private correspondence exhorted vigilance because the Germany military continued to grow in size, skill, and enthusiasm; the "manufacture of arms and tanks, and poison gas goes on day and night."[45]

Even as Hitler charmed the world with his peaceful rhetoric, Dodd watched a society being acculturated to conflict. Although he normally disdained the cinema, on 9 January 1936 he succumbed to the urgings of friends and attended a showing of the immensely popular *Unsere Wehrmacht* (Our Defense Force). Dodd painfully endured the hour-long display of "vast army fields with tanks and machine guns operating and soldiers falling to the ground, all shooting and some killed; great parades of heavy trucks and big cannon; air attacks with hundreds of flying machines dropping bombs on a city." At critical moments "Hitler, Goering and even Goebbels appeared" in the film, proclaiming "their approval of all that was going on." Thoroughly disgusted, Dodd cringed each time the audience went wild with applause. "I could hardly endure the scenes and what seemed to me the brutal performances."[46]

Less than a month later the Führer sponsored a mammoth equine display for the entertainment of Berlin's diplomatic community. At the climax German cavalry galloped into the arena and ignited a sham battle. Augmented by exploding cannons, blazing machine guns, and charging tanks, they created an impressive spectacle that sent one message to the German audience and another to the international dignitaries. The crowd of twenty thousand roared approval, thrust forward the Nazi salute, and gloried in Hitler and Goering's beaming response. Dodd easily discerned the other message. "Practically all Germany is behind [Hitler] in the policy of re-armament," he warned Under Secretary of State Phillips. "We need not deceive ourselves as to the urge for eastern expansion even to the Black Sea; nor may any western power assume the German population is not proud of appearing in uniform and marching wherever commanded." Nazi leaders expected to "dominate Europe as Napoleon tried to do," Dodd wrote, reflecting that "it is curious that Napoleon is a hero here."[47]

Dodd also witnessed firsthand Hitler's growing personality cult, a phenomenon made possible by mating intense nationalism with the modern techniques of mass psychological manipulation and communications. Along with other men of reason, however, he was slow to appreciate its significance. Writing to House in October 1933, Dodd described the Reich chancellor as little more than "a great boy," though "the world may yet suffer from that fact." Nonetheless, the omnipresence of the Hitler image struck him as peculiar. "His bust adorns great stores and art institutes." One was placed "on a high pedestal [with] Goethe's . . . on his right and Beethoven's on his left, both lower." By 1936 Dodd fully understood the phenomenon. He warned Roosevelt, Hull, and other high officials that Hitler had created a commanding personality cult, that his people embraced him as the living reincarnation of Luther, Joan of Arc, or Napoleon, and that millions even worshiped him as the second Messiah. Returning from the opera in September 1934, Dodd recalled with amazement that during each intermission people in the floor seats had turned to the Führer's private balcony and shouted "the Hitler greeting." The actors and singers had been equally "enthusiastic about the Chancellor's presence, more, I was told, than was evidenced when the Hohenzollerns used to sit in the royal box."[48]

Early in his tenure Dodd naively believed that he could encourage Germany's intellectuals to counter Hitler's growing totalitarianism. Speaking frequently before university audiences, he preached American democracy as practiced by his heroes—Jefferson, Wilson, and the contemporary Roosevelt—and came perilously close to undiplomatic critiques of his host government, a fact lamented by Hull as well as others in the foreign-service bureaucracy. As he watched Hitler consolidate his dictatorship, Dodd urged German professors to spread the democratic faith among the masses. Criticized for this course by the State Department, he responded with the assurance that although his association with university professors aligned him "with a liberal and somewhat unpopular element of Ger-

man life," he still thought himself "in fair relations with the dominant, if
. . . unwise, leadership of the country." Gradually, however, the National
Socialist Party asserted its control over every aspect of German life, which
finally led Dodd to admit the futility of his crusade. Any German advocat-
ing pacifism or democracy, he informed Roosevelt, "is imprisoned, sometimes sadly beaten." Thus, by 1936 he reluctantly concluded that "no
attention is paid to anything we say, except by poor University folk."[49]

Apparently, German intellectuals appreciated Dodd more than his own
government's foreign-service professionals did. Few in his embassy and
even fewer in the State Department found his view creditable. In Berlin
only Messersmith shared Dodd's insight. "I told the Ambassador," he
wrote in a private log dated 21–25 March 1935, "that next to death I
was sure of two things: First if this regime stays in power, . . . there is
going to be war; second, that if there is war we are going to be in it in
spite of all we shall do to keep out." Dodd "saw through all the Nazi
pretenses," Messersmith recalled after World War II. He "was never once
deceived by anything that any of them said to him. He certainly saw the
situation better than any of his colleagues among the chiefs of mission
in Berlin."[50]

In Washington, however, Secretary of State Hull and Assistant Secretary of State Moore chaffed at Dodd's reporting style, preferring the safe,
balanced prose of diplomatic jargon to the professor's straightforward
and, in their view, strident missives. When he received his account of
Dodd's tour of southern Germany, with its incriminating map, Moore
forwarded it to Roosevelt but appended an endorsement designed to
soften the message. "Dr. Dodd's letter presents a rather dark picture of
what is going on in Germany," he wrote, but he added that there were
alternative interpretations to his description of fully activated munitions
factories. They provided, after all, employment for a people burdened by
depression. Moore reminded Roosevelt that even Dodd habitually lectured about "what a hard task it has been from ancient times until now
to assure the mass of people a fair measure of the good things of life."[51]

Almost a year later Hull also evidenced weariness of the ambassador's
rhetoric. Thanking him for his most "vivid picture of conditions in Germany," Hull reminded Dodd that it merely "indicated how difficult it is
to make any long range forecasts." He assured Dodd that "we are watching the European situation very attentively, and I know that you will not
hesitate, when you think it necessary, . . . to let me have the benefit . . . of

your information and views." Irritated by yet another Dodd jeremiad, an exasperated Moore complained to the president's personal secretary in January 1937, "I cannot share his gloomy midnight belief that the world is now on the verge of another war."[52]

But Dodd confidently believed that war was almost inevitable. "Hitler has assumed a great responsibility in the pronouncement of his peace through armament thesis," he warned Hull in March 1935. "The fact remains that at the moment he is more powerful than ever in Germany, and by the same token he is more than ever a potential menace to the peace of Europe." In letter after letter Dodd tallied the threat. Germany was "arming to the teeth as fast as possible"; it was prepared to drill two million "volunteer soldiers" and had plans to train eight million more; it was constructing "a great navy . . . destined to dominate the Baltic and North Seas"; and it was manufacturing aircraft at an astonishing pace. "The Third Reich will at a strategic moment seize the [Polish] Corridor," and should that lead to war, then Hitler would conquer "Holland, north Switzerland, Austria and the Baltic coast," as well as win back from France regions sacred to Germany. The Führer also lusted for eastern territory. If German armies reached Leningrad, he speculated, "we should have such horrors that one can hardly imagine the consequences."[53]

Throughout the 1920s Dodd had lectured tirelessly praising Wilson's idealism, condemning short-sighted politicians who rejected the League of Nations, and calling for repentance, with America's entry into the world peace establishment. Now he was witnessing the catastrophic results of the anti-Wilson policies, and he lamented the world's impotence before an aggressive Germany, Italy, and Japan. Desperately Dodd urged the United States to live up to its international responsibilities. "No man who knows what happened in the Great War or understands the complexes of Europe and the Far East can fail to realize that American isolation will mean disaster everywhere," he wrote Roosevelt intimate Harry Hopkins in 1934. Encouraged by the president's tentative moves toward internationalism, Dodd supported his campaign to participate in the World Court and prayed that it would pave the way for America's full association with the League of Nations.[54]

Granted leave in December 1934, Dodd arrived in the United States in time to witness the Senate debate regarding America's entry into the World Court and the vote on 29 January 1935, which fell seven votes short of the two-thirds majority needed for approval. Having placed all his hopes on passage of the resolution, he was disconsolate. To him it was inconceivable that rational men could ignore Hitler's malignancy, that they could even admire and applaud his stated goals and remain passive before his threatened aggressions. In Dodd's mind, three ancient enemies and one former friend "were the outstanding opponents of" the World Court, which at best would have been "a mild move in the direction" of international cooperation. He raged privately at Senators William Borah and Hiram Johnson, long opponents of Wilson's League, and he particularly condemned William G. McAdoo, who had fallen so far from grace that he was now little more than a lackey for isolationist William Randolph Hearst. Dodd contemplated resignation, reasoning that it "would create a sensation" and would give him "the chance to say to the country how foolish it is for our people to denounce minority dictatorships in Europe" while allowing a minority of men, largely influenced by Hearst and the radio demagogue Father Charles Coughlin, "to rule the United States in such an important matter." [55]

While Dodd was in this agitated state he dined at Rexford Tugwell's splendid Georgetown residence. A member of the president's brain trust, Tugwell not only reveled in his exalted position but also enhanced his stature by issuing much coveted dinner invitations to other men of power and opinion. He chose isolationist Montana Senator Burton K. Wheeler as a foil to the internationalist Dodd and then rounded out his party with New Deal insiders Jerome Frank, John Carter, and Paul Appleby. Satisfied with the turbulent mix, Tugwell later savored the evening, recalling that it was "amusing and significant to confront Burt Wheeler," one of the World Court's chief enemies, "with Dodd who believes absolutely that this withdrawal of ours means war." [56]

Dodd found the evening anything but amusing. The personification of a magniloquent university professor, he lectured his fellow guests. Encouraged by the World Court rejection, Hitler would soon seize Austria, "producing a crisis which would compel England to withdraw her fleet from Asiatic waters." In the resulting vacuum Japan would attack Russia as the first step in her quest to conquer China and to control "strategic points in East Asia." When Pacific Ocean oil reserves became threatened, "the Standard Oil interest" would then drag the United States into war "against our will." In support of this thesis, Dodd produced Goering's map of Germany, pointed to its incriminating boundaries, and implored his listeners to accept the only reasonable conclusion: a second world war was imminent.[57]

Unimpressed, Wheeler dismissed the professor's arguments. Admitting his admiration of Germany and his dislike of France, he claimed that entry into the World Court, or certainly the League of Nations, was far more likely to lead the United States into war. He emphatically declared that it was not the function of the United States "to prevent the unification of Europe under Germany or any other power," nor was it the responsibility of the United States "to prevent the unification of Eastern Asia under Japan or any other power."[58]

Although Frank adamantly opposed Hitler, Carter largely agreed with Senator Wheeler, and none deemed Dodd's map impressive. Carter simply noted that the boundaries represented "strips of territory lost" in 1919 and perhaps encompassed a few areas in "neighboring countries, Switzerland included." But he dismissed the latter thought, arguing that it was an "optical effect" caused by the broad red line used to highlight Germany's natural boundaries. "My impression," he said the following day, "was that Dodd had been sold a pup in the argument that the red map was designed to suggest areas of German conquest." Wheeler simply huffed, "What of it?" In his view, "the natural thing to happen was for Germany to absorb Austria, Czechoslovakia, Hungary, and the Balkans."[59]

Dodd retired early, unable to countenance further the company of men who were ignorant "of the teachings of history" and "indifferent to the cultured appeals of such people as the English, the French and the Dutch, not to mention the great German intellectual element now so helpless." Following his departure, Tugwell assessed Dodd's mettle. The professor "was still suffering from a bad attack of Woodrow Wilson," he told his other guests. More the pity, because "the president seemed to be in general agreement with Dodd's thesis" and felt "compelled to build a billion dollars worth of warships which will be obsolete in ten years."[60]

Days later, lunching with Roosevelt, Dodd recounted the Tugwell dinner but refrained from divulging the senator's identity. The president easily guessed his name, blithely noted his alliance with the ruthless Huey Long of Louisiana, and then passed on to other pressing issues. At the end of February Dodd returned to his Berlin office, commissioned to the "delicate work of watching and do nothing." He saw better than most men what was happening in Germany but found it impossible to convince either his Berlin staff, with the exception of Messersmith, or his superiors in the State Department. "Just how the [German] people have been brought into the present attitude, I could not explain without writing the chapter of a book," he complained in a letter to the sympathetic Josephus Daniels. "To any real historian, however, it is fairly understandable."[61]

Surrounded by cautious advisers and isolationist politicians, Roosevelt stood virtually alone in his appreciation of his Berlin envoy. When Dodd threatened to resign unless he was granted a quarter's leave to teach at the University of Chicago in 1936, the president quickly approved his request. "We most certainly do not want him to consider resigning," he admonished Moore. "I need him in Berlin."[62]

Even as Dodd dedicated himself to diplomatic service he retained his commitment to scholarship, yearned for the lecture hall with its eager students, and held dear the interest of the University of Chicago history department, which had, after all, succored his career. He soon confided to Bessie Louis Pierce an abiding desire "to be restored to my work, simply for a quarter a year." International relations were "hopeless of improvement," he complained. "The writing of history is more to me than endless dinners and diplomatic technicalities."[63]

To be sure, Dodd initially had been optimistic, believing that his liberation from the classroom and especially from administrative duties would give him sufficient time to focus on his long-delayed history of the Old South. Carefully packing his notes, outlines, and rough drafts, he had set out for Germany mindful that less than a century before his distinguished predecessor George Bancroft had combined diplomatic protocol with historical research. Confident that he could quickly order the embassy to his liking, he had assured a former colleague that by "autumn, I shall have time to write chapters of my *Old South*—more time than I had when chairman at Chicago."[64]

To his disappointment, Dodd had soon learned that the Berlin embassy lacked facilities he had taken for granted as an academician. More than anything else, the embassy library was woefully unsuited to his needs. Other than a complete set of the Yale *Chronicles,* it contained little of academic value—only statute books, internal reports, and League of Nations resolutions. Gradually Dodd found additional volumes carelessly scattered about the building, some originating from Bancroft's tenure, but even so, "ready reference to American history is next to impossible." Further burdened with a professional staff ignorant of both American and German history, Dodd felt the need for "books of usable type" to instruct them and asked fellow Chicago historian Avery Craven to develop an appropriate bibliography of standard works. With rare humor, he assured his friend that he would then "call on some kindly American millionaire when he comes into the embassy to make good this deficiency."[65]

Endless diplomatic functions—formal dinners, receptions, weekend retreats—deflected Dodd's scholarly course. If "teaching at Chicago always limited time for research," he complained to Craven, then the work in Berlin was even more "strenuous. . . . It has to do with ceremonies and with controversies that require a lot of time but mean nothing constructive." With his staff far from ordered by autumn, Dodd suspected that a lifetime of scholastic preparation was in jeopardy. He confided to House that he was "doubtful of the wisdom of having intimated last spring that I might be of service in Berlin." Only the first of the projected four volumes of his *Old South* was near completion. "Now I am here," he complained, "sixty-four years old, and engaged ten to fifteen hours a day! Getting nowhere."[66]

In addition to his anguish over his personal dilemma, Dodd worried about threatened changes at the University of Chicago. For twenty-five years he had taken pride in his role as a prime mover in its development into one of the nation's top graduate programs. "I have long felt that Chicago is the place for best and least partisan work in the country," he told Bernadette Schmitt. "Harvard and Yale veer always to undergraduate and sectional history of the U.S." But in 1933 the department seemed threatened. The Great Depression necessitated budget cuts, and Dodd had little faith in the judgment of President Hutchins, whom he viewed as an autocrat devoid of concern for faculty opinion or respect for the discipline of history. Dodd well remembered that on one infelicitous occasion the university president had remarked that all his undergraduate "history work at Yale was worthless." Within weeks of Dodd's arrival in Germany, friends forwarded the rumor that Hutchins intended to abolish the history department and make its professors part of the Social Science faculty.[67]

Dodd exploded. Most social-science practitioners had little respect for history, he fumed. The greatest weakness of the Roosevelt administration was that it relied too heavily upon political scientists, economists, and sociologists, who had no real knowledge of human nature. For all their impressive social models and economic charts, these vaunted academicians knew little of practical experience. As historians, Dodd assured Bessie Louis Pierce, "you and I know that human nature is not logical, that neither ideals, actual self interest or even emotion determines great issues." Public men could never solve the nation's problems "if our universities allow the social sciences to deal merely with contemporary or near contemporary issues." Counting Hutchins among those misguided academicians who failed to appreciate "the value of history," Dodd grew ever more angry, and in early 1934 he considered resigning in protest should the president fail to work in concert with the faculty. Fortunately, he held back from this action just long enough to learn that Hutchins had refrained from dramatic changes. Only later did Dodd realize that his resignation would have pleased Hutchins more than it would have perplexed him.[68]

Unhappy in his Berlin exile, Dodd looked back with fondness upon the the classroom's safe and comfortable environs. In October 1933 he reminded Hull that Roosevelt had orally promised him occasional leave for the purpose of teaching and immediately requested an official absence for the spring quarter in 1934. The secretary of state tentatively gave his approval, provided affairs in Germany were "not too critical." In November Schmitt approved Dodd's proposed course on the colonial South, with its special emphasis on the rise of the first American aristocracy, but no sooner had he and Dodd come to final agreement than Hull informed Dodd that Germany's political instability required continued vigilance. Disappointed, the ambassador stoically accepted the decision, reluctantly canceling his course and reflecting sadly upon his fading contact with academia.[69]

Denied the opportunity to share his thoughts with students, he concentrated on his forthcoming presidential address before the American Historical Association. Scheduled for presentation in Washington D.C., on 27 December 1934, it would be delivered in the same city and on almost the same date as his first professional paper in 1901. J. Franklin Jameson would most certainly be there, along with perhaps a few others who had heard Dodd's initial assessment of the southern social structure.[70] If these scholars recalled Dodd's brief discussion of Nathaniel Macon, they would remember his lauding the North Carolina senator as a friend of common-man democracy and a bitter foe of the aristocratic establishment. Three decades later and more, Dodd's themes remained the same; all that had changed was his professional stature.

Throughout the 1920s Dodd had resisted requests to publish articles from his research into the Old South, promising instead to present them as a whole argument in his projected volumes. To be sure, he had readily used his notes in classroom lectures and in speeches before numerous general audiences, but these had only hinted at the content of his work. With the first volume of his manuscript almost finished, Dodd judged it appropriate to use the occasion of his presidential address to preview his principal ideas. Entitled "The First Social Order in the United States," it would summarize his interpretation of the process by which the aristocracy had emerged dominant in the colonial South.[71]

Working on the paper at odd moments snatched from his diplomatic obligations, Dodd drew his inspiration not only from his massive notes but also from ideas molded during a lifetime of discontent with the existing class structure. Resentment toward elitist privilege had seasoned his youthful intellect, and his entire adult experience had reenforced his mind-set. To him the past, the present, and the future merged, impacting both his historical interpretations and his contemporary perspectives. Having made heroes of Jefferson, Wilson, and Franklin Roosevelt, he consistently ignored or explained away their patrician origins. Typically, on 4 March 1934 he paused to reflect upon the first anniversary of Roosevelt's inauguration and concluded that the current president had emerged at a moment in American history every bit as critical as when Jefferson had confronted the aristocrats of his age. "Roosevelt sees this," he wrote in his diary, "in spite of the fact that his training at Groton and Harvard was faulty, even vicious, and the wealth of his family burdensome." Having embraced a task "quite as difficult as Jefferson's," Roosevelt had Dodd's prayers for success, being possessed, Dodd believed, of the opportunity to create an enlightened society "where slave-holders (big business chiefs) no longer rule."[72]

Dodd made little distinction between the southern aristocrats, who had oppressed the common man before and after the Civil War, and the business magnates, whom he deemed a curse on the contemporary age. "I have never been able to sympathize with the slave-owners and their group," he wrote in 1933, "or with the masterful industrialists who succeeded them in 1865, or with the bankers who did as much as any group

to wreck us in 1929." Because Dodd assumed that colleges and universities failed to expose these class enemies of democracy, he saw his presidential address as a salvo in the battle to enlighten future generations.[73]

"There have been two conscious or unconscious social orders in the
United States," Dodd maintained before the assembled historians. The
first, dominated by slave-owning aristocrats, "began with the Stuart Restoration and ended in 1865"; the second, comprising the robber barons,
"emerged slowly between 1823 and 1861, took definite economic form
in 1865, and reached the acme of its power, if not its end, in 1929." Now,
in the midst of the suffering brought on by the Great Depression, Dodd
optimistically proclaimed that "many serious thinkers in the American
intellectual realm . . . feel that a third social order is slowly emerging, that
democracy is going to be tried at last on a national scale." If 250 years
after Charles II liberty had at last triumphed over autocracy, the American
people needed to understand why victory had taken so long to achieve.
He proposed to lead his listeners through the tragic opening act of a New
World morality play, demonstrating that the earliest colonials had
yearned for freedom, struggled against the forces of oppression, but in
the end suffered the first of many bitter defeats.[74]

In Dodd's construction, mid-seventeenth-century America drew set-
tlers from two distinctive and antagonistic groups. "Out of the turmoil of
Stuart England . . . came hundreds of entrepreneurs who hoped to build"
on the "North American mainland ducal and manorial estates." Although they proposed to rely upon England's impoverished masses to
form the nucleus of a New World peasant class, these would-be nobles
soon discovered that few among their meaner contemporaries were willing to risk danger, disease, and death for the status of serfs. "Only the
bravest and most self-reliant of the unemployed . . . yielded to the persuasions of the entrepreneurs," Dodd insisted. And they demanded an excessive price: the guarantee of property and, with it, liberty.

As indentured servants, England's poor had come to Maryland, Virginia, and the Carolinas every bit as dedicated to success as their wealthy
masters. They sold their labor dearly, demanded and got land and goods
at the end of their service, and thereby anticipated the privileges of an
English freeholder. To be sure, their servant period was difficult, but "if
treatment was rough, pressure too great, and marriage among the servants punished too severely, they ran away to the frontier where they
could hunt and fish . . . and buy land from the Indians." Although the

master class passed stringent laws to punish miscreants, they were not often enforced in a country "where half the population sympathized with the runaways" and the executors of the law, the church vestry and the county justices, "were often ex-servants." Overwhelmed by the power of the common man, "the plantation areas [became] unruly democracies."

Dodd proclaimed that "self-guided democracies . . . defeated all efforts before 1660 to set up a landed social order reflective of the reactionary ideas of the well-to-do." This would soon change, however, when the newly restored Charles II commissioned colonial governors to maintain a properly stratified society. Beginning in 1663 Virginia's autocratic William Berkeley warmed to this commission: he canceled elections to the House of Burgesses, forced churches to make the vestry an appointive rather than elective office, and mandated that local justices and sheriffs would be commissioned by the governor's council. His rule became so arbitrary that in 1676 Nathaniel Bacon led a democratic rebellion supported by "four-fifths of the people." When Berkeley fled, they "then forced the election of a new house of burgesses and repealed all the control laws of the preceding thirteen years." Unfortunately, Bacon's untimely death left "no competent democratic leader available," and by year's end "the authoritarian governor was again on his throne."

Hardly shaken by Berkeley's death in 1677, his widow perpetuated the aristocratic creed. A child of the powerful Culpeper family, Lady Berkeley inherited her husband's immense wealth and employed it, along with her marriage to another well-connected man, to assume "a leadership of the Virginia gentry which was hardly less effective than the governorship itself." She set a standard for patrician domination that was happily emulated from Maryland to the Carolinas.

The successful efforts of Governor Berkeley, his widow, and scores of equally determined aristocrats, argued Dodd, combined with other influences to "hasten the social evolution desired by London." Throughout the southern colonies "large land grants, limited suffrage, and county oligarchies" ensured that only the elite families governed. "Carrolls, Talbots, and Taneys in Maryland; Washingtons, Carters, Byrds, and Blands in Virginia; [and] Barnwells, Middletons, and Rhetts in Carolina" were but the leading representatives of the rising aristocratic class. Some were the products of British nobility, others were the more fortunate descendents of former indentured servants, and all constituted "the beginnings of a social order which had taken definite form before Negro slavery became important."

Nonetheless, slavery played a seminal role. By providing an assured and renewable labor force, it liberated the upper classes from their dependence upon the ungovernable white underclass. No longer able to demand rights in exchange for their services, many lesser whites fled to the frontier, but most "became share-tenants or slowly degenerated into 'poor whites' whose descendents became more helpless and more numerous as the emerging aristocracy expanded westward." Considering slavery antagonistic to free labor's interests, German, Irish, and Scottish immigrants shunned the South and gravitated northward to William Penn's more enlightened dominion. "For fifty years the process continued," Dodd stressed, and the result was a new democratic experiment in Pennsylvania, and the more definite fixing of the slave system upon the South, the complete social control of the wealthier class. The southern slave masters constructed mansions that reflected their exalted status, erected educational institutions to school their sons in the ruling ethic, and contracted marriage alliances that perpetuated wealth and power. Victorious over democracy, this social order dominated until it "came to its tragic end when Robert E. Lee surrendered at Appomattox."

If Dodd had hoped his paper would stimulate new thoughts and create a greater appreciation of the southern class struggle, he was sadly disappointed. Years later one of his graduate students, who praised Dodd as a teacher and mentor, said that Dodd's "presidential address for the AHA embarrassed all of us. His cavalier and needless misinterpretation of Stuart England could have been corrected from any textbook in English history, but he somehow arrived at his own version of it and without troubling to verify he stood before God and all the experts and put it down in the record."[75]

There was of course a reason why Dodd arrived at a version of history that differed from that of "all the experts." He had been born into the lower ranks of society, which made him a rarity among American intellectuals. Most were the products of elitist homes in which wealth, culture, and family influence had paved the way to a quality education. They did not often come into contact with their less privileged contemporaries, and they assumed that they were society's natural leaders. When they were presented with evidence to the contrary, they dismissed class discontent as an emotional response of the uneducated masses stirred by malcontented demagogues.

Even as Dodd prepared his AHA address he bemoaned the fact that the next generation of historians, among them his own students, were out of sympathy with his interpretations, that fifteen years beyond the publication of *The Cotton Kingdom* few among them found much merit in its manifested spirit. "A really brilliant young scholar in my former field (Old South) does not for the moment occur to me," he reflected sadly in early 1934. To be sure, Frank Lawrence Owsley "at Vanderbilt is every way but one admirable"; another student had written much but was "quite social caste in interpretation"; and yet a third taught Old South at Tulane but had been "spoiled at Oxford."[76]

Vanderbilt historian Owsley exemplified the southern social and cultural dynamics that had led so many of Dodd's disciples to stray from his teachings. Born into a comfortable Alabama family, he was the product of an upwardly mobile yeoman father and an aristocratic mother. In his writings Owsley often drew upon the familial traditions of his paternal ancestors, successful farmers who fell just short of patrician status, but his historiographical perspective just as often echoed the values of his maternal relations, powerful and wealthy Montgomery aristocrats. As a youth he had enjoyed the exciting tales spun by grizzled Confederate veterans, and he had readily absorbed the anti-Yankee bias taught in textbooks scrutinized by the United Daughters of the Confederacy. Matriculating at the University of Chicago on the eve of World War I, he despised the northern climate and even more the perceived cold nature of the northern people, but he basked in the warmth of Dodd's seminars and the privilege of studying southern history under a master teacher. Emulating Dodd, he became a master teacher in his own right, and because his view of the South was more congenial than Dodd's to upper-class perspectives, his students more readily clung to his comfortable anti-Yankee, anti-Negro preachments.[77]

Initially Owsley repeated Dodd's class themes. His first article, "Defeatism in the Confederacy" (1926), reflected his master's touch, demonstrating the disillusionment of yeomen whites fighting a war that benefited the upper classes. Owsley soon repented of such youthful indiscretions, however, and by the early 1930s he had moved toward ideas more in agreement with those of the patrician South. In 1933 he congratulated Avery Craven on his recently published biography of Edmund Ruffin, the fire-eating Virginia advocate of southern nationhood. "More of this needs to be done for the South," he noted. "Dodd should have done more of it, I think, for he is a gifted writer." But on further reflection Owsley suggested that "it may be fortunate that he has not, for he has been very unsympathetic with what Ruffin[,] Calhoun[,] Rhett and others stood for." Owsley empathized with these antebellum chauvinists, defended the South against what he considered neoabolitionists, and charted in his own publications a path divergent from that of Dodd, the class-conscious son of a North Carolina yeoman.[78]

As a youthful scholar in 1900 Dodd had attended his first AHA meeting, become associated with the leading men of his discipline, and aspired to be counted among their number. Thirty-five years after that initial experience he had reached the pinnacle of his profession and should have gloried in the respect of his peers, but public, professional, and private tragedies robbed him of much of his joy. Just three days after his presidential address his mother-in-law died, plunging the family into mourning; this sad event only added to his other burdens.[79] Even as he stood preeminent among his fellow historians his new career as the American ambassador to Hitler's Germany diverted his attention from scholarly concentration on the past to an animated concern for the present. Distracted by the Senate's debate over the United States' entry into the World Court, in a few weeks he would be devastated by Congress's repudiation of its international responsibilities.

Professionally, Dodd not only bore the burdens of an unfinished lifework and of students apostatizing from his teachings; in late 1934 he also suffered the indignity of President Hutchins's arbitrarily retiring him from the University of Chicago's history department. "It was . . . the plain assumption by the President that my connection [with Chicago] ceased, or would automatically cease, next June or October" that angered me, he explained to Schmitt. "No resolution of the Trustees has been forwarded to me, no letter of the President suggesting the time and terms of my retirement." While Dodd protested that he had no desire to usurp opportunities for younger men, he had hoped that he "might render the Department a service in the graduate field by giving a course or two each summer on the Old South."[80] As much as anything else, Dodd felt insulted, cast out from his long-cherished position without thanks or appreciation.

Unlike Hutchins, Schmitt appreciated Dodd's emotional need for a positive parting experience. He pushed the administration to invite Dodd to return to deliver a valedictory course during the summer of 1936. Chicago proved far more amendable to the idea than the State Department. Dodd opened negotiations with R. Walton Moore in February 1935, wrote follow-up letters throughout the summer, and in September threatened resignation unless he was granted the appropriate leave. Roosevelt personally intervened, ordering the State Department to grant the request of his Berlin ambassador.[81]

Taught in June and July 1936, Dodd's course "Critical Moments of American History, 1763 to 1921" was for him a most satisfying experience. "To my surprise," he wrote Moore, "about 200 students, teachers and graduates" enrolled, overwhelming him with work gladly done. Nor was his success limited to the classroom. He spoke in response to several invitations, delivering his most notable address on the Chicago campus on 7 July. "There were about 2000 people present, hundreds standing and other hundreds unable to get into the hall," he told Josephus Daniels. "It was a sad occasion, for I could not avoid describing the causes of *The Dilemma of Modern Civilization* and the terrible dangers ahead of us all." *Time* magazine took note of the ambassador's lectures, recorded his appreciation of Woodrow Wilson, and quoted him saying, "I am not free to speak. . . . But if men knew their history, they certainly would not do a great many things they do."[82]

Refreshed, Dodd recorded his grades before embarking for Germany on 29 July. Teaching at Chicago "has been worth a great deal to me," he wrote in a letter of appreciation to Roosevelt. To Moore he added, "The work has been welcome—but now I must return to Europe—center of world troubles."[83] Dodd's somber assessment of Nazi autocracy complimented his negative opinion of seventeenth-century southern aristocrats and spurred his desire to finish his *Old South* manuscript.

Adding to his sense of urgency was Dodd's own sense of mortality, a grating fear that he might die before he completed his work. Frederick Jackson Turner's demise in 1935 frightened him, for he had long considered Turner both a friend and a model by which to assess his own scholarly progress. "I am very sorry that Turner's teaching burden was always so great and later his health so troublesome that he never finished his undertaking in the sense intended," Dodd lamented, knowing that the same thing might soon be said about his own career. To his friend Carl Sandburg he confided, "I hope your Lincoln work is soon to be completed. My half-completed *Old South* will probably be buried with me."[84]

Throughout 1934 and 1935 and into early 1936 Dodd despaired of drawing his work to a satisfying conclusion and thus jealously guarded those increasingly rare moments devoted to personal writing. "I have never done what I consider an adequate piece of work, everything thus far preliminary and now I am about to be defeated," he anguished in a letter to Bessie Louis Pierce. "My real work remains undone—and here it is very hard indeed to get a single uninterrupted week-end." Overwhelmed by this mood, he complained to Texas historian Eugene C. Barker that the "tenseness of the situation in Europe, especially in Berlin, keeps one on his nerves all the time—not the best thing for a person like me"; and as late as spring 1936 he complained to Josephus Daniels that "I only wish I could get back to my work about ten hours a day. At present I am too much engaged."[85]

Fortunately, Dodd's leave of absence to teach at the University of Chicago also freed him to concentrate at least briefly on his magnum opus. He returned to Germany in late summer with the manuscript of volume 1 virtually completed, deeming only a last polish necessary before submission to New York's Macmillan Company. On 2 November 1936 he mailed the volume, entitled *The Old South: Struggles for Democracy,* promising three more volumes. Upon the publication of volume 1 a year later, he explained to Bessie Louis Pierce that his book's "purpose was not to give all the facts, but to show what men hoped and risked their lives for during the 17th century." This first effort illustrated how "poverty-stricken Europeans and religious freedom people managed to get" to the southern colonies and demand democracy; the next volume would advance the story, focusing on the eighteenth century's "emerging slave aristocracy," and the final two volumes would continue the struggle between the advocates of liberty and the forces of human oppression up to the Civil War.[86]

In 1909, Dodd had publicly condemned Thomas Nelson Page's *Old Dominion and Her Makers* for its obvious bias in favor of Virginia's "colonial lords and ladies, or their close imitators."[87] Almost three decades later he made his own offering to the historiography of the colonial South. Like Page's work, *The Old South: Struggles for Democracy* was replete with heroes and villains, but Dodd clearly empathized with the region's struggling masses and cast its "first families" as the malefactors. Just under three hundred pages long, it largely followed themes outlined in his 1934 address before the American Historical Association but expanded on them and added in particular positive discussions of the Puritan parliamentarian Edwin Sandys and the Enlightenment philosopher John Locke, who Dodd argued had sowed the seeds of democratic faith first in Virginia and then in the Carolinas.

Dodd praised Sandys as one of America's earliest democratic heroes. A leader of the House of Commons, moral critic of James I, and shareholder in the Virginia Company, he displayed his disdain for privilege by heading "the committee of Commons to inquire into the wrong-doing of monopolies in 1604." From that point forward "he never ceased to oppose the granting of monopolies" and persisted in his hostility toward the king; in 1619 he crusaded for changes in Virginia's charter that in effect created "the first democratic constitution that was ever applied in North America." It authorized the House of Burgesses, a body made up of "representatives of the people, to sit in a Virginia legislature in every essential like the House of Commons in England." Sandys's efforts, Dodd argued, "encouraged the thought that men were to govern themselves in the new England. The free men were to be the rulers of the land." When in 1621 Virginia's House of Burgesses restricted the power of the royal governor by reserving to itself the right of taxation, this demonstrated "that Sandys had done his work well."[88]

If Sandys deliberately and openly stimulated democracy in Virginia, Dodd asserted that John Locke secretly but just as intentionally laid its foundations in the Carolinas. The colony's proprietors, men of high aristocratic faith, commissioned Locke to structure for their settlements a governmental system duplicating in America the political climate of late Stuart England. Seventeenth-century England restricted the franchise to responsible men of property, a tiny fraction of the land's population. Dodd noted that when the same standard was applied to the Carolinas, it had a democratizing effect. Thousands of indentured servants completed their obligations, received as payment "their little tracts of land," and were thereby granted the suffrage. "As the population increased the [Carolina] parliament would necessarily be dominated by the common men of the new country," Dodd explained. This was a situation "analogous to the terms on which Sir Edwin Sandys had authorized the assembling of the House of Burgesses." Locke's "perfect reproduction of Stuart England slowly became a crude and unruly democracy ignoring grand constitutions."[89]

According to Dodd, the democratic seed took root in the southern colonies, but it produced a fragile plant that was continually threatened by insidious advocates of patrician rule. His narrative chronicled the machinations of the privileged few, led by Lord and Lady Berkeley, their allies, and their minions. At the close of the seventeenth century England's southern possessions had matured into little more than "small farmer–trading colonies maintain[ing] their struggle for democratic governments." Dodd promised to reveal their fate in his next installment. To be entitled *The First American Social Order,* its objective would be "to describe the emergence of Negro slavery and its effects upon the system which Sir Edwyn [*sic*] Sandys and John Locke had hoped to see established in far-off North America."[90]

To Dodd's disappointment, *The Old South: Struggles for Democracy* received at best lukewarm reviews. Most commentators disparaged his descriptions of Stuart England and argued that his interpretations offered little that was new. Among these, the historian Paul H. Buck expressed profound disappointment. He had "expected a great book from Mr. Dodd," but this volume could only be classified as "a good book but . . . not a distinguished piece of scholarship." Nonetheless, hoped Buck, "this criticism will become irrelevant as the later volumes appear. Upon them and not upon the introductory chapters of the first volume final judgement will rest."[91] Tragically, neither Dodd's promise nor Buck's hope was fulfilled. The future volumes were tabled, for Dodd, the accomplished student of the past, had become overwhelmed by the crises of the present.

By birth a plebeian, by training a scholar, and by nature a strong-minded, uncompromising moralist, Dodd had entered upon a career in politics with personal characteristics that would be disastrous to his own well-being in such an environment. His affinity for the values of the common man made him ill at ease with diplomatic functionaries schooled in the genteel manners of the upper classes; his partisan writings praising Woodrow Wilson chaffed living politicians, who resented being condemned by a historian; and his open disdain for the Nazi Party offended a German government that had the power to make his life, as well as the lives of his overburdened staff, miserable. That his assessment of Adolf Hitler was perfectly accurate and his predictions of German aggression were acutely perceptive mattered little to scores of important people who viewed Dodd as a threat to the world order.

Although Roosevelt considered Dodd an admirable advocate of the democratic faith and appreciated his assessment of central European affairs, Dodd's own staff was far less impressed, finding his unflinching commitment to principle burdensome as they struggled to accomplish their pragmatic tasks. The Berlin government grudgingly tolerated Dodd's official protest against persecutions aimed at Jews, Christian ministers, and university professors, but it grew livid at his thinly veiled critiques of Hitler and his public disdain for Nazi symbols and retaliated against the American embassy with petulant delays in routine business.

Dodd's boycott of the Nürnberg rallies constituted his strongest personal challenge to the new German order. He followed his refusal to attend the 1933 party convocation with repeated absences in 1934, 1935, and 1936.[92] This not only infuriated Hitler, who considered these impressive gatherings of paramount importance, but also perplexed many prominent Americans, who considered Dodd's boycott an unnecessary insult to the German government. By 1936 two well-known academicians, the former Cornell president Jacob Gould Schurman and the American University historian Charles C. Tansill, had become highly vocal in their criticisms of Roosevelt's foreign policy, especially his actions toward Germany. Both attended the Nürnberg rally of 1936, determined to demonstrate the solidarity of at least some Americans of merit with Hitler's campaign to bring stability to central Europe.

Highly respected as both an educator and an expert in international affairs, Schurman had retired in 1920 after twenty-eight years as Cornell's chief executive to indulge his interest in Republican politics and foreign service. Having served President William McKinley as the first head of the Phillipine Commission in 1899, he was appointed the American minister to China by the newly elected President Warren G. Harding in 1921. Four years later he resigned to become Calvin Coolidge's ambassador to Berlin. Throughout his tenure there, from 1925 to 1929, he developed an intense empathy with the suffering German people, believing that they had been too harshly punished for their leaders' mistakes during the Great War. He judged the Weimar Republic a failure, predicted its collapse, and foresaw its replacement by a powerful totalitarian leader. Whatever misgivings he possessed concerning Hitler's fanaticism, he considered it the natural result of mistakes made by an American government led by the misguided Woodrow Wilson. Three days following Hitler's reoccupation of the Rhineland on 7 March 1936, Schurman urged British and French statesmen to accept this as an accomplished fact because the "one-sided demilitarization of the Rhineland was the least satisfactory part" of the postwar settlements. "Is another war, which may engulf all Europe and perhaps America, too, necessary because Germany has resumed her absolute sovereignty over the Rhineland?" he queried.[93] Such an attitude of appeasement hardly endeared him to the current American ambassador to Germany.

In late summer Schurman visited Berlin, where Dodd received him with the weary respect of a man whose predecessor is not welcome. Out of professional courtesy Dodd provided him with a temporary staff and an official automobile and chauffeur and then watched with disdain as the German government granted Schurman privileges normally reserved to serving diplomats. Hitler granted him a private audience on 3 August, and Goering and Goebbels honored him at formal dinners from which, Dodd complained, "representatives of all democratic countries were omitted." When on 14 August Foreign Minister Neurath employed Schurman to inflict a calculated insult, Dodd became even more incensed. Scheduled to meet with the minister at 12:30 P.M., Dodd sat in an anteroom for twenty minutes while Neurath casually prolonged his meeting with the former ambassador. An enraged Dodd received nothing more than a perfunctory apology, made even less satisfying by the knowledge that Schurman had accepted Hitler's invitation to the Nürnberg party rally.[94]

When Schurman returned to the United States shortly after the September party congress, he assured reporters that the "Nazi regime had been accepted whole-heartedly by the German people." They "emphasize the military life," he soothed, "based upon the conception that primarily it gives moral training and discipline and secondly it is for national defense." Little worried by Hitler and ever the loyal Republican, Schurman then endorsed Kansas Governor Alf Landon's presidential bid.[95]

If Schurman accepted Hitler's rise to power as the natural outgrowth of America's failed postwar policies, Charles C. Tansill embraced Hitler as a stalwart hero opposed to Soviet Communism. A well-respected diplomatic historian at American University in Washington D.C., Tansill was a vocal critic of Wilsonian idealism in general and William E. Dodd in particular. Even after the cataclysm of World War II, Tansill remained bitter toward the American ambassador, castigating him as "an American liberal [with] a deep-seated dislike for every aspect of the Nazi movement," a "second-rate mind that had mastered merely the dubious fundamentals of how to get ahead in the historical profession," and "a babe-in-the-woods in the dark forests of Berlin." From Tansill's perspective, Stalin constituted a greater threat than Hitler to world stability, and an intelligent American government would have been better served by cooperating with the Nazi regime.[96]

Invited to Germany as a guest lecturer for the Carl Schurz Society of Berlin, Tansill then journeyed to the 1936 Nürnberg rally. The Führer honored him as a special guest and conversed with him on several occasions; in turn Tansill was deeply impressed by the dictator's personal magnetism. "I consider Hitler one of the ablest orators of the modern age," the professor proclaimed on his return to the United States. "His power as a convincing public speaker has done much to strengthen his position in the country which under his leadership has regained law, order, hope, and self-respect." He described the Germans as a peace-loving people with "no ill feeling . . . toward any nation except Russia, and only toward that one because of its 'Red' menace."[97]

Tansill blamed Dodd for whatever ill will existed between the United States and Germany. Standing before an assembly of Presbyterian ministers in Washington, he related the German government's concern over unfriendly relations. "The principle reason for the feeling is that the American Ambassador . . . has openly denounced the government and continues to be unsympathetic," he declared. "But neither the attitude of our ambassador nor the protests of any group or groups in this country will affect Hitler's power in the least. . . . The people are solidly behind him, and are completely satisfied with the program he has planned."[98] Tansill's pro-Nazi rhetoric became an immediate embarrassment to American University, so much so that when he harshly criticized fellow faculty members in front of students, the chancellor summarily revoked his tenure, severing his relationship with the institution.[99]

Tansill's concern over Dodd's attitudes and their results was shared by State Department officials in both Germany and the United States. One disaffected Berlin officer pointedly blamed deteriorating relations on "the unfriendly mission of Ambassador Dodd." His conflicts with career officers both in his own embassy and in the Washington bureaucracy extended beyond mere disputes over diplomatic decorum. Given his aversion to aristocratic pretensions, he found the lavish protocol of state functions distasteful and the patrician habits of American foreign-service officials unacceptable. A weary Dodd admitted that the "atmosphere (in Berlin) is to a person of my social attitudes and political prejudices so tense that relaxation is almost impossible."[100]

Dodd, parsimonious by nature, took offense at ostentatious diplomatic displays. Repulsed by the outrageous waste represented by dinners and receptions at the English, French, and Dutch embassies, he lectured the State Department that the American foreign service "ought to no longer imitate Victorian or Louis XIV social pretense." He soon discovered that wealthy career officials diametrically opposed retrenchment efforts in his own embassy. Although Dodd had succeeded in changing his staff's work habits, he continued to confront their resistance. "I am Jeffersonian in this," he wrote to a Washington ally, "and hope you will ask the president to back me."[101]

Dodd's yeoman ethic did strike a positive chord with many in Washington's political establishment, but he admitted that his ideas were "not popular with [State Department] regulars." One gossiped to a friend in the Berlin embassy that the "extraordinary thing is the widespread ramifications of [Dodd's] opinions. . . . To a degree larger than generally realized, I think that they are responsible for the reduction in our Foreign Service appropriations." The writer went on to say that the ambassador "approves of your work, but there is no doubt that he feels . . . you are living on too elaborate a scale and is preaching this doctrine not only in relation to you but to a great many others."[102]

Cast into an adversarial relationship with his Berlin staff, Dodd misinterpreted their counsel to moderate his criticisms of the German government. He noted that several of his affluent officers owned stock in such American corporations as DuPont and Standard Oil, and he therefore assumed that they marched with "the ranks of privileged capitalists." Because Dodd speculated that these same companies profited from secret contracts to rearm Germany, he concluded that his own staff, along with foreign-service officers throughout Europe, harbored fascist proclivities.[103]

A class-conscious Dodd easily connected American business elites with Nazi leaders. He conceived that just as a slave-rich minority had subverted democracy in the Old South, a Nazi minority was crushing democracy in Germany and a capitalistic minority was challenging democracy in contemporary America. "Our President has the most difficult situation in the world," he confided to a friend in late 1936. "I fear Business will defeat him [just] as slavery minorities defeated all real reforms before 1860."[104]

In Dodd's mind, newspaper magnate William Randolph Hearst best symbolized the natural alliance between the American business elite and the new German order. The ambassador had long felt contempt for the wealthy publisher. During World War I Dodd had accused Hearst of being an agent for German propaganda and had publicly denounced his newspaper chain for its opposition to Wilsonian internationalism. Not surprisingly, in 1933 the Hearst press had commenced a campaign criticizing Dodd's ambassadorship. A paranoid Dodd concluded that newspaper spies lurked everywhere, even among Roosevelt's staff. "One experienced newspaper man" in Berlin, Dodd explained to the State Department, "told me that a confidential letter to the President was apt to be reported to the Hearst people by a woman in his office."[105]

Dodd's singular hatred of Hearst led him to chronicle rumors of an understanding between Hearst and Hitler. Basing his report to Roosevelt on information supplied by a disgruntled newspaper correspondent, Dodd maintained that in the summer of 1934 the German government had lavishly entertained the publisher and his mistress. Following an hour-long audience with Hitler and additional negotiations with Minister of Propaganda Joseph Goebbels, Hearst supposedly had struck a bargain: for an annual fee of two hundred thousand dollars Hearst would instruct his reporters to give only positive assessments of what was going on in Germany. In a letter to the majority leader of the U.S. Senate, Dodd complained that Hearst and "his libertine women" were impressed by the Nazi regime. "Hearst is an ally of dictatorship," he warned, expressing his concern that important senators continually praised him.[106]

Dodd ached to share his historical perspectives with those powerful political leaders who he believed could most benefit from his instruction. He lectured individual senators, calling their attention to two fateful occasions when antidemocratic minorities had frustrated the people's expressed desires. In the first instance southern aristocrats had defeated Jeffersonian democracy, and in the second a handful of willful senators, led by Idaho's William Borah, had aborted Wilsonian internationalism.

After more than thirty years as a college and university professor, Dodd seemed little aware of the differences between students in a seminar and U.S. senators in session. In 1934 he wrote Borah, cataloging the senator's sins in 1919 and urging him to embrace a more liberal perspective.[107] Months later Dodd lunched with the members of the Senate Foreign Relations Committee, after which he expressed his pleasure that they were genuinely interested in his views on foreign relations. He was nonetheless surprised that they did not appreciate his suggestion that they read an excellent work on "the history of American debts to other countries—a perfectly nonpartisan account which any Senator ought to be glad to read." Borah, he noted, "made a point of sending excuses that he could not be present."[108]

Although Dodd's lectures on internationalism irritated a few prominent senators, it was his arguments favoring Roosevelt's court-packing scheme that seriously diminished his political support. Without cautioning his correspondents to keep his views private, the ambassador wrote key senators proclaiming that the Supreme Court was by design an aristocratic institution. In his own interpretation of southern history he linked Chief Justice John Marshall's judicial policies with the slaveholders' successful campaigns against Jefferson and concluded that the actions of contemporary justices threatened Roosevelt's New Deal. In a direct affront to one anti-Roosevelt legislator, Dodd asked: "How can Senator Borah, so long in high position, fail to recognize the meaning of anti-Democratic judicial and Senate minority vetoes?"[109]

Senators responded with anger. Among them, a livid Borah declared that if Dodd "is against dictatorship and is for [Roosevelt's] court packing plan," then he "is crazy." Echoing this sentiment, newspapers across the country demanded Dodd's immediate recall.[110] A perplexed Dodd protested that his only desire had been to "render service to my country, even if Senators wished to abuse me for writing bits of truth about past blunders."[111]

Sensing Dodd's loss of face, his State Department enemies, chief among them the imperious Sumner Welles, seized the opportunity to make him lose favor with Roosevelt. Welles had long chaffed at what he considered the ambassador's plebeian arrogance and despised his unorthodox diplomatic style. Of impeccable patrician origins, Welles counted among his distinguished ancestors the Massachusetts abolitionist Senator Charles Sumner. A member of the Harvard class of 1914, Welles had gained entry to the State Department largely through the influence of a family friend, Assistant Secretary of the Navy Franklin D. Roosevelt. Serving in numerous Asian and South American postings, Welles had risen rapidly in the service's professional ranks, aided in large measure by his demonstrated brilliance as well as his exceptional wealth.[112]

Dodd first stirred Welles's animosity at a State Department conference in the spring of 1934. Expressing his opposition to millionaires in the foreign service, Dodd complained about a recent staff appointee who had charged the government three thousand dollars to move his household goods and then spent more than thirty thousand dollars above his salary to furnish his opulent residence with eight servants. "Sumner Welles was the only man who seemed perturbed at my description," Dodd reported to a friend. He "twisted and squirmed. I did not know that he lives in a mansion that rivals the White House."[113]

By late 1937 Welles basked in Secretary of State Hull's favor and was soon advanced over the more senior R. Walton Moore to become under secretary of state. Promoting a conciliatory attitude toward the German regime, he considered Dodd a burden. Valuing Welles's counsel, Hull took advantage of Dodd's furlough in America to order the Berlin embassy to send a representative to the Nürnberg rally. Dodd vigorously complained to Hull, and to his profound distress, his letter was leaked to the press. Welles was delighted. Following an appointment with Welles on 27 September, the German ambassador to Washington informed his superiors that Welles "frankly confessed that Dodd was as incomprehensible to him as to us."[114]

Chastened, Dodd returned Germany to find his authority undercut in his own embassy and his person unwelcome in the German Foreign Office. Politically embarrassed by Dodd's imprudent statements concerning the Supreme Court and fearing future impolitic utterances from him, Roosevelt distanced himself from his Berlin representative. On 1 October Welles confided to the German ambassador in Washington that the president had determined to recall Dodd. Although Dodd had anticipated retirement in the spring of 1938, on 23 November the State Department ordered him to leave Berlin no later than 31 December 1937.[115]

Dodd was despondent. The mission he had begun with hope more than four years earlier now seemed a dismal failure. In disgrace, he and Mattie packed their goods and prepared for a quiet retirement on their Virginia farm, consoled only by the thought that Dodd might at long last finish his *Old South* series and turn his meticulous diary into a memoir of his German years.[116]

Only a few Americans in Berlin shared Dodd's insight and, like him, looked to the future with fear. Among them, the journalist William Shirer assured Dodd that he "always felt *grateful* that you were there. It was integrity and moral and intellectual courage that was needed there in our representative, and you had it—completely. . . . Lesser men in your post—and Roosevelt was almost a genius in picking mediocre men for foreign posts—would have done the country untold harm."[117] Shirer's compliment was a harbinger of the American public's greater appreciation of the former ambassador. Much to his surprise, Dodd arrived in America a hero whose insight into the German menace would be greatly in demand. Unfortunately, his triumphal return would be followed by much tragedy.

CHAPTER SIX

"No Lectures Any More"

Martha Johns Dodd suffered a fatal heart attack shortly before midnight on 27 May 1938. For months she had accompanied her husband on his exhausting lecture tour as he warned audiences from Boston to Chicago that Adolf Hitler would soon cast the world into unimagined torment. Blighted by her husband's bleak images of Nazi Germany, she felt alienated from the horrible realities of her time. "This is such an unfortunate world, I would prefer to die," she lamented. Worn out by their efforts, in early May the weary couple finally paused for a month's rest at their Virginia farmstead. That fateful evening William retired at ten o'clock, leaving his troubled wife listening to the late news. The next morning he waited patiently at the breakfast table, little concerned at first because Martha had fallen into the habit of sleeping late. At nine he opened her bedroom door to find his companion of thirty-six years "lying across her bed, not undressed and cold and stiff." Dodd was swept into a greater void than he had ever thought possible. "Now I am alone," he grieved, "where we had expected to live at least ten . . . years more, she six years younger than myself."[1]

Dodd was a major player in a world in which grief had become precious coin; a civilization rushing to war paid little attention personal tragedies. Yet "the death of my wife has been such a calamity that my health has not been good," he wrote to Josephus Daniels in August. In spite of this, he had "lectured several times since June 6th because of appointments made before."[2] And he would continue to lecture until, in sad emulation of his hero Woodrow Wilson, he would suffer the collapse of his own body, ending his long and distinguished career. Dodd's last months were frenetic; he had glimpsed the future, and he had to warn the American people of the impending cataclysm.

Dodd and his family had sailed from Hamburg on 28 December 1937, leaving, in the words of an American press dispatch, "a cold silence on the part of Germany." Unheralded by the Nazi media, his departure also was not mourned by his frustrated underlings. Thoroughly glad to be rid of their bookish chief, they looked forward with anticipation to his replacement, Hugh Wilson, a State Department regular well schooled in traditional diplomatic protocol. "With the coming of Ambassador Wilson relations [with Germany] will improve," predicted one staffer; his professionalism was expected to salve "the bad effects of Mr. Dodd's outspoken criticisms."[3]

Although Dodd's contempt for Hitler and his minions was well known, he had never directly criticized the German government in public. To be sure, his private conversations and correspondences were replete with negative assessments of the Nazi leadership, and he frequently condemned totalitarian rule in oblique speeches couched as history lectures. But State Department regulations as well as the sensitive nature of his Berlin post largely muzzled Dodd, suppressing his desire to make open his critiques. However much the German Foreign Office disliked the American envoy, they could find no official cause to declare him unwelcome, so they consistently manifested their displeasure through diplomatic slights to him personally and with deliberate procrastinations in routine embassy business. Dodd's demise as ambassador came instead from the machinations of his State Department enemies, who had released to the press his private letter to Secretary of State Cordell Hull protesting American representation at the Nürnberg party rally of 1937. In Dodd's mind this confirmed his long-held suspicion that antidemocratic elites controlled the American foreign-service bureaucracy, sympathized with business magnates at home and fascist rulers abroad, and determined to subvert democracy everywhere.

Throughout the long, storm-driven passage to America Dodd fretted over his future course. He could formulate no plan and even doubted whether the American public would be interested in the opinions of a disgraced former ambassador. Dodd thus met the waiting press with more of an apology than a call for action. Landing in New York City on the evening of 6 January 1938, he refused to confirm rumors that he had resigned in protest over the official American presence at the recent Nürnberg rally and bitterly directed his petitioners to make "their inquiries at the State Department itself." But he steadfastly defended his refusal to attend "the ideological Nazi enclaves where democracy and its ideals were . . . ridiculed and attacked." No American loyal to the concept of democracy could in good conscious represent the United States in Hitler's Germany, he averred. But Dodd maintained that however evil the Nazi dictator was, his advent had been facilitated by powerful forces within the United States. Villainous "business and industrial groups" had created the world conditions leading to totalitarianism and potential war by failing "to recognize the need of international cooperation after 1920. Some of their chiefs defeated world peace efforts at Geneva more than once, because they thought the sale of arms and war materials more important than world peace." Still others had insisted in 1923 and again in 1930 "on trade barriers which made debt payments impossible."[4] With these words Dodd declared his personal war on Nazi Germany and reaffirmed his long crusade against class enemies at home.

Stung by Dodd's remarks, the German Foreign Office publicly denied his importance. "No formal notice will be taken of Mr. Dodd's observations inasmuch as they reflected the 'retiring Ambassador's habitual lack of comprehension of the new Germany.'"[5] Of course Dodd understood the "new Germany" in ways its Nazi overlords did not wish the world to know. He had returned to his native people cognizant of German horrors and desperate to enlighten his deeply divided nation. Many Americans admired Hitler's quest for Continental order, even more feared participation in deadly European affairs, and vast numbers more were simply ignorant. Sixty-eight years old and weary from the pressures of ambassadorship, Dodd disregarded his personal exhaustion, believing that to rally his fellow citizens against Hitler transcended his physical well-being.

If Dodd had no real plan of action, circumstances quickly swept him onto the speaker's podium, creating the opportunities he had so strongly desired. No longer fettered by State Department regulations, he was free to articulate publicly his deepest fears, to expose to the American people Hitler's evil intent. "Civilization as we know it is in grave danger unless Germany, Italy, and Japan are checked by the Democracies," he warned two hundred friends who had gathered to honor him at the Waldorf Astoria on 13 January. An uncooperative United States was "as much to blame" as any other country for an unstable Europe. American officials "and certain privileged business groups" had defeated Woodrow Wilson's League of Nations, and without the United States' influential presence, the League lacked the power to check "the renewal of ancient European annexation ideas." American businessmen had further exacerbated the situation first by pushing through Congress exorbitant tariffs that blocked European exports and destroyed European economies and then by selling war materials to would-be aggressors who advocated conquest as an antidote to national penury. Hitler promised prosperity through "a renewal of the ancient claims of German emperors to rule the Danube and Polish peoples" as well as "all of Italy." And six million unemployed Germans willingly acquiesced to his totalitarian policies. Dodd reminded his audience that "all the world knows, how [Hitler] denied religious, personal and press freedom, how universities and schools were put under party control, and how almost as many personal opponents were killed in five years as Charles II had executed in twenty years of the seventeenth century." Only a vigilant United States allied with equally determined democracies abroad could contain the Hitlerian cancer.[6]

Shaken by Dodd's 6 January interview and fearing his potential influence, the German foreign ministry quietly urged its American counterpart to restrict his rhetoric. Just hours before the Waldorf Astoria dinner a German foreign-service officer called upon the U.S. embassy in Berlin with the hope that "American authorities could see their way clear to prevent if possible . . . Mr. Dodd employing his official stay in Germany as a basis for attacks on Germany in any speeches or publications which he might have in prospect." Forewarned of this attempt to suppress American free speech, Secretary of State Hull was in a foul mood when the German ambassador to Washington entered his office early the following morning.[7]

Enraged that Dodd had "accused Chancellor Hitler of killing as many people in Germany as were killed by Charles II," the envoy propounded that such utterances by the man who "had been recognized until recently as Ambassador at Berlin" jeopardized friendly relations with his country, and he demanded that the U.S. government publicly announce "that it disapproved what Dr. Dodd had said." In a violation of diplomatic decorum, Hull interrupted the envoy's diatribe with a stinging rebuke. "We do have under our Constitution and Bill of Rights freedom of speech," he lectured. The German ambassador knew Dodd personally, was "acquainted with his ideas," and was familiar with "his disposition to give expression to them wherever he goes." Since Dodd had resigned from his post in Berlin, said Hull, he no longer represented the views of the State Department, and "now being a private citizen," he had complete freedom to express his views. Sweetly salting the wound, Hull then asked whether the German ambassador knew "how many men Charles II killed." He did not, and neither did Hull. The two men agreed that they "were not certain that Charles II was especially notorious in this regard."[8]

That afternoon Hull called a press conference in which he outlined the essential elements of the morning's conversation, highlighted his discussion of fundamental American freedoms, and then concluded that Dodd, no longer officially tied to the American government, was free to express his private opinions. Whether by accident or by skilled intent, Hull had elevated Dodd to the role of a popular champion of American democracy in a world threatened by fascist aggressors. Dodd, in turn, played the roll well, feigning surprise that the German ambassador would object to his right to critique Nazi rule. In all fairness, Dodd explained to reporters, he should have as much right to criticize the German administration as German officials had to condemn the U.S. government. Surely Hitler's ambassador knew "that in September, 1936, two of the highest officials of Germany ridiculed and attacked democracies and in September, 1937, three similar attacks were made at the same place—Nuremburg." He "must have heard these unfriendly speeches, or at least have read about them in the German papers."[9]

Speaking invitations immediately inundated Dodd. "I have received more than thirty letters a day including telegrams," he informed Daniels. These included "invitations to make lectures all the way to Minn.[,] Texas and California." Without pausing to organize his schedule, Dodd plunged ahead, speaking before audiences ranging from the Southern Women's National Democratic Organization to a Jewish temple gathering, to scholars assembled at universities. Everywhere he repeated familiar themes: the United States had erred in not joining Wilson's league, and business elites, spiritual heirs to the South's slave-rich aristocracy, had put corporate profits before World peace; such mistakes had made Germany's, Italy's, and Japan's murderous aggressions easy. Hitler's bold annexation of Austria in mid-March and his threats toward Czechoslovakia and Poland validated Dodd's predictions, enhanced his reputation, and generated still more lecture requests.[10] Throughout February, March, and April Dodd darted from one engagement to the next, spreading his message of impending conflict, hoping to galvanize a nation to action, and grieving that the American people had not awakened to their proper course.

His initial effort climaxed on 27 April, when, exhausted, Dodd participated in New York City's fifth annual Student Strike for Peace. At Columbia University's South Field he passionately warned a crowd of one thousand that unless the world democracies united against fascist aggressors, mankind would be plunged into a second and greater world war. Even as he spoke sophomoric students unfurled a huge Nazi banner from a dormitory adjacent the speaker's podium. Unaware of the action, Dodd reacted with confusion to the scattered boos that suddenly arose from the assembly. Always the stern and humorless professor, Dodd had never tolerated undergraduate immaturity; now, when he believed that the fate of nations as well as the lives of millions depended on his getting his message across, he found such behavior reprehensible. Shaken and distraught, Dodd finally acknowledged his need for rest, a time to reflect on his country's condition and to plan an even more purposeful and effective campaign. On 6 May he retreated to his Virginia farm, desperate for a brief respite.[11]

Gifted with a keen insight into the past, Dodd easily read the omens of the present and fearfully glimpsed the baleful future. This foreknowledge more than frightened him; it placed upon him an emotional load greater than he could bear. Soon personal tragedies and disappointments compounded this burden, overwhelming him emotionally and diminishing his capacity to make rational judgments. George S. Messersmith, who had been recalled to Washington after Germany's annexation of Austria, visited with Dodd several times during the summer and fall. Each conversation saddened Messersmith: "It was pitiful to see [Dodd's] mental deterioration."[12] Yet Dodd was a man of will and courage who did not drift easily into helplessness. From May 1938 to July 1939 he rebounded, at least in part, from each personal setback, until only physical collapse stilled a frantically racing mind intensely focused more upon a world in crisis than upon the vicissitudes of his own circumstances.

Even when Martha's sudden death cast Dodd into intense grief, he fulfilled his speaking obligations. Just eleven days after the shock of discovering her body he stood before the graduating class of the Virginia Polytechnic Institute predicting that its members soon would be thrown

into a war-shadowed environment. He then took a train to Massachusetts
for a weekend lecture series. There on the evening of 10 June he injected
a more ominous thought into his standard presentation. Everyone was
familiar with Hitler's "hostility toward the Jews," he told Boston's Harvard Club; what few realized was that he intended "to kill them all."[13]

Dodd returned to his northern Virginia farm, empty of wife and children but filled with "bundles of letters," which arrived every day. "Letter
writing is too burdensome," he complained to a former Chicago colleague. "I must lecture occasionally and the letters from all sorts of people
pile up while I am gone." Driven to spread his message, Dodd appeared
before the University of Virginia's Institute of Public Affairs on 10 July.
His severe message remained unaltered: "in the present international dilemma" mankind was "threatened by grave dangers, for which the United
States is as much to blame as any other country"; "the saving of democracy and World civilization, after the World War, depended on the League
of Nations and the application of President Wilson's Fourteen Points";
"the people of practically all countries hoped for and prayed for Woodrow Wilson's success, yet the governments and certain privileged business
groups defeated them."[14]

Dodd's lectures reflected his unwavering faith in democracy, his belief
that in a fair contest an enlightened public would always support candidates dedicated to the public weal. In his view, the events that had been
most disastrous to his world—the bloody Civil War, the rejection of Wilsonianism, the rise of Adolf Hitler—stemmed from the subversion of the
people's will by malignant minorities such as slave-rich aristocrats, greedy
capitalists, and bullying Nazis. Ever the liberal intellectual, he proclaimed
the gospel of democracy, urged its untarnished practice within the American political system, and prayed that a democratic America would soon
unite with other democratic nations to undermine European totalitarianism.

Even as Dodd shared his thoughts with audiences across the country
his son, William Edward Dodd Jr., was beginning what he hoped would
be a meaningful political career. Casting himself as a Democrat loyal to
Roosevelt, he challenged veteran Congressman Howard W. Smith in Virginia's August primary. A neophyte pitted against a seasoned campaigner,
Dodd was clearly the underdog, and yet he had reason to hope. Roosevelt
had castigated Smith as one of the many party conservatives who had

resisted New Deal reforms. Indeed, few Democrat's had taken as strong an anti-Roosevelt position as Smith had. He had opposed Public Works Administration appropriations, railed against Roosevelt's quest to liberalize the Supreme Court, voted against legislation to end farm tenancy, and, most galling to the president, led the campaign against the Fair Labor Standards Act. Committed to Smith's demise, Roosevelt sent Secretary of the Interior Harold L. Ickes and Assistant Attorney General Robert N. Anderson, a native Virginian, to young Dodd's aid. But neither their assistance nor Dodd's pledged fidelity to the New Deal proved sufficient. On the appointed day Smith easily polled three votes to every one for his opponent.[15]

Stunned by his son's electoral humiliation, Dodd slipped into a brief but deep depression. For months he had endured horrific shocks—his precipitous recall from Berlin, his many confrontations with an indifferent American public unsure of its response to the European crisis, Martha's death, and now William Jr.'s awful rejection by Virginia voters enamored with a political reactionary. Each incident was powerful enough to challenge the strongest constitution. Burdened by their cumulative impact, Dodd collapsed into a confused and unresponsive state. "I am distressed about you," wrote a worried North Carolina relative. "I fear you are not taking care of yourself at all." Similarly concerned, Secretary of Commerce Daniel C. Roper determined to lift his friend's spirit. On 16 August he and his wife cordially included Dodd in an afternoon lawn party at their Washington home. "I am very anxious to see you and hope you will be with us," Roper wrote. "I think that the kind of informal party that we hope to have . . . will be helpful rather than detrimental to your nervous strain."[16]

The late August gathering cheered Dodd immensely. He thoroughly enjoyed the fellowship of important Washington figures who shared his international concerns and who encouraged his crusade. Returning to his farm at Round Hill, he wrote Roper thanking him for the kindness and then asked for a second and greater favor. Dodd felt the call to return to his mission. He would soon leave for speaking engagements in North Carolina followed by a circuit of Kansas, Oklahoma, and Texas and scattered appearances in the Midwest and Northeast. But before Dodd could commence such a grueling schedule, he needed further encouragement; he desperately desired Roosevelt's endorsement, a surety that his efforts

were more than a lonely cry in the wilderness. "When the President re-
turns I wish you would ask him if I may not see him about the 5th or 6th
of September," he petitioned.[17]

Roosevelt considered a visit with Dodd politically inexpedient. Cautiously campaigning for preparedness while both the general public and
powerful politicians accused him of warmongering, he dared not openly
embrace Dodd or his message. Dodd, who had once considered himself
one of the president's confidants, did not appreciate Roosevelt's political
dilemma and resented being rejected by the man for whom he had literally
sacrificed his scholarly career. Rebuffed in his effort to reach Roosevelt
through Roper, Dodd wrote directly to the President's secretary. If at all
convenient, he begged, could *the President . . . see me before the end of
the month. . . .* I would like to know what the President thinks on the
most important matters for us." Roosevelt again disappointed his former
ambassador. "I am sorry you have not found a moment's time to see me,"
Dodd scolded on 29 September. "Certain things I wished very much to
have your opinion about before delivering my series of lectures in the
Southwest."[18]

Putting this disappointment behind him, Dodd traveled to Kansas,
where he spoke to crowds in Manhattan, Hutchinson, and Topeka. He
then dropped southward, presenting postprandial talks in Amarillo,
Texas, on 8 October and in El Paso three days later. October and November then dissolved into a collage of railroad terminals, hastily consumed
meals, and repetitious lectures, all of which were physically and emotionally draining. When Dodd ran into difficulty arranging transportation to
the University of Cincinnati, his insistent host suggested that he fly from
Pittsburgh to Washington and catch the overnight train to the Cincinnati,
where he would arrive just in time for the appointment. By such drastic
means Dodd fulfilled this and other obligations. "I served as ambassador
in Berlin for four and a half years," he told his Cincinnati audience. "And
I would rather be dead than see the principles of Nazi-fascists control
our land and the whole world."[19] Ironically, his fast-paced efforts were so
destructive of his personal weal that the pledge's fulfillment was assured.

In late November Dodd boasted to Josephus Daniels that "I have been
lecturing again since October 1st all the way from Ohio to southwestern
Texas and . . . all over the Middle West, even in Chicago (where . . . 7,000
[came] to hear me once . . .)." These appearances had become Dodd's
opiate, blotting out all other considerations, as he was consumed by his

own message, a familiar formula that condemned the enemies of Wilsonianism, railed against the threat of Nazism, and considered both analogous to another and earlier war-mongering cabal. The United States "has now substituted for the slave holders a more complete substitution of a government by holders of great estates," he preached before a Virginia Baptist convention. These latter-day villains had devoted more than five million dollars "to defeat America's entry into the League of Nations," and their victory adumbrated the destruction of European democracy by Hitlerites.[20]

By the end of November little mattered to Dodd but his fearful jeremiad. He sacrificed his own health to this crusade, speaking before audiences great and small, responding whenever and wherever he was beckoned. His determination to deliver two speeches in tiny McKinney, Virginia, on 5 December proved fateful. Driving to the engagement, he approached Hanover Court House, a community not far from where he had held his first teaching post, Randolph-Macon College. Dodd's thoughts may have drifted back nearly forty years to his early professorial career, to happy days with his bride, or to the delights of his first eager students. Whatever the distraction, he failed to notice four-year-old Gloria Grimes, a Negro girl who suddenly darted into his path. Dodd swerved, unsure whether he had hit or missed the child. Looking into his rear-view mirror, he saw another motorist slowing down to give aid. Gratified, he continued on. He was the crusading former American ambassador to Germany and the McKinney Rotary Club awaited him.[21]

Adolf Hitler was only the worst of the demons that tormented Dodd. For decades he had campaigned against those he considered to be the people's enemies: southern aristocrats and their haughty postbellum descendents, northern capitalists, corrupt and reactionary politicians, insensitive academicians, Prussian Junkers, and, most recently, German Nazis. Together they had carved away at his soul, rendering him in his last frantic months incapable of appreciating the seriousness of his crime. He was guilty of fleeing the scene of an accident, of leaving on the side of the road a seriously injured child, an impoverished Negro girl whose status at birth was far less propitious than his own. Six witnesses recorded his automobile license number as he drove from the scene.[22]

When he completed his talks in McKinney, Dodd returned to his Round Hill farm, where, on 8 December, a Virginia State policeman delivered an arrest warrant charging that William Edward Dodd "did unlaw-fully and feloniously operate a motor vehicle . . . over the highways in a careless and reckless manner and in doing so did strike one Gloria Grimes causing personal injuries . . . and did fail to stop and take account of said accident." The officer told Dodd that the little girl was hospitalized in critical condition with a fractured skull, cerebral concussion, and other assorted injuries, that his automobile would be confiscated pending dis-position of the case, and that he would be immediately escorted to Han-over Court House for a bail hearing. Not fully grasping the gravity of the situation, Dodd resented its inconvenience as he focused upon the speech he was to deliver the following evening, a New York City engagement with Mayor Fiorello La Guardia.[23]

Stirred by a small glimpse of reality, Dodd scribbled a tepid letter of apology to Gloria Grimes's mother, an action that only added to the grief he had already inflicted. "The reason I did not stop to talk things over," he explained, "was that I thought that the child had escaped. Besides I did not want the newspapers all over the country to publish a story about the accident. You know how newspapers love to exaggerate things of this sort. I hope your child recovers." He enclosed a check for twenty-five dol-lars to defray medical expenses. Their attorney advised the Grimeses to return the check uncashed and prepared a civil suit for twenty-five thou-sand dollars.[24]

However much Dodd had hoped to avoid publicity, his leaving the scene of an accident, his unsagacious letter, and his public persona guar-anteed him maximum embarrassment. Dodd's attorney, Leon M. Bazile, secured postponements of the arraignment first to 10 January and again to 17 January, when, suffering from acute laryngitis, Dodd stood ner-vously before a Hanover Court House judge to plead not guilty. When he attempted to whisper an explanation, Bazile tugged firmly on his arm, pulling him into his seat. The attorney rose and moved for an indefinite delay. Dodd was sixty-nine years old, "in very poor physical condition," and "in no condition to stand trial in the near future." Unmoved, the judge set the date for 2 March.[25]

Dodd's throat condition worsened. On 20 January he checked into the Georgetown University Hospital, where he stayed for three weeks of tests and recuperation, leaving in no better condition than when he had en-tered. Throughout his physical confinement he remained preoccupied with world affairs. "Hitler . . . is bent on dominating Europe," he wrote

Roosevelt. But this need not have occurred, he said: "what a world we would have had if Wilson's policy had been applied." Instead American politicians had foolishly followed the big industrialists and the arms manufactures, whose legacy was "millions unemployed, world debts far greater than ever imagined," and a blighted international arena "where the dictators have influence." Sinking into a deeply morose state, Dodd shared a like lamentation with Josephus Daniels. "The world seems to have gone mad," Daniels agreed. "Our good friend Woodrow Wilson can not be happy in Heaven, when he sees that the people who shattered his dream are reaping the whirlwind."[26]

If inwardly Dodd bewailed the fate of millions, outwardly he remained accountable for the injury he had inflicted upon a single child. Bazile carefully reviewed with him the evidence of his guilt: unimpeachable witnesses were prepared to identify Dodd and his automobile, to swear that he had struck Gloria Grimes and dragged her more than 150 feet, and to state that he "stopped only long enough to straighten in the road and to continue on his way." He then carefully explained to his barely comprehending client that neither his status as the former ambassador to Germany nor the urgency of his message mitigated the seriousness of his actions.[27]

The trial was a media circus. Photographers' cameras flashed as the principals entered the courtroom, one New York journalist chartered a private airplane to rush pictures to meet his deadline, and two representatives of African-American newspapers jostled with their white colleagues to telegraph their stories over a specially constructed Western Union line. Having been informed that Dodd would change his plea, the judge ordered the indictment read and then called for the aging dignitary's response.

"Well," Dodd began with hesitation. Bazile quickly stood, placed his hand on Dodd's shoulder, and whispered, "Just say guilty, nothing more."

"Do you plead guilty?" the judge demanded.

"Yes, but I did stop." Before Dodd could continue, Bazile pushed him into his seat, fearful that he would further incriminate himself.

At the judge's order, the prosecutor outlined the essential elements of the case, after which Bazile made a plea for leniency. Dodd's daughter testified to her father's debilitating anguish over Mattie's death, and Gloria Grimes's physician acknowledged that Dodd had taken full responsibility for the victim's medical expenses. Dodd's doctors described his throat difficulties and his general state of nervous exhaustion, and finally R. Walton Moore, of the State Department, recounted Dodd's recent service to the country and lauded him for his honesty and integrity.[28]

Following an hour's consideration, the judge returned to pronounce sentence. Considering Dodd's diminished mental capacity and his poor physical health, he dispensed with a mandatory confinement of one year and instead ordered Dodd to pay a $250 fine and court costs. He also revoked Dodd's driver's license and noted that "being convicted of a felony [Dodd] cannot hereafter exercise the right of suffrage unless his political disabilities are removed."[29]

More than anything else, the last clause devastated Dodd. Famous for his advocacy of pure democracy and appalled by its destruction in Germany, he could not countenance his personal disenfranchisement. With a civil suit still pending, Bazile feared that in his confused state his client might respond to hounding reporters with statements prejudicial to his cause. He urged Dodd to accept a friend's invitation to visit California, adding that his doctor agreed and also demanded that Dodd refrain from public speaking for at least six months.[30]

Following his attorney's advice, on 8 March Dodd left for a month's stay in the West. His throat condition was deteriorating; still, he could not resist the lecture podium. Hitler had stirred within him an urge that overrode all considerations of health. He succumbed to speaking invitations in the Los Angeles area, and on 22 March he traveled to Claremont to deliver what was probably his last public address. Laboring "under a speech handicap before an audience of 1200," reported a local journalist, "Dodd painted a grave picture of the war clouds which are forming over Europe."[31]

Throughout April, May, and June Dodd's health continued to decline. Even though he blamed the weather in Los Angeles—"there was a fog every day"—for his failure to improve, upon his return to Virginia he finally heeded his doctor's admonition to rest. Too ill to attend his civil trial on 6 May, he allowed Bazile to settle out of court with the Grimes family, paying them thirty-five hundred dollars in addition to medical and legal expenses. "The child recently returned to her home," reported the *New York Times.* "Doctors are hopeful she will recover entirely from the accident." But Dodd's condition worsened. "I have been ill four months," he wrote Josephus Daniels days after the trial. "It is a nervous throat trouble which gets worse every month. To-day it took 1 ½ hours for me to eat luncheon."[32]

Physically unable to speak out against Hitlerism, Dodd turned inward, focusing on what he considered his recent persecutions, and his grip on reality seemed less than secure. On 7 June he wrote R. Walton Moore urging him to intercede with Virginia's governor for the restoration of his citizenship rights and driving privileges. He emphasized that he resented the fact that his attorney and the judge had forced him to declare himself guilty of injuring a young child. "You know the girl was the sole cause of the accident," he flatly declared. "I could not understand why they thought I was guilty." Perhaps, he mused, the real cause of his misfortunes was opposition to the Confederate societies in 1907, or his unmasking of the sins of the Martin Machine so many years before, or even his early support for Woodrow Wilson when almost every Virginia politician opposed him.[33]

Although these events had occurred too long before to have anything to do with his current problems, Dodd's status was of concern to politicians at the highest levels. "Dodd, former Ambassador to Germany, is dying at Mt. Sinai Hospital, New York City," an aide informed President Roosevelt on 10 July. Dodd had recently traveled to the city to visit his daughter, and his condition had become critical. His physicians believed that Dodd's ailments were exacerbated by severe melancholia, caused by the "feeling that the White House felt that he had fallen down in Germany." At his aide's suggestion, Roosevelt immediately telegraphed: "Distressed to learn of your illness. Trust you may recover quickly and take up again the valuable work in which you have been engaged." However much this may have cheered Dodd, he would have been distressed to learn of a disclaimer attached to the copy of the telegram placed in the president's personal file. "Valuable work," the aide explained, referred not to the former ambassador's recent lectures but "to Prof. Dodd's history of the South on which he has been engaged for years." Two days later Virginia's governor issued Dodd a partial pardon, restoring his citizenship rights. Dodd's current illness, he noted, "substantiated assertions made at his trial, that he was ill and not entirely responsible at the time of the accident."[34]

However much the president's telegram and the governor's magnanimity may have lifted Dodd's spirits, there was little the doctors could do for his physical condition. Deeming his throat blockage inoperable, they inserted a feeding tube into his stomach and sent him back to Virginia to await the inevitable. Finally cognizant of his fate, Dodd accepted it. "I am still ill," he wrote to his friend Bessie Louis Pierce on 6 October, "can not speak a word to my family. . . . No lectures any more. I'm afraid no books." Many other farewell letters went out to those who had shared his fervent crusades. "I have papers convenient to keep my mouth clean and I have to use them every minute," he told Josephus Daniels on New Year's Day. Clearly the end was at hand. "Ten years would be good for me," he lamented. "I wish to write my other two or three volumes." But it would not be, and there was more to regret as well. "Our world did not learn anything from the last war," he reflected. "I am sorry, for that method of keeping the peace would have been effective. But your life and mine can't last much longer." Dodd died on 9 February 1940 at 3:30 P.M. President and Mrs. Roosevelt were among those who sent flowers.[35]

Eight years following Dodd's passing, Frank Lawrence Owsley, one of his more successful students, stood to deliver the prestigious Walter Lynn-wood Fleming Lectures at Louisiana State University. Reading from a manuscript that would soon become his highly acclaimed *Plain Folk of the Old South,* he propounded ideas that would have been anathema to Dodd. Owsley hypothesized a harmonious southern culture in which yeomen and aristocrats resided felicitously together as neighbors. "To deal with the plain folk as a class-conscious group, bitter and resentful toward the aristocracy because of exploitation and neglect," he told his receptive audience, "is far from reality." As proof, he confidently asserted that older southern historians, those "born before 1890," had "a firsthand acquaintance with one and often two generations who had lived before 1860." Such worthies as J. G. de Roulhac Hamilton of North Carolina, Charles W. Ramsdell of Texas, and George Petrie and Walter Lynnwood Fleming of Alabama could personally attest to antebellum harmony. Conspicuously absent from his selected canon was his Chicago mentor, William Edward Dodd.[36]

Owsley's oversight could hardly have been accidental. Scions of the South's "best families," Hamilton, Ramsdell, Petrie, and Fleming viewed southern society from the top down and presented a historical ideology that was congenial to the region's upper classes. Owsley too viewed the

South's plain people from a patrician perspective.[37] Ironically, by ignoring Dodd Owsley highlighted his uniqueness.

A product of North Carolina's common folk, Dodd understood from personal experience their values, hopes, and fears, and as a scholar he proclaimed themes that were unacceptable to apologists for the Old South. Thus, when in 1920 Emory University offered him an honorary doctorate in recognition of his "notable contributions to Southern history," Dodd forlornly hoped that it signaled the acceptance of themes critical of the region's oppressive minority. But his views were not accepted. The South's elite establishment had no desire to allow the region's underclass a voice, and Dodd became a lonely scholar crying in the wilderness. His ideas were obscured, buried beneath the writings of historians whose image of the antebellum epoch complimented the South's powerful aristocracy.

Dodd's life was an intellectual and cultural odyssey. He traveled far beyond his impoverished North Carolina origins in quest of broadening goals. Combining intelligence and drive, he became the peer of great historians, the confidant of presidents, and the often disregarded prophet of impending world disaster. Though it all, however, a central theme permeated Dodd's existence. From his youthful experiences he developed a bitterness toward the aristocracy of his native soil, and from his adult observations he fashioned a resentment toward all privileged classes—southern patricians, northern industrialists, Prussian Junkers, German Nazis. His historical writings and many lectures became the means through which he warned his contemporaries against the dangers of elitist rule and preached the egalitarian ideals of Thomas Jefferson and the internationalist vision of Woodrow Wilson. Had the South won in 1865, he once wrote, it would have meant the "repudiation of the Declaration of Independence and . . . the explicit recognition of social inequality." The planters would have formed "a State in which the laboring class should be the property of the capitalists," and in which "every man should have a place and should keep his place."[38] Yeoman born, Dodd found that vision intolerable.

NOTES

PREFACE

1. Stephenson, *The South Lives in History*, 28–57; Dallek, *Diplomat and Democrat*.

2. Dallek, *Diplomat and Democrat*, viii.

CHAPTER ONE: The Genesis of a Class-Conscious Scholar

1. Theodore H. Jack to Dodd, 15 May 1920, and Dodd to Jack, 20 May 1920, Dodd Papers, LC; *New York Times*, 9 June 1920. Having guided Jack through his doctoral degree at the University of Chicago, Dodd recommended him for the post of chair of the history department at Emory in 1916 (Dodd to Warren A. Candler, 10 April 1916, Candler Papers).

2. Dodd to Jack, 20 May 1920, Dodd Papers, LC. For a list of Dodd's published works see Williams, "A Bibliography of the Printed Writings of William Edward Dodd."

3. Dodd to Adams, 12 January 1914, Dodd Papers, LC.

4. Stephenson, *The South Lives in History*, 28–57; Dallek, *Democrat and Diplomat*, 95–98; Hofstadter, *Progressive Historians*, 28. In a historiographic discussion of the South's common folk, Randolph B. Campbell noted briefly the contrast between Dodd's themes of class conflict and their denial by his graduate student Frank L. Owsley (Campbell, "Planters and Plain Folk: The Social Structure of the Antebellum South," in Boles and Nolen, *Interpreting Southern History*, 48–51).

5. Dodd to W. W. Cook, 22 March 1912, Dodd Papers, LC.

6. Dodd to Frederic Bancroft, 20 June 1908, Bancroft Papers.

7. Dodd, *Cotton Kingdom*, 31–32.

8. The information in this and the following paragraphs is from Escott, *Many Excellent People*, 2–8, 15–19.

9. Ibid., 7–10. The relationship between social classes in the antebellum South has long been debated by southern historians. Dodd began this discussion in *The Cotton Kingdom*, arguing that slave-rich planters dominated the region's social, political, and economic institutions. A generation later one of his graduate students would take exception to this. In his seminal work, *Plain Folk of the Old South*, Frank L. Owsley assumed that the southern yeomen were rarely class-conscious and that social harmony existed between them and the aristocrats. Several students of the South supported his views, including Blanche Clark (*Tennes-*

see Yeomen), Herbert Weaver (*Mississippi Farmers, 1850–1860*), Clement Eaton
("Class Differences in the Old South," 357–58), Eugene Genovese ("Yeomen
Farmers in a Slaveholders' Democracy," 341–42), and Forrest McDonald and
Grady McWhiney ("The Antebellum Southern Herdsman," 166). Some recent
scholars have pointed to latent class antagonism associated with the antebellum
and Civil War eras: Emory Thomas (*The Confederacy as a Revolutionary Experience*, 102–5), Paul Escott (*After Secession*, 94–135), Phillip Paludan (*Victims*),
Orville Burton (*In My Father's House Are Many Mansions*), Steven Hahn (*Roots
of Southern Populism*), and Fred Arthur Bailey (*Class and Tennessee's Confederate Generation*). To these should be added the older work of Roger Shugg, *Origins of Class Struggle in Louisiana*.

10. Owsley, "Defeatism in the Confederacy"; Tatum, *Disloyalty in the Confederacy*; Escott, *After Secession*, 94–135; Bailey, *Class and Tennessee's Confederate Generation*, 99–104. Stephen V. Ash's "Poor Whites in the Occupied South,
1861–1865," explores at length the disloyalty of the Southerners impoverished
during the Civil War.

11. Roark, *Masters without Slaves*, 54–67; Bailey, "The Textbooks of the
'Lost Cause.' "

12. Hahn, *Roots of Southern Populism*, 137–43.

13. Heritage of Johnston County Book Committee, *Heritage of Johnston
County*, 32, 54.

14. Dodd to Martha Johns Dodd, 2 July 1923, Dodd Papers, LC.

15. Heritage of Johnston County Book Committee, *Heritage of Johnston
County*, 54.

16. Herman H. Horne, "Ashley Horne"; Dodd to H. C. Nixon, 25 March
1936, Dodd Papers, LC; Satterfield, "Ashley Horne," in Heritage of Johnston
County Book Committee, *Heritage of Johnston County*, 220.

17. Diary of William E. Dodd, 13 August 1919, Dodd Papers, RM (hereinafter
cited as Dodd Diary). Several pertinent examples of Dodd's class attitudes were
deleted from the published version of this diary. Cf. Mabry, "Professor William
E. Dodd's Diary, 1916–1920," 67 (hereinafter cited as "Professor Dodd's Diary").

18. Dodd to Nellie, 6 December 1922, Dodd Papers, LC.

19. Seventh United States Census, 1850: Wake County, North Carolina, Popu-
lation Schedule, 225; Eighth United States Census, 1860: Wake County, North
Carolina, Population Schedule, 21; Dodd genealogy, typescript ca. 1951, Martha
Dodd [Stern] Papers. The Dodd genealogy was prepared by a professional genea-
logical researcher, Daisy Bailey-Waitt, hired by Martha Dodd Stern in 1951 (see
Daisy Bailey-Waitt to Martha Dodd Stern, 17 December 1951, Martha Dodd
[Stern] Papers).

20. Clipping from *Raleigh News and Observer*, 14 June 1933, Dodd Papers,
LC; Ross and King, *Marriage Records of Johnston County*, 33; Dodd genealogy,
Martha Dodd [Stern] Papers.

21. E. D. Dodd to Wendell H. Stephenson, 28 February 1952, and "The Dodd
I Knew," typescript, ca. 1951, 11, Stephenson Papers. A Dodd graduate student

and longtime friend of Dodd's daughter, Martha, the author of "The Dodd I Knew" chose not to sign his remembrances.

22. William E. Dodd, "Autobiography," unpublished manuscript, ca. 1933, Dodd Papers, LC (hereinafter cited as Dodd, "Autobiography").

23. Dodd genealogy, Martha Dodd [Stern] Papers.

24. Eighth United States Census, 1860: Johnston County, North Carolina, Population Schedule, 2; Horne, "Ashley Horne."

25. Tarver, "Samuel Ruffin Horne," in Heritage of Johnston County Book Committee, *Heritage of Johnston County,* 221; Dodd genealogy, Martha Dodd [Stern] Papers.

26. Seventh United States Census, 1850: Johnston County, North Carolina, Population Schedule, 150; Eighth United States Census, 1860: Johnston County, North Carolina, Slave Schedule, 1; Branson, *North Carolina Business Directory,* 133.

27. Bejah Horne Will. Horne's first name is spelled in various ways, but the most common spelling is "Benajah."

28. Dodd to J. Franklin Jameson, 7 February 1913, Jameson Papers; Dodd to Thomas J. Watson, 3 December 1935, Dodd Papers, LC.

29. Dodd, "Autobiography"; Dodd to Nixon, 25 March 1936, Dodd Papers, LC.

30. Dodd, "Autobiography"; Dodd to Stark Young, December 1932 (fragment), Dodd Papers, LC; Horne, "Ashley Horne."

31. Dodd, "Autobiography."

32. Dodd to Michael Singer, 14 August 1919, Dodd Papers, LC.

33. Dodd, "Autobiography."

34. Dodd to Nellie, 6 December 1922, Dodd Papers, LC; Dodd, "Autobiography."

35. Dodd, "Autobiography"; Horne, "Ashley Horne"; William E. Dodd, "Early Virginia Years," ca. 1933, unpublished manuscript, Dodd Papers, LC (hereinafter cited as Dodd, "Early Virginia Years").

36. Stephenson, *The South Lives in History,* 29; Dodd to George H. Denny, 24 May 1902, Dodd Papers, LC; Dodd to Josephus Daniels, 29 July 1927, Daniels Papers; "Professor Dodd's Diary," 53; Dodd and Dodd, *Ambassador Dodd's Diary,* 178.

37. Dodd to Denny, 24 May 1902, and Teacher's First Grade Certificate, 11 December 1891, 12 August 1893, Dodd Papers, LC.

38. Clipping from the *Monganton (N.C.) New Herald,* 13 June 1933, and Dodd to Denny, 24 May 1902, Dodd Papers, LC.

39. Dodd, "Autobiography." Some confusion exists concerning when Dodd first enrolled at VPI. In his unpublished autobiographical sketches he stated that he had entered in February 1891, but McBryde did not assume the presidency until September, and Dodd's transcript lists him as beginning in the fall semester (Dodd, "Autobiography"; *Catalogue of the Virginia Agricultural and Mechanical College, 1891–92,* 9; "Copy of Grades for Dodd, William E.," in Clarie Slusher

to Wendell Stephenson, 6 October 1951, Stephenson Papers [hereinafter cited as "Dodd's Grades"]).

40. "Dodd's Grades"; *Catalogue of the Virginia Agricultural and Mechanical College, 1892–93*, 9, *1893–94*, 8, *1894–95*, 6; *Catalogue of the Virginia Agricultural and Mechanical College and Polytechnic Institute, 1895–96*, 6.

41. *Catalogue of the Virginia Agricultural and Mechanical College, 1891–92*, 6; Dodd, "Freedom of Speech in the South," 383; Edward E. Sheib Vertical File; Green, *A History of the University of South Carolina*, 455. Having left VPI in 1898, Sheib applied to return in 1903. The board denied the request, noting that he was "not popular in every quarter" (Virginia Agricultural and Mechanical College Unofficial Board of Trustees Minutes, 4 August 1898, 47; Virginia Agricultural and Mechanical College Board of Visitors Minutes, 16 June 1903, 2:12).

42. Dodd, "Autobiography"; *Catalogue of the Virginia Agricultural and Mechanical College and Polytechnic Institute, 1895–96*, 56.

43. Dodd, "Young Men's Christian Association."

44. Dodd, "Y.M.C.A.," 55; Dodd, "Young Men's Christian Association," 74–75.

45. Dodd and Dodd, *Ambassador Dodd's Diary*, 244–45.

46. "Dodd's Grades"; Dodd, "Autobiography."

47. Herman Horne to Dodd, 6 August 1897, 27 February 1898, 19 July, 18 August 1899, Dodd Papers, LC; Dodd, "Autobiography"; Dodd, "Early Virginia Years."

48. "Dodd's Grades"; Dodd, "Autobiography"; *Catalogue of the Virginia Agricultural and Mechanical College and Polytechnic Institute, 1895–96*.

49. Dodd to Daniels, 14 May 1934, Daniels Papers.

50. Edward Sheib to Dodd, 23 March 1900, Dodd Papers, LC.

51. Dodd, "Autobiography."

52. Ibid.; Samuel R. Horne to Dodd, 10 January 1899, Dodd Papers, LC.

53. *Wohnungs-Meldeschein, Leipzig* [Registry of residence], 17 July 1897, Dodd Papers, RM; A. H. Drinkard to Dodd, 20 August 1897, Dodd Papers, LC.

54. Clippings from *New York World Telegram*, 14 June 1933, and *New York Post*, 15 May 1937, Dodd Papers, LC.

55. Dodd to Denny, 24 May 1902, and Dodd to Sihler, 13 August 1919, Dodd Papers, LC; Dodd, "Autobiography."

56. Hofstadter, *Progressive Historians*, 314–16.

57. Dow, "Features of the New History"; Dodd, "Karl Lamprecht and *Kulturgeschichte*"; Dodd, review of *Zur jüngsten Vergangenheit*, by Von Karl Lamprecht.

58. "The Dodd I Knew," Stephenson Papers.

59. Dodd to Trevelyan, 19 May 1915, Dodd Papers, LC. For examples of Dodd's comparing German and southern aristocrats see Dodd, "Social Philosophy of the Old South," 746; Dodd, *Cotton Kingdom*, 16–17; Dodd to Maurer, 11 November 1914, Dodd to Stephenson, 23 September 1919, Dodd to Patterson, 23 September 1919, and Dodd to Teacher and Friend, 2 January 1920, Dodd Papers, LC.

60. Dodd, "Autobiography."

61. Dodd to Maurer, 11 November 1914, Dodd Papers, LC; Dodd, *Statesmen of the Old South*, 2, 55.

62. Dodd, "Autobiography."

63. Ibid.; Dodd to Martha Johns, 21 August 1898, Dodd Papers, LC.

64. Dodd, "Autobiography."

65. Dodd to Sihler, 13 August 1919, Dodd Papers, LC.

66. Dodd, "Autobiography"; Dodd to Isabel [Goodwin], 19 February 1931, Dodd Papers, LC. For another example of Dodd's friendship with an American graduate student in Germany and their mutual trials at Leipzig see Elliot H. Goodwin to Dodd, 30 April 1899, Dodd Papers, LC.

67. Dodd, "Autobiography."

68. Ibid.; *Abgangszeugniss, Universitat Leipzig* [Transcript of classes, Leipzig University], 27 June 1899, Dodd Papers, RM.

69. Dodd, "Autobiography"; Erich Marcks to Sir, 13 November 1899, Dodd Papers, LC.

70. Dodd, "Autobiography"; Dodd to Martha Johns, 12 December 1898, Dodd Papers, LC.

71. Dodd, "Autobiography."

72. Ibid.

73. Sheib to Dodd, 23 March 1900, Dodd Papers, LC.

74. John T. Morse to Dodd, 30 December 1899, and Jameson to Dodd, 9 January 1900, Dodd Papers, RM.

75. Dodd, "Autobiography."

76. Sheib to Dodd, 23 March 1900, Dodd Papers, LC. The nature of Sheib's conflict with the board is unclear. In the fall of 1900 he secured a chair in education at Tulane University in New Orleans. He died in 1903 (Edward E. Sheib Vertical File; *New Orleans Picayune*, 29 March 1903).

77. Sheib to Dodd, 23 March 1900, Dodd Papers, LC.

CHAPTER TWO: A Plebeian Scholar in the Old Dominion

1. Dodd to McKinley, 24 October 1919, Dodd Papers, LC; Dodd to Samuel N. Harper, 24 October 1919, Harper Papers; Dodd to Frederick Jackson Turner, 11 October 1911, Turner Papers, HEH.

2. Bailey, "The Textbooks of the 'Lost Cause'"; *New Orleans Times-Democrat,* 31 December 1903.

3. John Spencer Bassett to Dodd, [ca. August 1902], Dodd Papers, LC.

4. Kemp P. Battle to Dodd, 30 November 1900, Dodd to Herman Horne, 13 December 1918, 11 February, 9 June 1919, and Dodd to Ashbel B. Kimball, 4, 18 December 1918, Dodd Papers, LC; W. P. Trent to Dodd, 20 February 1900, Dodd Papers, RM.

5. Charles W. Dabney to J. M. McBryde, 16 January 1900, and Dabney to Dodd, 22, 31 January, 19 February, 17, 22 March 1900, Dodd Papers, LC.

6. Mrs. L. H. Bisham to Dodd, 13 December 1899, 9 January 1900, Stephen

B. Weeks to Dodd, 16 December 1899, 2 January 1900, J. Franklin Jameson to Dodd, 9 January 1900, Henry Adams to Andrew H. Allen, 17 January 1900, Allen to Henry Cabot Lodge, 18, 23 January 1900, Henry C. Cameron to Dodd, 27 April 1900, A. C. Haynes to Dodd, 5 May 1900, J. H. McAdams to Dodd, 5 May 1900, and Battle to Dodd, 11 May 1900, Dodd Papers, RM; Dodd to Thomas M. Pittman, 25 July 1900, Briggs Papers; Dodd, "Autobiography."

7. Dodd, "Autobiography"; Guest membership card, Cosmos Club, Washington D.C., 3 July 1900, Dodd Papers, LC.

8. Dodd to Herbert Baxter Adams, 21 July 1900, Herbert Baxter Adams Papers.

9. Dodd, "Early Virginia Years."

10. Josephus Daniels to Dodd, 25 October 1900, Dodd Papers, LC; Daniels to Dodd, 12 January 1934, and Dodd to Daniels, 9 May 1939, Daniels Papers.

11. Dodd, "Early Virginia Years."

12. Dodd to Martha Johns, 12 April 1896, 28 January, 22 May, 1 June, 12 December 1898, 18 March, 1 August 1899, Dodd Papers, LC.

13. Dodd, "Early Virginia Years."

14. William G. Starr to Dodd, 18 August 1911, Resolution of the Randolph-Macon College Board of Trustees, [September 1900], and Dodd to George H. Denny, 24 May 1902, Dodd Papers, LC; Dodd to Oswald Garrison Villard, 3 July 1906, Villard Papers.

15. Scanlon, *Randolph-Macon College,* 152–53.

16. Ibid., 10, 33–57, 126, 145, 210.

17. The information in this and the following paragraphs is from Dodd, "Early Virginia Years."

18. Dodd to Walt Holcomb, 27 January 1927, Dodd Papers, LC.

19. Dodd, "Early Virginia Years"; Dodd to Albert Bushnell Hart, 10 December 1907, McLaughlin Papers.

20. Dodd, "Early Virginia Years." To save money, Dodd stayed in the home of a University of Michigan professor who had been a fellow student at Leipzig (J. C. Hildren to Dodd, 24 October 1900, Dodd Papers, LC).

21. Bassett to Dodd, 1 December 1901, Dodd Papers, LC; Dodd, "Early Virginia Years."

22. Daniels to Dodd, 30 January, 5, 6 June 1901, F. P. Venable to Daniels, 31 January 1901, Edwin W. Bowen to J. D. S. Riggs, 27 April 1901, and Bowen to Venable, 13 May 1901, Dodd Papers, LC; *The University of North Carolina Catalogue, 1901–1902,* 17. Eighteen years after Dodd's failure to secure the university posting, he explained to a friend, "When I was a youngster and briefless, the University of North Carolina needed a man in history. I was informed by an ex-President then influential that if A. B. Andrews recommended me I would be appointed" (Dodd to Walter Clark, 9 May 1919, Clark Papers).

23. Richard Irby to Dodd, 24 May 1901, Dodd Papers, LC; Dodd, "Early Virginia Years."

24. Dodd, "Early Virginia Years."

25. Dodd to Hart, 10 December 1907, McLaughlin Papers; Dodd, "Early Vir-

ginia Years"; Dodd to Martha Johns, 4 January–17 Decemeber 1901 passim, Dodd Papers, LC.

26. Bassett to Dodd, 1 December 1901, Dodd Papers, LC; Dodd, "Early Virginia Years." The Dodd-Johns wedding announcement illustrates much about the South's class consciousness: "We take pleasure in announcing the marriage of Miss Mattie, daughter of Mr. and Mrs. Thomas Johns to Mr. William Edward Dodd at Auburn, Dec. 24, 1901. Miss Johns is an accomplished daughter of one of our best Wake County families. Mr. Dodd is Professor of History in Randolph Macon College, Va. and is well known in North Carolina. We wish them all happiness" (undated newspaper clipping, Dodd Papers, LC).

27. Dodd, "Early Virginia Years."

28. Ibid.

29. Dodd, "The Place of Nathaniel Macon in Southern History," 663.

30. Dodd, "Early Virginia Years."

31. Dodd to Pittman, 8 July 1902, Pittman Papers; Dodd to Charles Francis Adams Jr., 3 July 1902, Charles Francis Adams Jr. Papers.

32. For a sampling of these men's efforts see McGuire, "School Histories in the South"; Cussons, *United States "History" As the Yankee Makes and Takes;* and Christian, *The Confederate Cause and Its Defenders* and "Official Report of the Grand Camp, C. V., Department of Virginia."

33. Stuart McGuire, "Sketch of the Life of Hunter Holmes McGuire, M. D., L.L.D.," typescript, McGuire Papers; clipping from *Richmond Times-Dispatch*, 12 January 1912, Cussons Papers; Wyndham R. Meredith, "Judge George L. Christian," in *Proceedings of the Thirty-Fifth Annual Meeting of the Virginia State Bar Association*, 90–91; Christian, *The Confederate Cause and Its Defenders*, 4; Bailey, "Free Speech and the 'Lost Cause' in the Old Dominion." For examples of the historiographic views of the Virginia Confederate Veterans and especially the ideas of George L. Christian see McGuire and Christian, *Confederate Cause and Conduct in the War between the States.*

34. Houghton, Mifflin and Company to Dodd, 6 June 1902, Dodd Papers, LC; Jones, *Fiske's False History;* McGuire and Christian, *Confederate Cause and Conduct in the War between the States*, 12–28; Virginia State Board of Education Minutes, 28 May 1902, 7–8; Dodd to editor, *Richmond News*, 4 November 1902, and *Richmond Times-Dispatch*, 6 November 1902. In this letter to the editor Dodd concluded that "some of the effort expended by" the Confederate patriotic societies "to expel the northern writer from the south might be better applied to the training of our public school teachers to the raising of their salaries, to the betterment of our colleges and to the endowment of some university, where the verities of history both northern and southern might be taught."

35. B. F. Johnson to Dodd, 5 October 1901, Dodd Papers, LC; Dodd, "The Status of History in Southern Education," 111.

36. Ibid., 109–11.

37. Dodd, response to C. Meriwether in *Nation* 75 (1902): 150; John H. Latane to Dodd, 9 August 1902, and Dodd to Harry P. Judson, 30 November 1920, Dodd Papers, LC; Dodd to William L. Cheney, 20 June 1932, Dodd Papers, RM.

38. *Richmond News,* 23 October 1902; Bassett to Dodd, [ca. August 1902], Dodd Papers, LC.

39. Dodd, "Some Difficulties of the History Teacher in the South," 119.

40. Sledd, "The Negro"; Reed, "Emory College and the Sledd Affair of 1902."

41. Andrew Sledd to Dodd, 21 July 1902, Dodd Papers, LC.

42. L. R. Vaughn to editor, *Richmond News,* 27 October 1902; *Richmond Times,* 8, 10, 21 August 1902.

43. William A. Dunning to Dodd, 9 March 1903, and Bassett to Dodd, 25 March 1903, Dodd Papers, LC.

44. Bassett, "Stirring Up the Fires of Racial Antipathy," 299; Hamilton, *Fifty Years of the South Atlantic Quarterly,* 53–61.

45. Bassett to Dodd, 9, 24 November, 3 December 1903, and Edwin Mims to Dodd, 21, 22 November, 8 December 1903, Dodd Papers, LC; Dodd to Charles Francis Adams Jr., 10 November 1903, 3 May 1906, Charles Frances Adams Jr. Papers; Stephenson, *Southern History in the Making,* 105, 126–30.

46. Bassett to Dodd, 9 November 1903, 2 February 1904, Dodd Papers, LC.

47. American Historical Association, *Annual Report . . . for the Year 1903,* 1:26; "Meeting of the American Historical Association at New Orleans," 443–44; Dodd, "Some Difficulties of the History Teacher in the South," 118–21; Bassett to Dodd, 2, 27 February 1904, Dodd Papers, LC. Dodd's essay is reprinted in Hamilton, *Fifty Years of the South Atlantic Quarterly,* 73–92.

48. Dodd to Howard K. Beale, 2 December 1932, Dodd Papers, LC; Bassett, "Task of the Critic," 297. This essay is reprinted in Hamilton, *Fifty Years of the South Atlantic Quarterly,* 79–83.

49. Dodd to Jameson, 8 January 1906, Jameson Papers; Bassett to Dodd, 28 April 1907, Dodd Papers, LC.

50. Bassett to Dodd, 7 May 1907, Dodd Papers, LC.

51. Dodd, "Freedom of Speech in the South," 383.

52. Ibid., 383–84. See also Dodd to Charles Francis Adams Jr., 26 June 1906, Charles Francis Adams Jr. Papers.

53. W. Leconte Stevens to Dodd, 28 April 1907, and Bassett to Dodd, 28 April 1907, Dodd Papers, LC.

54. Denny to Dodd, 22 May 1907, Dodd Papers, LC.

55. Dodd to Hart, 10 December 1907, McLaughlin Papers; Bassett to Dodd, 17 December 1908, Dodd Papers, LC.

56. Dodd to Joseph Hetherington McDaniel, 27 June 1905, McDaniel Papers; Dodd to William Roscoe Thayer, 3 July 1905, Thayer Papers; Hart to Dodd, 11 July 1905, Dodd Papers, LC.

57. Dodd to Turner, 14 October [1919], Turner Papers, HU; Dodd to Woffin, 9 November 1920, Dodd Papers, RM.

58. Billington, *Frederick Jackson Turner,* 65–66, 124–31.

59. Dodd to Jane [Addams], 29 January 1919, Jane Addams Memorial Collection.

60. Daniels to Dodd, 4 April 1901, and Daniels to Sir, 18 June 1903, Dodd Papers, LC; Daniels to Dodd, 4 May 1939, and Dodd to Daniels, 9 May 1939, Daniels Papers; Dodd to H. G. Connor, 30 March 1903, and Daniels to Connor,

20 June 1903, Connor Family Papers; clipping from the *Raleigh Progressive Farmer*, [August 1903], Dodd Papers, RM; Dodd, *Life of Nathaniel Macon*, ix.

61. Dodd, *Life of Nathaniel Macon*, 16–18, 47.

62. Ibid., 9–11, 29–40, 56–57, 64, 69–70, 298, 345, 370, 401.

63. Reviews of *The Life of Nathaniel Macon* in *Nation*, in *New York Times*, 19 December 1903, and by Peirce in *American Historical Review*, 191–92.

64. Andrew C. McLaughlin to Dodd, 25 February, 26 May 1904, Dodd Papers, LC.

65. See Dodd's reviews of the following: *The Life of James Madison*, by Gaillard Hunt; *The American Republic and Its Government*, by Albert Woodburn; *The Cambridge Modern History: The United States*, vol. 7, ed. A. W. Ward, G. W. Prothero, and Stanley Lenthes; *History of the United States from the Compromise of 1850*, vol. 5, by James Ford Rhodes; *The Political History of Virginia during the Reconstruction*, by Hamilton James Eckenrode; *Reminiscences of Peace and War*, by Mrs. Roger A. Pryor; *Forty Years of Active Service*, by Charles T. O'Ferrall; *Memoirs with Special Reference to Secession and Civil War*, by John H. Reagan; and *Seventy-five Years in Old Virginia, with Some Accounts of the Life of the Author and Some History of the People against Whom His Lot Was Cast*, by John Herbert Claiborne.

66. Bassett to Dodd, 2 February 1904, Dodd Papers, LC; Dodd to Connor, 26 August 1906, Connor Family Papers; Dodd to Charles Francis Adams Jr., 28 September 1904, 15 August, 3 November 1908, Charles Francis Adams Jr. Papers; Dodd to William K. Boyd, 15 April 1908, Boyd Papers.

67. Dodd originally envisioned a larger and more detailed biography suitable for the Macmillan Company of New York, but he readily accepted the contract offered by the George W. Jacobs Company with its guarantee of publication (Dodd to Charles Francis Adams Jr., 28 July 1908, Charles Francis Adams Jr. Papers).

68. Dodd to Charles Francis Adams Jr., 18 September 1904, Charles Francis Adams Jr. Papers; Dodd to Frederic Bancroft, 2 June 1908, Bancroft Papers; Dodd to Connor, 1, 3 February 1905, Connor Family Papers; Dodd to Yates Snowden, 4 September 1905, Snowden Papers; Dodd, quoted in George W. Duncan, "Report of Historical Committee," *Minutes of the Eleventh Annual Reunion of the United Sons of Confederate Veterans*, 197–98.

69. Duncan, "Report of Historical Committee," *Minutes of the Eleventh Annual Reunion of the United Sons of Confederate Veterans*, 197; Dodd to Robert E. Lee Jr., 24 October 1904, Lee Family Papers; Dodd to Charles Francis Adams Jr., 3 May 1906, Charles Francis Adams Jr. Papers.

70. The information in this and the following paragraphs is from Dodd, *Jefferson Davis*, 51–52, 56, 167, 180, 198–99, 208–9, 217, 239, 339, 340, 345.

71. Dodd to Charles Francis Adams Jr., 28 July 1908, Charles Francis Adams Jr. Papers; Mrs. James Mercer Garnett, "Report of Historical Committee," *Virginia Division, U.D.C., Minutes of the Thirteenth Annual Convention*, 14.

72. Reviews of *Jefferson Davis* in *Nation* and *New York Times* and by Charles Francis Adams Jr. in *American Historical Review*.

73. Dodd to Charles Francis Adams Jr., 28 July 1908, Charles Francis Adams

Jr. Papers; Dodd to Bancroft, 29 May 1908, Bancroft Papers; T. L. Mabie to Dodd, 13, 28 March 1908, Dodd Papers, LC.

74. Dodd to Bancroft, 29 May 1908, Bancroft Papers.

75. Dodd, "The Principle of Instructing United States Senators"; Dodd, "Chief Justice Marshall and Virginia, 1813–1821," 776–87; Dodd to Clark, 7 September 1906, Clark Papers.

76. Dodd, *Jefferson Davis*, 210–11.

77. Dodd to Childers, 21 April 1916, House Papers.

78. Dodd, "Autobiography."

79. Dodd to Andrew Jackson Montague, 11 May 1908, Montague Papers.

80. Dodd to Theodore Roosevelt, 28 May 1906, Dodd Papers, LC; Dodd to Montague, 16 May 1906, Montague Papers; *Raleigh News and Observer,* 14 June 1933; Roosevelt to Dodd, 31 January 1907, reprinted in Roosevelt, *Letters of Theodore Roosevelt,* 5:575; Mowry, *The Era of Theodore Roosevelt and the Birth of Modern America,* 170–71.

81. Dodd to Montague, 16 May 1906, Montague Papers; Dodd, memorandum, 5 March 1908, Dodd Papers, LC; "Professor Dodd's Diary," 69. Dodd shared his excitement with J. Franklin Jameson, who was less than impressed and thereafter wrote sarcastically to a friend: "It appears that the President of these United States . . . read [Dodd's] book—or said that he had—and with so much satisfaction that he invited the blushing author to come and have luncheon with him at the White House. I did not see Dodd after, but presume that he enjoyed himself" (Jameson to Waldo G. Leland, 18 February 1908, reprinted in Donnan and Stock, *An Historian's World,* 116).

82. Dodd to Julian S. Mason, 31 October 1912, Dodd Papers, LC.

83. Ibid.; Dodd to Connor, 11 January 1908, Connor Family Papers; Dodd to Montague, 29 June, 27 July 1908, Montague Papers; Dodd to Turner, 5 October 1908, Turner Papers, HEH; Dodd to Bancroft, 18, 28 September, 3, 10 October 1908, Bancroft Papers; Dodd to Charles Francis Adams Jr., 3 November 1908, Charles Francis Adams Jr. Papers.

84. Larsen, *Montague of Virginia,* 3–7, 39–46.

85. Dodd to Montague, 14 October 1904, Montague Papers; Larsen, *Montague of Virginia,* 216–24.

86. Montague to Dodd, 25 March, 13 May 1908, Montague Papers.

87. Dodd to Anderson, 13 October 1919, Dodd Papers, RM.

88. Dodd to Bancroft, 18, 27 October 1908, Bancroft Papers; Dodd to Charles Francis Adams Jr., 3 November 1908, Charles Francis Adams Jr. Papers; Dodd to Press of Richmond, 12 July 1911, Montague Papers; *Richmond Times Dispatch,* 5 July 1911.

89. Dodd to Hart, 10 December 1907, McLaughlin Papers; *University of Chicago Annual Register, 1907–08,* 23.

90. Dodd to Hart, 10 December 1907, McLaughlin Papers.

91. *University of Chicago Annual Register, 1907–08,* 21–22; McLaughlin to Dodd, 3 April 1908, Dodd Papers, LC.

92. McLaughlin to Dodd, 24 April 1908, Dodd Papers, LC.

93. Dodd to McLaughlin, 16 April 1908, and McLaughlin to Dodd, 24 April 1908, Dodd Papers, LC.

94. Dodd to Bancroft, 20 June 1908, Bancroft Papers. In an earlier letter Bancroft had acknowledged Dodd's difficulty working in a southern environment (Bancroft to Dodd, 15 June 1908, Dodd Papers, LC).

95. University of Chicago Board of Trustees Minutes, 16 June 1908, 6:217; T. W. Goodspeed to Dodd, 22 June 1908, Dodd Papers, LC.

96. Dodd to Turner, 25 June, 1 July 1908, Turner Papers, HEH; Dodd to Montague, 29 June 1908, Montague Papers; Roper, *U. B. Phillips*, 81–82.

97. Dodd to Montague, 27 July 1908, Montague Papers.

98. Ibid.; Ashley Horne to Dodd, 19 December 1908, Dodd Papers, LC.

99. Harry Morris Stephens to Dodd, 5 November 1908, and Bassett to Dodd, 17 December 1908, Dodd Papers, LC.

100. Ashley Horne to Dodd, 19 December 1908, Dodd Papers, LC.

101. Dodd to Bancroft, 12 February 1910, Bancroft Papers. In the fall of 1909 Dodd wrote Ulrich B. Phillips telling him of his discontent with the city of Chicago. Phillips replied with sympathy, "I fully appreciate your sectional quandary. I was troubled, of course, by very much the same dilemma and decided to return South largely because I preferred to live and work among Southern people" (Phillips to Dodd, 28 September 1909, Dodd Papers, LC).

102. Dodd, review of *The Old Dominion: Her Making and Her Manners*, by Thomas Nelson Page, 182–83; Jameson to Dodd, 10 August 1908, Dodd Papers, LC.

CHAPTER THREE: A Southern Scholar in Chicago

1. Dodd, "History and Patriotism," 119; Dodd, "Fight for the Northwest," 784.

2. Dodd, "History and Patriotism," 119; Dodd, "Josephus Daniels," 791.

3. Dodd to [Mary Shannon] Smith, 9 May 1919, Dodd Papers, LC; Dodd to Walter Clark, 9 May 1919, Clark Papers.

4. Woodward, *The Burden of Southern History*, 109–40.

5. "Professor Dodd's Diary," 28; Dodd to Patterson, Dodd Papers, LC; Dodd, "History and Patriotism," 110.

6. Dodd to Waldo G. Leland, 9 May 1909, American Historical Association Papers; Dodd to Frederic Bancroft, 17 January 1909, Bancroft Papers.

7. "Professor Dodd's Diary," 49; Dodd to Andrew Jackson Montague, 9 January 1909, Montague Papers; Dodd to Bancroft, 12 February, 7 September 1910, Bancroft Papers.

8. Dodd to Montague, 3 May 1909, Montague Papers; Dodd to Frederick Jackson Turner, 3 February, 8 April 1909, Turner Papers, HEH; Dodd to Bancroft, 21 February 1910, Bancroft Papers; Leland to Dodd, 14 June 1909, American Historical Association Papers; University of Chicago Board of Trustees Minutes, 23 March 1909, 6:334.

9. Dodd to Bancroft, 21 February, 12 March 1910, Bancroft Papers.

10. Dodd to Bancroft, 12 March 1910, Bancroft Papers.

11. Dodd to Bancroft, 21 February, 12, 26 March 1910, Bancroft Papers.

12. Dodd to Bancroft, 19 August 1910, Bancroft Papers.

13. Dodd to Bancroft, 25 November 1910, Bancroft Papers.

14. Dodd to [Martha Johns Dodd], 3 July 1911, Dodd Papers, LC.

15. Dodd to Bancroft, 18 September, 17 October 1912, Bancroft Papers; Dodd to Ashley Horne, 23 November 1912, and Dodd to Henry [Ellis], 14 December 1912, Dodd Papers, LC.

16. Dodd to Bancroft, 18 September 1912, Bancroft Papers; Dodd to Ashley Horne, 23 November, 23 December 1912, Dodd Papers, LC; Dodd to William K. Boyd, 20 October 1914, Boyd Papers.

17. Dodd to Bancroft, 23 June, 16 August 1913, Bancroft Papers; Dodd to Andrew C. McLaughlin, 30 August, 18 October 1913, and McLaughlin to Dodd, 3 October 1913, Department of History Records, University of Chicago.

18. Dodd to Page, 7 September 1919, Dodd Papers, LC.

19. Carl Becker to Dodd, 22 May 1917, Becker Papers; Dodd to Teacher and Friend, 27 April 1915, Dodd to Hoyt, 29 June 1912, Dodd to Patterson, 23 September 1919, and Dodd to Max Farrand, 25 January 1921, Dodd Papers, LC.

20. Dodd to Bancroft, 11 November 1913, Bancroft Papers; Dodd to Becker, 12 December 1914, Becker Papers; Dodd to Edward M. House, 4 June 1916, 22 September 1918, House Papers; "Professor Dodd's Diary," 43.

21. "Professor Dodd's Diary," 49.

22. William A. Dunning to Dodd, 4 June 1914, and Dodd to Dunning, 8 June 1914, Dodd Papers, LC.

23. Craven, "William E. Dodd: As Teacher," 7; Frank L. Owsley to George Petrie, 19 February 1917, Owsley Papers.

24. Nixon, *Lower Piedmont County*, xix.

25. Wiebe, *The Search for Order*, 121; Billington, *Frederick Jackson Turner*, 337–38.

26. Ibid.

27. James T. Shotwell to Dodd, 22 October 1909, Dodd Papers, LC; Dodd, "Fight for the Northwest," 774.

28. Ibid., 775, 781–84.

29. Ibid., 786–88.

30. Dodd to Montague, 1 January 1910 [1911], Montague Papers; Charles A. Beard to Dodd, 27 September 1911, Dodd Papers, LC; Dodd to Bancroft, 8 January 1911, Bancroft Papers.

31. American Historical Association, *Annual Report . . . for the Year 1910*, 40–41.

32. Dodd to Theodore Roosevelt, 24 February 1912, Dodd to [Ellis], 14 December 1912, and Dodd to Ashley Horne, 23 December 1912, Dodd Papers, LC.

33. American Historical Association, *Annual Report . . . for the Year 1912*, 38.

34. Dodd, "Profitable Fields of Investigation in American History," 522–24.

35. Ibid., 522–25.

36. Ibid., 527–36.

37. Ulrich B. Phillips, "On the Economics of Slavery, 1815–1860," American Historical Association, *Annual Report . . . for the Year 1912,* 150–51; Roper, *U. B. Phillips,* 101–2.

38. J. Franklin Jameson to Dodd, 5 February 1913, and Dodd to Charles H. Ambler, 5 January 1913, Dodd Papers, LC.

39. Dodd to Jameson, 9 March 1914, Jameson Papers; Dodd to Bancroft, 15 March 1914, Bancroft Papers.

40. Billington, *Frederick Jackson Turner,* 337–38; Billington, "Tempest in Clio's Teapot."

41. Dodd to Bancroft, 22 January 1914, Bancroft Papers; Theodore D. Jervey to Dodd, 7 January 1914, Dodd Papers, LC.

42. Dodd to Dunbar Rowland, 13 March 1914, Dodd Papers, LC; Dodd to Jameson, 9 March 1914, Jameson Papers; Cooke, *Frederic Bancroft,* 98–102.

43. Bancroft to Dodd, 23 March 1914, Dodd Papers, LC; Jameson to Dodd, 24 March 1914, Jameson Papers.

44. Dodd to Bancroft, 7 July 1914, Bancroft Papers.

45. Dodd to Bancroft, 21 December 1914, Bancroft Papers; American Historical Association, *Annual Report . . . for the Year 1914,* 14, 18, 20; Bancroft to Dodd, 10 March 1915, and Dodd to Ambler, 28 April 1915, Dodd Papers, LC.

46. Bancroft, Latane, and Rowland, *The Attempt to Seize the American Historical Review;* Dodd to Boyd, 7 May 1915, Boyd Papers.

47. Dodd to Boyd, 7, 21 May 1915, Boyd Papers; Dodd to Ambler, 28 April 1915, Dodd Papers, LC.

48. Bancroft to Dunning, 6 January 1915, Dunning Papers; Bancroft to J. G. de Roulhac Hamilton, 24 March 1915, J. G. de Roulhac Hamilton Papers; Bancroft to Dodd, 10 March 1915, Dodd Papers, LC.

49. Dodd to Bancroft (not mailed), 14 March 1915, Dodd Papers, LC; Dodd to Bancroft, 13 April 1915, Bancroft Papers.

50. Becker to Dodd, [1915], Becker Papers.

51. Ambler to Dodd, 14 May 1915, Dodd to Rowland, 2 June 1915, and Dodd to Jameson, 1 June 1915, Dodd Papers, LC; Dodd to Boyd, 13 June 1915, Boyd Papers; Billington, *Frederick Jackson Turner,* 342–43.

52. American Historical Association, *Annual Report . . . for the Year 1915,* 54, 69–75, 83.

53. "Professor Dodd's Diary," 32 and 55; secretary of the American Historical Association to Dodd, 31 December 1917, American Historical Association Papers.

54. Dodd to Turner, Turner Papers, HEH; Dodd to Ambler, 6 December 1932, Dodd Papers, LC.

55. Dodd, "History and Patriotism," 109; Dodd to Becker, 8 April 1917, Becker Papers.

56. Dodd to Woffin, 9 November 1920, Dodd Papers, RM; Dodd, "Economic Interpretations of American History," 489; Dodd, "History and Patriotism," 110.

57. Dodd, "History and Patriotism," 118.

58. Dodd, reviews of *Early Life and Letters of General Thomas J. Jackson,*

"Stonewall Jackson," by Thomas Jackson Arnold; *The Life of John Caldwell Calhoun,* by William M. Meigs; and *J. L. M. Curry: A Biography,* by Edwin Anderson Alderman and Armistead Churchill Gordon.

59. "Report: Before the Virginia State Board of Education in the Matter of the Re-adoption for Four Years of 'Virginia's Attitude towards Slavery and Secession' by Beverley B. Munford," [1919], Executive Records: Governor Westmoreland Davis; Beverley B. Munford to Armistead C. Gordon, 6 November 1906, and Gordon to Munford, n.d., Gordon Papers; W. Gordon McCabe, eulogy of Beverley B. Munford, *Proceedings of the Virginia Historical Society Annual Meeting held December 29, 1910,* Beverley B. Munford Scrapbook.

60. Munford, *Virginia's Attitude toward Slavery and Secession,* vii, 15–33, 6–76, 82–103, 164, 176–77, 304.

61. Dodd to Bancroft, 17 April 1910, Bancroft Papers; Dodd, review of *Virginia's Attitude toward Slavery and Secession,* by Beverley B. Munford.

62. Dodd to Bancroft, 17 April 1910, Bancroft Papers; Reamuer Coleman Stearnes to Munford, 17 January 1910, and Munford to J. Taylor Ellyson, 10 March 1910, Munford Family Papers; "Report: Before the Virginia State Board of Education in the Matter of the Re-adoption for Four Years of 'Virginia's Attitude towards Slavery and Secession' by Beverley B. Munford," [1919], Executive Records: Governor Westmoreland Davis; A. P. Hill to Mary Munford, 22 September 1926, Mary Cooke Branch Munford Papers.

63. Dodd to Hoyt, 29 June 1912, 12 December 1914, Dodd Papers, LC; Dodd to Bancroft, 25 November 1910, 13 November 1911, Bancroft Papers; Dodd to Becker, 14 August 1915, Becker Papers.

64. Dodd to Bancroft, 29 November 1909, 12 February 1910, Bancroft Papers; Dodd to Turner, 4 November 1909, Turner Papers, HEH; Dodd to Boyd, 24 June 1909, 5 January, 17 February 1913, Boyd Papers; Dodd to Montague, 4, 30 November 1909, 15 February 1911, Montague Papers.

65. Dodd, "Social Philosophy of the Old South," 735, 746; Dodd, *Statesmen of the Old South,* 232.

66. Dodd, "History and Patriotism," 115.

67. Dodd, *Cotton Kingdom,* 24, 72–73, 84, 111, 114, 120–21; Dodd, *Expansion and Conflict,* 136–40, 213–15; Dodd, "Social Philosophy of the Old South," 736.

68. Dodd, *Cotton Kingdom,* 51–53, 56–57, 60–62, 64–65; Dodd, *Expansion and Conflict,* 187; Dodd, *Statesmen of the Old South,* 136–37; Dodd, "Social Philosophy of the Old South," 735–39, 742–45.

69. Dodd, *Expansion and Conflict,* 145; Dodd, *Cotton Kingdom,* 102–3.

70. Dodd, *Cotton Kingdom,* 42, 123–24; Dodd, *Statesmen of the Old South,* 205–6.

71. Dodd, *Cotton Kingdom,* 41–42, 47, 95–96; Dodd, *Expansion and Conflict,* 215; Dodd, *Statesmen of the Old South,* 199.

72. Dodd, *Cotton Kingdom,* 10–20, 30–35; Dodd, *Expansion and Conflict,* 141–42, 146.

73. Carter G. Woodson to Dodd, 13 June 1928, 11 May, 7 June, 15, 27 Au-

gust, 30 September 1929, 28 May, 24 October 1931, and Dodd to Woodson, 19 June, 1 July, 1, 3 October 1929, 5 June, 20, 28 October 1931, Dodd Papers, LC.

74. Dodd to [Ellis], 14 December 1912, Dodd Papers, LC.

75. Dodd to Bancroft, 25 November 1910, Bancroft Papers.

76. Avery O. Craven, "William Edward Dodd," *Dictionary of American Biography*; Dodd to Childers, 21 April 1916, House Papers.

77. Dodd to Montague, 3 August 1909, and Dodd to Press of Richmond, 12 July 1911, Montague Papers; Dodd to [Ellis], 14 December 1912, and Dodd to J. Rion McKissick, 20 December 1925, Dodd Papers, LC; *Richmond Times-Dispatch*, 5 July 1911.

78. Shelton, "William Atkinson Jones," ii–iv, 251.

79. Dodd to Montague, 8 May 1911, Montague Papers.

80. Christopher B. Garnett to Dodd, 15 May, 15 June 1911, Dodd Papers, LC.

81. Shelton, "William Atkinson Jones," 251–60.

82. *Richmond Times-Dispatch*, 5 July 1911.

83. Ibid.

84. George W. Denny to Dodd, 15 July 1911, and Garnett to Dodd, 22 July 1911, Dodd Papers, LC; Dodd to Montague, 19 August 1911, Montague Papers; Shelton, "William Atkinson Jones," 260.

85. Shelton, "William Atkinson Jones," 265–97.

86. *Richmond Times-Dispatch*, 5 July 1911.

87. Link, *Wilson*, 1–3; Blum, *Woodrow Wilson*, 5–7; Mulder, *Woodrow Wilson*, 3–28; Dodd, *Woodrow Wilson and His Work*, 7.

88. Blum, *Woodrow Wilson*, 11–22.

89. Ibid., 23–29; Mulder, *Woodrow Wilson*, 188–96.

90. Blum, *Woodrow Wilson*, 29–33; Mulder, *Woodrow Wilson*, 196–203. For an example of a contemporary journalist interpreting the "Battle of Princeton" as a democratic crusade against aristocracy see White, *Woodrow Wilson*, 145–48.

91. Blum, *Woodrow Wilson*, 36–47, 57–58; Mulder, *Woodrow Wilson*, 225–29, 263–77.

92. "Professor Dodd's Diary," 9; Dodd to Turner, 3 October 1919, Turner Papers, HU; Dodd, "Josephus Daniels," 793; Dodd to Bancroft, 2 November 1910, 30 April 1911, Bancroft Papers.

93. Dodd to Bancroft, 3 October 1908, Bancroft Papers; Dodd, "Democracy and Learning," 430–31.

94. Woodrow Wilson to Dodd, 4 May 1910, in Wilson, *Wilson Papers*, 20:408–9; Dodd, *Woodrow Wilson and His Work*, 60.

95. Dodd to Wilson, 9 September 1911, in Wilson, *Wilson Papers*, 23:311–12; Wilson to Dodd, 1 April 1912, Dodd Papers, SHC.

96. Dodd to Josephus Daniels, 17 December 1912, Dodd Papers, LC; Findling, *Dictionary of American Diplomatic History*, 368–69. The rumor of Page's appointment to Great Britain apparently began with an editorial in the *Nashville Banner*. Long a patron of Virginia's Martin machine, he had quickly wearied of opposition from the "so-called 'progressive faction'" of the Democratic Party (clipping from *Nashville Banner*, [November 1912], enclosed in Marcus J. Wright

to Thomas Nelson Page, 25 November 1912, Thomas Nelson Page Papers; Thomas Nelson Page to Gordon, 14, 17 March 1913, Gordon Papers).

97. Dodd to Daniels, 11 November 1913, Daniels Papers; Dodd to [Ellis], 14 December 1912, Dodd Papers, LC.

98. Dodd to Martha Johns Dodd, 25 August 1914, Dodd Papers, LC.

99. Dodd to Maurer, 11 November 1914, and Dodd to Trevelyan, 19 May 1915, Dodd Papers, LC; Dodd to Yates Snowden, 10 March 1916, Snowden Papers; Dodd, "Social Philosophy of the Old South," 746.

100. Dodd to Daniels, 6 January 1915, Daniels Papers.

101. Dodd to William Jennings Bryan, 17 May 1916, Bryan Papers.

102. Dodd, *Woodrow Wilson and His Work*, 177; "Professor Dodd's Diary," 14–15; Dodd to House, 17 August 1916, House Papers; Dodd to Oswald Garrison Villard, 27 January 1917, Villard Papers.

103. "Professor Dodd's Diary," 59; Dodd to House, 20 December 1916, House Papers; Dodd, *Woodrow Wilson and His Work*, 177; Holme, *Life of Leonard Wood*, 1–11, 14, 81–153.

104. "Professor Dodd's Diary," 9–11; Dodd to Villard, 4 October 1916, Villard Papers.

105. "Professor Dodd's Diary," 11; Dodd to Millard E. Tydings, 13 January 1936, Moore Papers; Dodd to Ray Standard Baker, 20 March 1936, Dodd Papers, LC. In the letters to Baker and Tydings Dodd mistakenly lists his first meeting as August 1915.

106. Dodd to Villard, 4 October 1916, Villard Papers; "Professor Dodd's Diary," 17–23.

107. Dodd to Maurer, 11 November 1914, Dodd Papers, LC.

CHAPTER FOUR: A Wilsonian Scholar in the Republican Interlude

1. Dodd to H. L. Mencken, 3 October 1924, Dodd Papers, LC.

2. W. Swearingen to Walter Presscott Webb, 24 February 1924, Webb Papers; Dodd to Wallace Notestein, 23 February 1920, Notestein Papers; Dodd to Carl Becker, 15 July 1920, Becker Papers.

3. Dodd to McLean, 9 April 1923, Dodd Papers, LC.

4. Childers, "A Friend's View of Colonel House," 553–63; George and George, *Woodrow Wilson and Colonel House*, 75–104; Neu, "In Search of Colonel Edward M. House."

5. Dodd to Sir, 6 April 1916, Dodd to Henry Herbert Childers, 21 April 1916, Dodd to Edward M. House, 17 May 1916, and House to Dodd, 4 June 1916, House Papers; Childers, "A Friend's View of Colonel House," 553–63.

6. Dodd to Oswald Garrison Villard, 12 January 1917, and Villard to Dodd, 1 February 1917, Villard Papers.

7. "Professor Dodd's Diary," 39.

8. Dodd to Josephus Daniels, 5 April 1917, Daniels Papers.

9. Murray, *Red Scare*, 12–15.

10. Dodd, *Woodrow Wilson and His Work*, 222–24.

11. "Professor Dodd's Diary," 49–50; *New York Times*, 4, 5 November 1917.

12. "Professor Dodd's Diary," 48–49; Dodd to House, 3 February 1918, House Papers; Gelfand, *The Inquiry*, 45, 339.

13. [Dodd], "The Present Status of the Monroe Doctrine," n.d., The Inquiry Papers.

14. "Professor Dodd's Diary," 53, 54; Dodd to House, 24 December 1917, 3 February 1918, House Papers.

15. Dodd, *Woodrow Wilson and His Work*, xiv.

16. Dodd, review of *John Harlan*, by Johnson Brigham.

17. Dodd to House, 3 September 1917, 22 September 1918, House Papers.

18. Dodd to McKinley, 24 October 1919, Dodd Papers, LC; Dodd to Frederick Jackson Turner, 3 October 1919, Turner Papers, HU; Dodd to Samuel N. Harper, 24 October 1919, Harper Papers.

19. Dodd to Henderson, 17 August 1919, Dodd Papers, LC; Dodd to House, 15, 18 September 1919, House Papers.

20. Dodd, "Josephus Daniels," 823, 825.

21. Dodd, "Roosevelt," 1140.

22. Ibid., 1141.

23. "Professor Dodd's Diary," 60; Dodd to Anderson, 13 October 1919, Dodd Papers, RM.

24. "Professor Dodd's Diary," 68–69; Dodd to Teacher and Friend, 2 January 1920, Dodd Papers, LC; Dodd to Gamaliel Bradford, 29 January 1931, Bradford Letterbook.

25. "Professor Dodd's Diary," 69; Dodd, "Woodrow Wilson and Democracy," typescript, [ca. 1926], Dodd Papers, LC.

26. "Professor Dodd's Diary," 78.

27. Ibid., 70–71, 74, 76.

28. Ibid., 77; Dodd to Anderson, 13 October 1919, Dodd Papers, RM.

29. "Professor Dodd's Diary," 81–82.

30. Ibid., 82.

31. Ibid., 59; Dodd, "British-American Difficulties," 572–74.

32. Dodd to House, 3 February, 11 March 1919, House Papers.

33. Dodd to House, 12 October 1919, House Papers.

34. Dodd to Anderson, 3 October 1919, Dodd Papers, RM.

35. Dodd to House, 12 October 1919, House Papers.

36. Turner to Dodd, 6 October 1919, Turner Papers, HU.

37. Turner to Dodd, 6 October 1919, and Dodd to Turner, 3 October 1919, Turner Papers, HU; Wilson, "Mr. Goldwin Smith's 'Views' on Our Political History," 489–99.

38. Turner to Dodd, 9 October 1919, Turner Papers, HU.

39. Dodd to Turner, 14 October 1919, Turner Papers, HU.

40. The information in this and the following paragraphs is derived from Dodd, *Woodrow Wilson and His Work*, 14, 52, 67, 80, 83, 98, 109–10, 121, 127, 200, 281, 289–91, 300, 321–22, 354, 370–71, 375–79, 385.

41. Dodd to Notestein, 23 February 1920, Notestein Papers.

42. Dodd to Becker, 14 June 1920, Becker Papers; clipping from *New York Times,* 12 September 1920, Dodd Papers, RM.

43. Dodd to Becker, 14 June 1920, Becker Papers; Dodd to John White, 17 June 1920, Dodd Papers, LC.

44. Dodd to Becker, 14 June 1920, Becker Papers.

45. Ibid.

46. Becker to Dodd, 17 June 1920, and Dodd to Becker, 15 July 1920, Becker Papers.

47. Dodd to Claude Bowers, 24 December 1922 [photostat], Claude Bowers file, Holman Hamilton Papers (hereinafter cited as Bowers Photostats); Dodd to Miss Wilson, 5 January 1921 (draft on back of notes for Wilson lecture), Dodd Papers, RM.

48. Edwin S. Corwin, review of *Woodrow Wilson and His Work;* Dodd to J. G. de Roulhac Hamilton, 22 January 1922, J. G. de Roulhac Hamilton Papers.

49. Dodd to Becker, 14 June 1920, Becker Papers.

50. Dodd's correspondence between 1920 and 1932 includes hundreds of letters negotiating speaking appointments. For a sampling of his commitments see Dodd to House, 12 March 1920, 10 November 1930, House Papers; Dodd to Daniels, 23 November 1922, 30 April 1927, Daniels Papers; Becker to Dodd, 24 March 1923, Becker Papers; Dodd to Charles W. Ramsdell, 18 April 1923, Ramsdell Papers; Dodd to A. Merkle John, 31 October, 29 December 1922, Dodd to Priddy, 6 October 1922, Dodd to Woodrow Wilson, 23 November 1922, Dodd to Nellie, 6 December 1922, Dodd to Willoughby Walling, 22 January 1923, Daniel C. Roper to Dodd, 25 January 1923, 23 February, 13 October, 19 November 1926, Dodd to Mr. President, 3 April 1923, Dodd to Martha Johns Dodd, 27 April 1923, 13 December 1926, 25 March 1927, 24 January, 6, 18 March 1928, 9 March 1929, clipping from Laramie, Wyoming, newspaper, ca. 1924, Dodd to William G. McAdoo, 8 February 1924, Albert H. Lylyer to Dodd, 19 February 1926, C. A. Ives to Dodd, 18 February, 24 May, 9 July 1926, Roosevelt P. Walker to Dodd, 8 November 1926, Margaret Banister to Dodd, 23 November 1926, Dodd to Roper, 12 November 1926, Daniels to Dodd, 7 December 1926, Louis H. Gibson to Dodd, 10 December 1926, Dodd to John, 20 December 1926, A. P. Brogan to Dodd, 28 January 1927, Dodd to Martha Dodd, 21 March 1927, Charles A. Messner to Dodd, 27 July 1928, S. G. Riley to Dodd, 6 February 1929, M. Estes Cocke to Dodd, 24 September 1929, Louis A. Bowman to Dodd, 14 January 1930, Elmer Scott to Dodd, 8 April 1930, William S. Webb to Dodd, 10 April 1930, Dodd to George Fort Milton, 6 February 1931, Dodd to F. W. Smithers, 25 April 1932, Dodd to Richard Crane, 2 August 1932, Dodd to Louis Howe, 2 October 1932, and Dodd to Carlyle Campbell, 8 October 1932, all in Dodd Papers, LC.

51. Dodd to Bowers, 1 July 1922, Bowers Photostats; John Spencer Bassett to Dodd, 1, 24 October, 9 November 1923, Dodd to Merriam, 27 October 1923, and Dodd to Martha Johns Dodd, 12 November 1923, 25 March 1928, Dodd Papers, LC.

52. Dodd to House, 28 October 1930, House Papers.

53. Dodd, "The Passing of the Old United States" (address to the Institute of Public Affairs, University of Virginia, 7 August 1929), House Papers.

54. Clippings from *St. Louis Star,* 15 January 1922, and *Garnett, Kansas, Review,* 23 February 1922, and Dodd, "Woodrow Wilson and Democracy," Dodd Papers, LC; untitled Chicago newspaper clipping, 15 July 1921, Dodd Papers, RM.

55. Mencken to Dodd, 7 October [1924], and Clarence Ayres to Dodd, 9 October 1924, Dodd Papers, LC; Charles Seymour to Dodd, 21 December 1928, 26 January 1932, and Dodd to Seymour, 5 January 1929, Seymour Papers; House to Dodd, 30 December 1930, Dodd Papers, LC.

56. Dodd to Bowers, 3 April 1924, 21 January 1925, Bowers Photostats; Dodd to House, 2 April 1924, 20 May 1925, 14 June 1926, House Papers; Dodd to Roper, 12 November 1926, Dodd to Bowers, 3 April 1924, Ray Standard Baker to Dodd, 1923, 21 May 1923, 23 June 1924, 7 July 1925, 1 December 1927, Dodd to Baker, 27 May 1924, 28 November 1927, 2 June 1930, Edith Bolling Wilson to Dodd, 25 November 1924, 13 January 1926, Dodd to Hurley, 7 December 1926, and Dodd to B. B. Jones, 29 May 1930, Dodd Papers, LC; Dodd to Miss Wilson, 5 January 1921, Dodd Papers, RM; Dodd and Baker, *Public Papers of Woodrow Wilson.*

57. Bowers to Dodd, 17 January 1923, Dodd Papers, LC. For a sampling of Dodd's interactions with Daniels, Roper, Bowers, and House see Dodd to Daniels, 7 April 1925, 30 September, 10 October 1926, and Daniels to Dodd, 22 January, 6 October 1926, 9 January 1932, Daniels Papers; Roper to Dodd, 17 December 1927, 18 January 1929, 25 April, 18 May 1932, and Dodd to Roper, 21 December 1927, 14, 26 April, 13 May 1932, Roper Papers; Dodd to Bowers, 5 November, 24 December 1922, 17 August 1923, 16 May, 4 June 1924, 30 September 1926, 12 March 1931, Bowers Photostats; Dodd to Seymour, 5 January 1929, Seymour Papers; House to Dodd, 6 July 1926, 22 December 1930, 13 December 1932, and Dodd to House, 22 October 1921, 17 May 1922, 6 February 1924, 20 October 1925, 14 June, 12 October 1926, 8 January 1931, 6 January 1932, House Papers; Roper to Dodd, 7 March 1923, Bowers to Dodd, 20 May, 5 August 1923, 9 February 1924, Dodd to Bowers, 24 January, 25 February 1923, Dodd to Milton, 24 November 1926, and Dodd diary, 12 January 1928, Dodd Papers, LC.

58. "Professor Dodd's Diary," 84; Dodd, *Woodrow Wilson and His Work,* 409, 415.

59. Dodd, *Woodrow Wilson and His Work,* 26.

60. Dodd to Bowers, 5 November 1922, Bowers Photostats; Dodd to Woodrow Wilson, 29 December 1922, Dodd Papers, LC.

61. Dodd to McLean, 9 April 1923, Dodd to Roper, 14 April, 17 December 1923, and Dodd to Mrs. John Gwin, 17 December 1923, Dodd Papers, LC.

62. Dodd to Bowers, 17 August 1923, Bowers Photostats.

63. Dodd to John D. Dodd, 30 April 1924, and Dodd to J. A. Woodburn, 19 October 1924, Dodd Papers, LC.

64. Dodd to John D. Dodd, 30 April 1924, Dodd to Bassett, 9 May 1924, and Dodd to Woodburn, 19 October 1924, Dodd Papers, LC.

65. Dodd to McAdoo, 8 February 1924, Dodd to John D. Dodd, 30 April 1924, Dodd to Bassett, 9 May 1924, and Dodd to Woodburn, 19 October 1924, Dodd Papers, LC; Dodd to Bowers, 11 February 1924, Bowers Photostats.

66. Dodd to Bowers, 20 July 1924, Bowers Photostats.

67. Dodd to John D. Dodd, 30 April 1924, and Dodd to Johnson, 9 May 1924, Dodd Papers, LC; Dodd to Bowers, 3 April 1924, Bowers Photostats.

68. Dodd to Thomas J. Woodhouse, 8 June 1924, Bowers Photostats.

69. Dodd to J. Niles Wheeler, 4 November 1922, and Dodd to Bowers, 24 January 1923, Dodd Papers, LC.

70. Dodd, *Woodrow Wilson and His Work*, 109.

71. Dodd to Bowers, 20 July 1924, Dodd to John J. McMahon, 16 May 1924, and Dodd to Woodhouse, 8 June 1924, Bowers Photostats; Dodd to Charles Horne, 7 June 1924, and Dodd to Mrs. John Gwin, 9 June 1924, Dodd Papers, LC.

72. Dodd to Roper, 31 July 1924, Dodd Papers, LC.

73. Dodd to Bowers, 31 October 1924, Bowers Photostats; Dodd to Albert Beveridge, 7 November 1924, Dodd Papers, LC.

74. Dodd to Daniels, 7 April 1925, Daniels Papers; Dodd to Bowers, 4 June 1927, Bowers Photostats; Dodd to Theodore D. Jervey, 27 July 1927, and Dodd diary, 18 March 1928, Dodd Papers, LC.

75. Dodd to Roper, 21 September 1928, Roper Papers; Dodd to Daniels, 23 May 1928, Daniels Papers; Dodd to Bowers, 4 June 1927, Bowers Photostats; Frank L. Polk to Dodd, 15 August 1928, and Dodd to Polk, 18 August 1928, Dodd Papers, LC.

76. Dodd to Ralph Gabriel, 14 August 1928, Gabriel Papers; Dodd to Roper, 2 November 1928, Roper Papers; Dodd to Seymour, 5 January 1929, Seymour Papers; Dodd to Lady Astor, 31 August 1928, Theodore Morison to Dodd, 20 October 1928, and Robert McElroy to Dodd, 30 [November] 1928, Dodd Papers, LC.

77. Dodd to Patterson, 23 September 1919, Dodd to Hewitt H. Howland, 9 March 1927, and Dodd to Newton D. Baker, 24 June 1932, Dodd Papers, LC; Dodd to Wilbur Cross, 25 January 1919, *Yale Review* Papers.

78. Dodd to Wheeler, 4 November 1922, Dodd Papers, LC.

79. Dodd to Becker, 14 June 1920, Becker Papers; Dodd to Patterson, 23 September 1919, Dodd Papers, LC.

80. University of Chicago Board of Trustees Minutes, 14 February 1922, 12:334.

81. Dodd to Ramsdell, 3 January, 3 February, 5 March 1923, Ramsdell Papers; Dodd to Andrew C. McLaughlin, 3 February 1923, Dodd Papers, LC.

82. Bailey, "Free Speech and the Lost Cause in Texas."

83. Dodd to Ramsdell, 3 February, 5 March, 11 May 1923, Ramsdell Papers; Dodd to McLaughlin, 3 February 1923, Dodd Papers, LC.

84. Dodd to [Dellett?], 22 December 1926, Dodd Papers, LC.

85. Dodd to J. Franklin Jameson, 9 February 1923, Dodd Papers, LC.

86. Dodd to House, 5 November 1923, House Papers.

87. Mencken to Dodd, 8 April, 12 November 1924, and Dodd to Mencken, 30 November 1923, Dodd Papers, LC; Dodd, "When Washington Tried Isolation"; Dodd, "Napoleon Breaks Thomas Jefferson."

88. Dodd, "When Washington Tried Isolation," 345–46, 348, 352.

89. Dodd, "Napoleon Breaks Thomas Jefferson," 305–6.

90. Dodd to Charles A. Beard, 21 July 1927, Dodd Papers, LC.

91. See the following published in *Century Magazine:* "The Making of Andrew Jackson"; "Andrew Jackson and His Enemies"; "The Rise of Abraham Lincoln"; "Lincoln or Lee"; "Lincoln's Last Struggle"; "Shall Our Farmers Become Peasants"; "Our Ingrowing Habit of Lawlessness"; and "The Passing of the Old United States." And see the following published in the *New York Times:* "A Document That Changed the World"; "Samuel J. Tilden—A Prophet Unheeded"; "Epic of the Embattled Farmer"; "The Great Wilson Adventure"; and "The Epic of Wilson: Again It Resounds."

92. Dodd, *Lincoln or Lee;* Dodd to Allen Tate, 9 June 1928, Dodd Papers, LC. See also Gabriel to Dodd, 2 May 1929, Gabriel Papers.

93. Dodd, "The Dilemma of Democracy in the United States," 350–51, 353.

94. Jameson, "The Meeting of the American Historical Association at Richmond," 476; Historical News, 185; Dodd to Martha Johns Dodd, 31 December 1927, Dodd to John D. Dodd, 2 January 1931, and Beard to Dodd, 30 November [1930], Dodd Papers, LC.

95. University of Chicago Board of Trustees Minutes, the University of Chicago, 10 February 1927, 17:43; Dodd to Daniels, 18 June 1927, Daniels Papers; Dodd to J. Fred Rippy, 16 April, 11 May 1926, and Frank L. Owsley to Rippy, 8 May 1926, Rippy Papers; Dodd to W. K. Boyd, 15 February 1927, Boyd Papers; Dodd to Rippy, 8 May 1927, Dodd to Erich Marcks, 27 May 1928, and Dodd to B. Barnett, 11 July 1928, Dodd Papers, LC.

96. Dodd to Dumas Malone, 24 March 1928, Dodd to Becker, 10 July 1928, Charles E. Merriam to Dodd, 14 July 1928, Becker to Dodd, 28 September 1928, and Dodd to Barnett, 11 July 1928, Dodd Papers, LC; Dodd to Roper, 11 July 1928, Roper Papers.

97. Dodd to Dellett, 22 December 1926, and Dodd to Arnett, 13 October 1927, Dodd Papers, LC.

98. Dodd to Arnett, 13 October 1927, and Dodd diary, 12 February 1931, Dodd Papers, LC; Dodd to Roper, 18 May 1928, 19 December 1932, Roper Papers. See also Dodd to Tufts, 25 October, 2 November 1925, Dodd to Malone, 1 March 1928, Dodd to Barnett, 11 July 1928, Dodd to Marcks, 25 December 1930, and Dodd to Merriam, 27 August 1932, Dodd Papers, LC; Dodd to Mark Anthony De Wolfe Howe, 8 January 1925, Howe Papers; and Dodd to Eugene C. Barker, 10 December 1932, Barker Papers.

99. Dodd and Dodd, *Ambassador Dodd's Diary,* 9–10; Dodd to House, 15 October 1932, 25 February 1933, House Papers.

100. For a sampling of Dodd's expressions of his intense contempt for business elites and the Republican Party see Dodd, "The Passing of the Old United States" (address to the Institute of Public Affairs, University of Virginia, 7 August 1929),

House Papers; and Dodd, "What Is the Matter with This Country" (speech delivered in Cincinnati, 27 January 1933), Roper Papers.

101. Dodd to Daniels, 5 November 1930, 30 April 1932, and Dodd to H. C. Nixon, 6 May 1931, Dodd Papers, LC.

102. Dodd to Franklin D. Roosevelt, 21, 29 August 1931, and Roosevelt to Dodd, 26 August 1931, Dodd Papers, LC.

103. Beard, *American Foreign Policy in the Making,* 72–76; Roosevelt to Dodd, 23 March 1932, Dodd Papers, LC.

104. Dodd to House, 28 May 1932, House Papers.

105. House to Dodd, 2 June 1932, House Papers; Roosevelt to Dodd, 7 June 1932, and Dodd to Louis Howe, 2 October 1932, Dodd Papers, LC.

106. Dodd to Roper, 24 August, 1 September 1932, and Roper to Dodd, 29 August 1932, Roper Papers.

107. Dodd to Roper, 15 December 1932, Roper Papers; Dodd to House, 25 February 1933, and House to Dodd, 27 February 1933, House Papers.

108. Dodd to Roper, 4 March 1933, and Dodd to House, 4 March 1933, Roper Papers.

109. Dodd to Dear Friend, 15 March 1933, and Dodd to Martha Johns Dodd, 25 March 1933, Dodd Papers, LC; Dodd to Bernadette E. Schmitt, 30 March 1933, Schmitt Papers.

110. Dodd to Martha Johns Dodd, 25 March 1933, Dodd Papers, LC; Cordell Hull to Roper, Roper Papers; Hull, *Memoirs of Cordell Hull,* 1:182.

111. William Phillips to Roosevelt, 18 May 1933, Roosevelt Papers, POF; Marvin H. McIntyre to Dodd, 3 June 1933, Dodd Papers, LC; Roper to Schmitt, 12 June 1933, Roper Papers; House to Dodd, 10 June 1933, House Papers; George S. Messersmith, "Some Observations of the Appointment of Dr. William Dodd as Ambassador to Berlin" (typed manuscript, n.d.), Messersmith Papers (hereinafter cited as Messersmith, "Observations on Dodd"); Dodd and Dodd, *Ambassador Dodd's Diary,* 3, 9–10; Drummond, *The Passing of American Neutrality,* 72–73.

CHAPTER FIVE: An American Scholar in Hitler's Court

1. Jane Addams to Dodd, 16 June 1933, Carl Becker to Dodd, 11 June 1932 [1933], H. L. Mencken to Dodd, 13 June 1933, and Dodd to Carl Sandburg, 21 November 1934, Dodd Papers, LC; Dodd to Maude H. Woodfin, 23 June 1933, Woodfin Papers; Dodd and Dodd, *Ambassador Dodd's Diary,* 4, 7; Helen C. Beachamp to Dodd, 24 June 1933, Dodd Papers, RM.

2. Dodd to Franklin D. Roosevelt, 13 October 1933, Roosevelt Papers, PSF.

3. Jay Pierrepont Moffat to John Campbell White, 31 March 1934, White Papers; Dodd to Oswald Garrison Villard, 26 February 1923, Villard Papers.

4. "Their Excellencies, Our Ambassadors," 108–9.

5. Dodd to Bessie Louis Pierce, 3 February 1934, Pierce Papers.

6. Dodd to Herman Horne, 23 September 1933, Dodd Papers, LC.

7. "Their Excellencies, Our Ambassadors," 115; Shirer, *Rise and Fall of the*

Third Reich, 183–84, 194, 198–200; Messersmith, "Observations on Dodd," 1.

8. Dodd and Dodd, *Ambassador Dodd's Diary,* 3.

9. Ibid., 3–4; University of Chicago Board of Trustees Minutes, 14 September 1933, 23:173.

10. Dodd to Roosevelt, telegram, 9 June 1933, Roosevelt Papers, POF; Dodd and Dodd, *Ambassador Dodd's Diary,* 5.

11. Roosevelt to Dodd, telegram, 12 June 1933, Roosevelt Papers, POF; Dodd and Dodd, *Ambassador Dodd's Diary,* 4–6.

12. Dodd and Dodd, *Ambassador Dodd's Diary,* 6.

13. Ibid., 6–7; Dodd to Pierce, 2 September 1933, Pierce Papers.

14. Dodd to Pierce, 27 June 1933, 4 May, 6 June, 4 October 1934, Pierce Papers; Dodd and Dodd, *Ambassador Dodd's Diary,* 7; Mrs. George E. Sevey to Roosevelt, Roosevelt Papers, POF.

15. Dodd and Dodd, *Ambassador Dodd's Diary,* 8; clipping from *Raleigh News and Observer,* 14 June 1933, Dodd Papers, LC.

16. Dodd and Dodd, *Ambassador Dodd's Diary,* 8–10; Dodd to Edward M. House, 23 June 1933, and Dodd to William L. Cheney, 21 July 1933, Dodd Papers, LC; House to Dodd, 5 July, 6 December 1933, House Papers.

17. William Phillips to George A. Gordon, 12, 27 June 1933, and Gordon to Phillips, 26, 28 June 1933, State, *Foreign Relations, 1933,* 2:381–84.

18. Gordon to Phillips, 26, 28 June 1933, State, *Foreign Relations, 1933,* 2:381–84.

19. Phillips to Gordon, 27 June 1933, and Gordon to Phillips, 28 June, 1 July 1933, State, *Foreign Relations, 1933,* 2:382–85.

20. "Their Excellencies, Our Ambassadors," 116; Messersmith, "Observations on Dodd," 2–3.

21. Messersmith, "Observations on Dodd," 2–4.

22. Ibid., 3; Dodd and Dodd, *Ambassador Dodd's Diary,* 12; Dodd to Samuel N. Harper, 15 July 1933, Harper Papers.

23. William J. Carr, memorandum on conversation with Raymond H. Geist, 5 June 1935, Carr Papers; Dodd to R. Walton Moore, 11 March, 6 June 1935, Moore Papers.

24. Dodd to Cordell Hull, 19 May 1934, Moore Papers.

25. Dodd to Moore, 23 May 1934, Moore Papers.

26. Dodd to Daniel C. Roper, 1 August 1933, Dodd to House, 16 August, 22 September, 31 October 1933, and Byrill to House, 13 September 1933, House Papers; Dodd to Harper, 11 August 1933, Harper Papers; Dodd to Moore, 19 May 1934, 26 September 1935, Moore Papers; Dodd to Roosevelt, 30 July 1933, Roosevelt Papers, POF; Dodd to Roosevelt, 23 December 1933, Roosevelt Papers, PSF; Dodd to Roper, 18 October 1936, Dodd Papers, LC; Dodd and Dodd, *Ambassador Dodd's Diary,* 17, 183.

27. Messersmith, "Observations on Dodd," 4, 8; Dodd to Roper, 1 August 1933, House Papers.

28. Byrill to House, 23 September 1933, and Dodd to House, 16 August, 21 November 1933, House Papers; Phillips to Dodd, 18 September 1933, Dodd Pa-

pers, LC; Dodd to Moore, 21 June 1934, Moore Papers; Dodd and Dodd, *Ambassador Dodd's Diary*, 15–16.

29. Dodd to Hull, 18, 20 August 1933, State, *Foreign Relations, 1933*, 2:256, 258; Phillips to Dodd, 1933, and Dodd to George S. Messersmith, 17 June 1934, Dodd Papers, LC; Dodd and Dodd, *Ambassador Dodd's Diary*, 24–26, 28; Dodd to House, 25 August 1933, House Papers.

30. Dodd and Dodd, *Ambassador Dodd's Diary*, 46–47.

31. *New York Times*, 13 October 1933; Dodd and Dodd, *Ambassador Dodd's Diary*, 46–47.

32. Dodd to Addams, 16 October 1933, Dodd Papers, LC; Dodd and Dodd, *Ambassador Dodd's Diary*, 47; Messersmith to Phillips, 19 October 1933, Messersmith Papers.

33. House to Dodd, 21 October 1933, Dodd to House, 20, 24 October, 4 December 1933, and Dodd to Phillips, 17 November 1933, House Papers; Dodd to Roosevelt, 13 October 1933, Roosevelt Papers, PSF; Dodd to Bernadette E. Schmitt, 30 October 1933, Schmitt Papers; Dodd to Phillips, 4 December 1933, Dodd Papers, LC.

34. Phillips to Dodd, 27 November 1933, Dodd Papers, LC; Dodd to Schmitt, 16 November 1934, Schmitt Papers.

35. Roosevelt to Breckinridge Long, 19 September 1935, Roosevelt Papers, PSF.

36. Dodd and Dodd, *Ambassador Dodd's Diary*, 50, 126.

37. Messersmith to Phillips, 6–7 December 1934, Messersmith Papers.

38. Dodd and Dodd, *Ambassador Dodd's Diary*, 48–49.

39. Ibid., 49–50.

40. Ibid., 88–89; Department of State, "Memorandum by the Ambassador in Germany (Dodd)," n.d., and Hull to Dodd, 7 February 1934, State, *Foreign Relations, 1934*, 2:218–21, 530–31; Dodd, memorandum of conversation with Chancellor Hitler, 7 March 1934, Dodd Papers, LC; White to Moffat, 8 March 1934, White Papers.

41. Dodd and Dodd, *Ambassador Dodd's Diary*, 90–91.

42. Ibid., 90–91, 276.

43. Dodd to Roosevelt, 5 November 1934, and Dodd to Moore, 5 November 1934, Roosevelt Papers, PSF; Messersmith, "Observations on Dodd"; clipping from *New York Post*, 15 May 1937, Dodd Papers, LC; Dodd to Avery O. Craven, 19 December 1933, Craven Papers; Dodd and Dodd, *Ambassador Dodd's Diary*, 22–23, 60–62, 160–61, 181–82, 325–26.

44. Dodd to Roosevelt, 5 November 1934, and Dodd to Moore, 5 November 1934, Roosevelt Papers, PSF; Dodd and Dodd, *Ambassador Dodd's Diary*, 181–82.

45. Dodd to Roosevelt, 5 November 1934, 9 May 1935, and Dodd to Moore, 5 November 1934, Roosevelt Papers, PSF; Dodd and Dodd, *Ambassador Dodd's Diary*, 182; Hull, *Memoirs of Cordell Hull*, 1:527; Ickes, *Secret Diary*, 2:90–91.

46. Dodd and Dodd, *Ambassador Dodd's Diary*, 296, 304.

47. Ibid., 306–7; Dodd to Moore, 10 February 1936, Moore Papers; Dodd to Phillips, 29 May 1936, Dodd Papers, LC.

48. Dodd to House, 20 October 1933, House Papers; Dodd to Roosevelt, 29 July 1935, 1 April 1936, Roosevelt Papers, PSF; Dodd to Hull, 7 May 1935, and Dodd to Long, 23 March 1936, Dodd Papers, LC; Dodd and Dodd, *Ambassador Dodd's Diary,* 56, 164–65, 225.

49. Messersmith to Phillips, 19 October 1933, Messersmith Papers; Dodd to House, 20 October 1933, and Dodd to Phillips, 17 November 1933, House Papers; Phillips to Dodd, 27 November 1933, Dodd to Erich Marcks, 26 July 1933, Dodd to Robert M. Hutchinson, 19 July 1935, Dodd to Abraham Flexner, 17 September 1935, Dodd to Phillips, 29 May 1936, and Dodd to Frank Graham, 23 November 1936, Dodd Papers, LC; Dodd to Roosevelt, 13 October 1933, 9 May 1935, Roosevelt Papers, PSF; Dodd to Thomas V. Smith, 18 October 1933, Smith Papers; Cordell Hull, "Memorandum by the Secretary of State," 5 August 1937, State, *Foreign Relations, 1937,* 2:377–78.

50. Messersmith, memorandum, 21–25 March 1935, Messersmith Papers; Messersmith, "Observations on Dodd," 11.

51. Moore to Roosevelt, 20 November 1934, Roosevelt Papers, PSF.

52. Hull to Dodd, 10 October 1934, Dodd Papers, LC; Moore to Marguerite LeHand, 25 January 1937, Roosevelt Papers, POF.

53. State, *Foreign Relations, 1935,* 2:319; Dodd and Dodd, *Ambassador Dodd's Diary,* 239, 241, 245–46, 263, 287, 307; Dodd to Hull, 5 April 1935, Dodd to Lord Lothiem, 19 June 1935, and Dodd to Moore, 5 October 1934, 27 June, 17 November 1935, 17 August, 29 May 1936, Moore Papers; Dodd to House, 14 February 1935, House Papers; Dodd to Roosevelt, Roosevelt Papers, PSF.

54. Dodd to Harry L. Hopkins, 26 July 1934, Dodd Papers, LC; Dodd and Dodd, *Ambassador Dodd's Diary,* 209–10.

55. Cole, *Roosevelt and the Isolationists,* 120–27; Dodd and Dodd, *Ambassador Dodd's Diary,* 210–11.

56. Rexford Tugwell, Diary, 2 February 1935, John F. Carter, memorandum of conversation at Tugwell's house, evening of 1 February 1935, and [Paul Appleby], untitled memorandum, [2 February 1935], Tugwell Papers; Dodd and Dodd, *Ambassador Dodd's Diary,* 212–13. Dodd recorded that Senator Josiah Bailey of North Carolina was in attendance, but this is not substantiated by Tugwell, Carter, or Appleby.

57. Tugwell, Diary, 2 February 1935, Carter, memorandum of conversation at Tugwell's house, evening of 1 February 1935, and [Appleby], untitled memorandum, [2 February 1935], Tugwell Papers.

58. Carter, memorandum of conversation at Tugwell's house, evening of 1 February 1935, Tugwell Papers.

59. Ibid.

60. Dodd and Dodd, *Ambassador Dodd's Diary,* 213; Carter, memorandum of conversation at Tugwell's house, evening of 1 February 1935, Tugwell Papers.

Tugwell recalled that immediately after the negative vote Roosevelt had shown him a draft letter thanking Senate Majority Leader Joseph T. Robinson for his pro–World Court campaign and adding: "As for the others, . . . I hope they may go to heaven because there they will have so much explaining to do—that is if God is in favor of peace, and I believe he is" (Tugwell, Diary, 2 February 1935, Tugwell Papers).

61. Dodd and Dodd, *Ambassador Dodd's Diary*, 213–14, 216; Dodd to Josephus Daniels, 31 August 1935, Daniels Papers.

62. Dodd to Pierce, 1 September 1935, Pierce Papers; Dodd to Moore, 3 September 1935, and Moore to Roosevelt, 10 September 1935, Moore Papers; Roosevelt to Moore, 11 September 1935, Roosevelt Papers, POF; Ickes, *Secret Diary*, 1:494.

63. Dodd to Pierce, 12 January 1934, Pierce Papers.

64. Dodd to Pierce, 14 July 1933, Pierce Papers; Dodd to Craven, 10 November 1933, Craven Papers; Dodd to Harper, 11 August 1933, Harper Papers.

65. Dodd to Craven, 29 July, 10 November 1933, Craven Papers.

66. Dodd to Craven, 10 November 1933, Craven Papers; Dodd to House, 31 October 1933, House Papers.

67. Dodd to Schmitt, 16 November 1934, Schmitt Papers; Dodd to Harper, 11 August 1933, Harper Papers; Dodd to Pierce, 2 September, 1, 25 October 1933, Pierce Papers; Dodd to John D. Rockefeller Jr., 20 February 1934, Dodd Papers, LC.

68. Dodd to Pierce, 2 September, 1, 25 October 1933, 17 February, 26 March 1934, Pierce Papers; Dodd to Craven, 19 February 1934, Craven Papers. Looking back on his unhappy relationship with the Hutchins administration, Dodd complained that he had not had much "influence with the authorities there: never had much, because I was too democratic in a 'democratic' country" (Dodd to Pierce, 16 September 1937, Pierce Papers).

69. Dodd to Hull, 4 October 1933, House Papers; Dodd to Pierce, 1 October 1933, 17 February 1934, Pierce Papers; Dodd to Schmitt, 3, 30 October, 28 November, 9 December 1933, 30 January 1934, Schmitt Papers.

70. "The Fiftieth Anniversary Meeting," 425.

71. Dodd and Dodd, *Ambassador Dodd's Diary*, 171–72; Dodd to House, 27 September 1934, House Papers.

72. Dodd and Dodd, *Ambassador Dodd's Diary*, 85, 171–72.

73. Dodd to Cheney, 21 July 1933, Dodd Papers, LC; Dodd to Moore, 14 January 1937, Moore Papers.

74. The information in this and the following paragraphs is from Dodd, "First Social Order," 217–20, 222–31.

75. Dodd and Dodd, *Ambassador Dodd's Diary*, 207; "The Dodd I Knew," typescript, ca. 1951, Stephenson Papers.

76. Dodd to Pierce, 3 February 1934, Pierce Papers.

77. Fred Arthur Bailey, "*Plain Folk* and Apology: Frank L. Owsley's Defense of the South," in Cobb and Wilson, *Perspectives on the American South*, 101–4; Owsley, *Frank Lawrence Owsley*, 35–42.

78. Owsley, "Defeatism in the Confederacy"; Frank L. Owsley to Craven, 27 April 1933, Craven Papers.

79. Dodd to Daniels, 14 March 1935, Dodd Papers, LC; Dodd and Dodd, *Ambassador Dodd's Diary,* 208–9.

80. Dodd to Schmitt, 22 October, 16 November 1934, Schmitt Papers; University of Chicago Board of Trustees Minutes, 9 May 1935, 25:45.

81. Dodd to Moore, 10 February, 6 June, 5 August, 3 September 1935, and Moore to Roosevelt, 10 September 1935, Moore Papers; Moore to Dodd, 19 August 1935, Dodd Papers, LC; Roosevelt to Moore, 11 September 1935, Roosevelt Papers, POF.

82. Dodd to Moore, 30 June 1936, Moore Papers; Dodd to Daniels, 5 August 1936, Daniels Papers; clipping from *Time* magazine, 6 July 1936, Dodd Papers, LC.

83. Dodd to Roosevelt, 28 July 1936, Roosevelt Papers, PSF; Dodd to Moore, 19 July 1936, Moore Papers.

84. Dodd to Max Farrand, 8 April 1935, and Dodd to Sandburg, 21 November 1934, Dodd Papers, LC.

85. Dodd to Pierce, 6 June 1934, Pierce Papers; Dodd to Eugene C. Barker, 30 July 1935, and Dodd to Daniels, 26 March 1936, Dodd Papers, LC. See also Dodd to Daniels, 14 March 1935, and Dodd to Moore, 26 September 1935, Dodd Papers, LC; Dodd to Pierce, 8 December 1934, 22 February, 10 December 1935, Pierce Papers; Daniels to Dodd, 20 April 1936, Daniels Papers; Dodd to House, 13 December 1935, House Papers; Dodd to Schmitt, 16 November 1934, Schmitt Papers; Dodd to Moore, 3, 26 September 1935, Moore Papers; and Dodd and Dodd, *Ambassador Dodd's Diary,* 216, 238.

86. Dodd to George Brett, 2 November 1936, Dodd Papers, LC; Dodd to Pierce, 17 December 1937, Pierce Papers.

87. Dodd, review of *The Old Dominion: Her Making and Her Manners,* by Thomas Nelson Page.

88. Dodd, *The Old South,* 30–32, 35, 54.

89. Ibid., 181, 224.

90. Ibid., vii, 297.

91. Paul H. Buck, review of *The Old South: Struggles for Democracy.* See also the reviews by David Y. Thomas and Curtis Nettles.

92. Dodd and Dodd, *Ambassador Dodd's Diary,* 164, 168; Dodd to Roper, 12 December 1936, Roper Papers; Dodd to Roosevelt, 22 January 1938, Roosevelt Papers, PSF.

93. *New York Times,* 10 March 1936, 13 August 1942.

94. Dodd to Moore, 17 August 1936, Dodd Papers, LC; Dodd to Roper, 12 December 1936, Roper Papers; *New York Times,* 4 August 1936.

95. *New York Times,* 16 October 1936.

96. Tansill, *Backdoor to War,* 46; *New York Times,* 14 November 1964.

97. Clipping from *Washington Post,* 17 November 1936, Dodd Papers, LC.

98. Ibid.; Dodd to Roper, 12 December 1936, Roper Papers; Dodd to Moore, Moore Papers.

99. Joseph M. M. Gray to Charles C. Tansill, 23 November 1936, Gray Papers.

100. Geist to Messersmith, 24 October 1937, 15 February 1938, and Geist to Moffat, 1 March 1938, Messersmith Papers; Dodd to Moore, 18 July 1935, Moore Papers; Dodd to Pierce, 12 January 1934, Pierce Papers.

101. Dodd to Hull, 19 May 1934, and Dodd to Moore, 18 January, 5 October 1934, Moore Papers; Dodd to House, 16 August, 31 October 1933, and Dodd to Phillips, 8 October 1933, House Papers.

102. Dodd to Moore, 26 July 1936, Moore Papers; Moffat to White, 12 January 1935, White Papers.

103. Dodd to Daniels, 8 February 1936, Dodd to House, 26 October 1936, Dodd to Moore, 17, 31 August 1936, Dodd to Roper, 18 October 1936, and untitled typescript, ca. 1938, Dodd Papers, LC; Dodd to Moore, 10 February, 26 July, 29 October 1936, 14 January 1937, Moore Papers; Carr, memorandum on conversations with Raymond H. Geist, 5 June 1935, Carr Papers.

104. Dodd to Moore, 19 October 1936, Moore Papers. For examples of Dodd's comparing the business elite to Old South slaveholders see Dodd, "A Troubled World, a Speech before the Y.M.C.A., Bremen, Germany," 9 September 1934, and Dodd to Moore, 19 November 1934, 5 August 1935, 21 June 1937, Moore Papers; Dodd to Richard Whitney, 1 March 1935, Dodd to Thomas J. Watson, 3 December 1935, clipping from *Greensboro Daily News*, 2 June 1936, Dodd to Newton D. Baker, 28 July 1936, Dodd to Daniels, 6 January 1937, and clipping from *Blue Ridge, Virginia, Herald*, 26 August 1937, Dodd Papers, LC.

105. Dodd, *Woodrow Wilson and His Work*, 173, 175; Dodd to House, 12 February 1919, House Papers; Dodd to Hull, 25 March 1933, and Dodd to Phillips, 4 December 1933, Dodd Papers, LC; Dodd to Roosevelt, 13 October 1933, Roosevelt Papers, PSF; Dodd to Moore, 26 September 1935, Moore Papers.

106. Dodd to Roosevelt, 20 March 1935, Roosevelt Papers, PSF; Dodd to Joseph T. Robinson, 30 January 1935, Moore Papers.

107. Dodd to William Borah, 10 January 1934, Roosevelt Papers, POF.

108. Dodd to Daniels, 14 March 1935, Daniels Papers; Dodd and Dodd, *Ambassador Dodd's Diary*, 214–15.

109. Dodd to Roosevelt, 8 February 1934, 7 January 1936, Roosevelt Papers, PSF; Dodd to Watson, 3 December 1935, Dodd to Baker, 28 July 1936, Dodd to James Couzens, 15 October 1936, Dodd to Daniels, 8 March 1937, clipping from *Richmond Times-Dispatch*, 11 May 1937, and clipping from *Raleigh News and Observer*, 28 September 1937, Dodd Papers, LC; Dodd to Daniels, 21 August 1935, 6 January, 9 February 1937, Dodd to Harry F. Byrd Sr., 8 February 1937, and Dodd, memorandum, [November 1936], Daniels Papers; Dodd to Robinson, 9, 30 April 1937, Robinson Papers.

110. Clippings from *Chicago Tribune*, May 1937, *New York Times*, 13 May 1937, *Philadelphia Inquirer*, [1937], and *Richmond Times-Dispatch*, 11 May 1937, Dodd Papers, LC.

111. Dodd to House, 5 June 1937, Dodd Papers, LC.

112. *New York Times*, 25 September 1961.

113. Dodd to House, 8 April 1934, House Papers.

114. Dodd and Dodd, *Ambassador Dodd's Diary,* 425, 427, 434; clippings from *New York Times,* 3 September 1937, and *International Herald-Tribune* (Paris), 5 September 1937, and unidentified newspaper clippings, 3 September, 7 December 1937, Dodd Papers, LC; Hull to Roosevelt, 25 January 1938, Roosevelt Papers, PSF; State, *Documents on German Foreign Policy, 1918–1945,* 1:630–31.

115. State, *Documents on German Foreign Policy, 1918–1945,* 1:632; Dodd and Dodd, *Ambassador Dodd's Diary,* 427, 433–34; Sumner Welles, "Memorandum by the Under Secretary of State," 1 October 1937, State, *Foreign Relations, 1937,* 381–83; untitled typescript, ca. 1938, Hull to Dodd, 23 November 1937, Dodd to Hull, 23 November 1937, and clipping from *Evening Standard,* 8 December 1937, Dodd Papers, LC; Dodd to Roper, 30 November 1937, Roper Papers; Messersmith, "Observations on Dodd," 15.

116. William Shirer to Dodd, 30 December 1937, Dodd Papers, LC. Dodd had been discussing the possibility of retirement for several months, noting to Roosevelt his desire to "finish my history of the *Old South*" (Dodd to Roosevelt, 24 May 1937, Roosevelt Papers, PSF).

117. Shirer to Dodd, 30 December 1937, Dodd Papers, LC. Shirer first met Dodd in Berlin in September 1934 and assessed him as "a blunt, honest, liberal man with the kind of integrity an American ambassador needs here" (Shirer, *Berlin Diary,* 15).

CHAPTER SIX: "No Lectures Any More"

1. Dodd to Franklin D. Roosevelt, 29 May, 18 September 1938, Roosevelt Papers, PPF; Dodd to Josephus Daniels, 30 May 1938, Daniels Papers; Dodd to Bessie Louis Pierce, 20 June 1938, Pierce Papers; Dodd to Rose J. West, 2 July 1938, Dodd Papers, LC; Dodd and Dodd, *Ambassador Dodd's Diary,* 446.

2. Dodd to Daniels, 14 August 1938, Daniels Papers.

3. *New York Times,* 10 February 1940; Raymond H. Geist to George S. Messersmith, 15 February 1938, and Geist to Jay Pierrepont Moffat, 1 March 1938, Messersmith Papers.

4. *New York Times,* 7 January 1938.

5. Ibid., 9 January 1938; Prentiss B. Gilbert to Cordell Hull, 13 January 1938, State, *Foreign Relations, 1937,* 383–84.

6. *New York Times,* 14 January 1938.

7. Gilbert to Hull, 13 January 1938, State, *Foreign Relations, 1937,* 384; *New York Times,* 15 January 1938.

8. Hull, "Memorandum by the Secretary of State," 14 January 1938, State, *Foreign Relations, 1937,* 384–85; Hull, *Memoirs of Cordell Hull,* 1:572–73.

9. *New York Times,* 15, 16 January 1938.

10. Dodd to Daniels, 30 January 1938, Daniels Papers; *New York Times,* 16, 30, 31 January, 22, 28 February, 15 March 1938; clipping from *Richmond Times-Dispatch,* 26 February 1938, Dodd Papers, LC.

11. *New York Times,* 28 April 1938; Dodd to Daniels, 30 May 1938, Daniels Papers.

12. Messersmith, "Observations on Dodd," 15.

13. *New York Times,* 5 June 1938; Dodd to Daniel C. Roper, 7 June 1938, Roper Papers; Dodd, "Dinner Discussion on Germany," Harvard Club, Boston, typescript, 10 June 1938, Dodd Papers, LC.

14. Dodd to Samuel N. Harper, 13 July 1938, Harper Papers; *New York Times,* 10 July 1938.

15. Dierenfield, *Keeper of the Rules,* 68–73.

16. Annie to Dodd, 17 August 1938, Dodd Papers, LC; Roper to Dodd, 16 August 1938, Roper Papers.

17. Dodd to Roper, 22, 23 August 1938, Roper Papers.

18. Dodd to Marvin H. McIntyre, 3 September 1938, and Dodd to Roosevelt, 29 September 1938, Roosevelt Papers, PPF.

19. Clippings from *El Paso Times,* 4 October 1938, *Topeka, Kansas, Daily Capital,* 5 October 1938, unidentified newspaper, 7 October 1938, *Hutchinson, Kansas, News,* [October] 1938, *El Paso Knife and Forker,* October 1938, and *Cincinnati Enquirer,* 3 November 1938, untitled program, Amarillo, Texas, 8 October 1938, and V. H. Drufner to Dodd, [October] 1938, 28 October 1938, Dodd Papers, LC.

20. Dodd to Daniels, 20 November 1938, Daniels Papers; clipping from *World News,* 8 November 1938, Dodd Papers, LC.

21. Untitled newspaper clippings, 5 December 1938, Dodd Papers, LC, and 9 December 1938, Bazile Papers; *New York Times,* 9, 10 December 1938.

22. *New York Times,* 10 December 1938. Gloria Grimes, her mother and father, and six siblings lived with her grandmother in a house described by one reporter as "a small, two-room shack near Hanover Court House" (untitled newspaper clipping, [ca. 2 March 1939], Bazile Papers).

23. Untitled newspaper clipping, [ca. 8 December 1938], Bazile Papers; *New York Times,* 10 December 1938.

24. *New York Times,* 9, 10 December 1938; untitled newspaper clipping, [ca. 2 March 1938], Bazile Papers.

25. *New York Times,* 10, 17 January 1939.

26. Dodd to Roosevelt, 28 January 1939, Roosevelt Papers, PPF; Dodd to Daniels, 13 February 1939, and Daniels to Dodd, 20 February 1939, Daniels Papers; Dodd to Carl Becker, 14 February 1939, Becker Papers.

27. Untitled newspaper clippings, [ca. 2 March 1939], Bazile Papers.

28. Ibid.

29. Ibid.; *New York Times,* 3 March 1939.

30. Dodd to Fred H. Harrison, 7 March 1939, William Buttrick to Claude Bowers, 17 March 1939, George A. Knapp to Dodd, 20 March 1939 (Dodd notations at bottom of letter), and G. E. Carr to Dodd, 27 March 1939 (Dodd notations at bottom of letter), Dodd Papers, LC.

31. Program, First Congregational Church, [March 1939], clipping from Los

Angeles newspaper, 13 March 1939, and clipping from *Pomona, California, Progress-Bulletin*, 23 March 1939, Dodd Papers, LC.

32. Dodd to Miss Robertson, 2 April 1939, Dodd Papers, LC; *New York Times*, 7 May 1939; untitled newspaper clipping, [ca. 7 May 1939], Bazile Papers; Dodd to Daniels, 9 May 1939 (fragment), Daniels Papers.

33. Buttrick to Nathan L. Rock, 24 March 1939, Dodd Papers, LC; Dodd to R. Walton Moore, 7 June 1939, Moore Papers.

34. Memorandum to Roosevelt, 10 July 1939, and telegram, Roosevelt to Dodd, 10 July 1939, Roosevelt Papers, PPF; *New York Times*, 11–13 July 1939.

35. Dodd to Pierce, 6 October 1939, Pierce Papers; Dodd to Daniels, 1 January 1940, Daniels Papers; clipping from *Washington Star*, 12 February 1940, and Martha Dodd Stern, William E. Dodd Jr., and Alfred K. Stern to Curtis, 21 February 1940, Dodd Papers, LC.

36. Owsley, *Plain Folk of the Old South*, 5, 133.

37. Fred Arthur Bailey, "*Plain Folk* and Apology: Frank L. Owsley's Defense of the South," in Cobb and Wilson, *Perspectives on the American South*, 101–14; Owsley, *Frank Lawrence Owsley*, 78–79, 134–35.

38. Dodd, *Cotton Kingdom*, 146.

BIBLIOGRAPHY

Primary Sources

MANUSCRIPT COLLECTIONS

Adams, Charles Francis, Jr. Papers. Massachusetts Historical Society, Boston.

Adams, Herbert Baxter. Papers. Milton S. Eisenhower Library, The Johns Hopkins University, Baltimore.

Addams, Jane. Memorial Collection. The University Library, University of Illinois at Chicago.

American Historical Association Papers. Library of Congress, Washington D.C.

Bancroft, Frederic. Papers. Special Collections, Columbia University Library, New York.

Bazile, Leon M. Papers. Virginia Historical Society, Richmond.

Becker, Carl. Papers. John M. Olin Library, Cornell University, Ithaca NY.

Boyd, William K. Papers. Duke University Archives, William R. Perkins Library, Durham NC.

Bradford, Gamaliel. Letterbook. Houghton Library, Harvard University, Cambridge MA.

Briggs, William G. Papers. North Carolina State Library and Archives, Raleigh.

Bryan, William Jennings. Papers. Library of Congress, Washington D.C.

Candler, Warren A. Papers. Robert W. Woodruff Library, Emory University, Atlanta GA.

Carr, William J. Papers. Library of Congress, Washington D.C.

Clark, Walter. Papers. North Carolina State Library and Archives, Raleigh.

Connor Family. Papers. Southern Historical Collection, University of North Carolina, Chapel Hill.

Craven, Avery O. Papers. Dunn Library, Simpson College, Indianola IA.

Cussons, John. Papers. Virginia Historical Society, Richmond.

Daniels, Josephus. Papers. Library of Congress, Washington D.C.

Department of History Records, University of Chicago. Joseph Regenstein Library, University of Chicago.

Dodd [Stern], Martha. Papers. Library of Congress, Washington D.C.

Dodd, William Edward. Papers. Library of Congress, Washington D.C.

———. Randolph-Macon College Library, Ashland VA.

———. Southern Historical Collection, University of North Carolina, Chapel Hill.

Dunning, William A. Papers. Special Collections, Columbia University Library, New York.

Gabriel, Ralph. Papers. Sterling Memorial Library, Yale University, New Haven CT.

Gordon, Armistead C. Papers. Virginia Historical Society, Richmond.

Gray, Joseph M. M. Papers. American University Archives, American University, Washington D.C.

Hamilton, Holman. Papers. Kentucky Historical Society, Frankford.

Hamilton, J. G. de Roulhac. Papers. Southern Historical Collection, University of North Carolina, Chapel Hill.

Harper, Samuel N. Papers. Joseph Regenstein Library, University of Chicago.

Horne, Bejah. Will. Typescript. Johnston County Library, Smithfield NC.

Horne, Herman H. "Ashley Horne." Typescript. Johnston County Library, Smithfield NC.

House, Edward M. Papers. Sterling Memorial Library, Yale University, New Haven CT.

Howe, Mark Anthony De Wolfe. Papers. Houghton Library, Harvard University, Cambridge MA.

The Inquiry. Papers. Sterling Memorial Library, Yale University, New Haven CT.

Jameson, J. Franklin. Papers. Library of Congress, Washington D.C.

Lee Family. Papers. Virginia Historical Society, Richmond.

McDaniel, Joseph Hetherington. Papers. Houghton Library, Harvard University, Cambridge MA.

McGuire, Hunter Holmes. Papers. Virginia Historical Society, Richmond.

McLaughlin, Andrew C. Papers. Joseph Regenstein Library, University of Chicago.

Messersmith, George S. Papers. Special Collections, University of Delaware Library, Newark.

Montague, Andrew Jackson. Papers. Virginia State Library and Archives, Richmond.

Moore, R. Walton. Papers. Franklin Delano Roosevelt Presidential Library, Hyde Park NY.

Munford, Beverley B. Scrapbook. Virginia Historical Society, Richmond.

Munford, Mary Cooke Branch. Papers. Virginia State Library and Archives, Richmond.

Munford Family. Papers. Virginia Historical Society, Richmond.

Notestein, Wallace. Papers. Sterling Memorial Library, Yale University, New Haven CT.

Owsley, Frank Lawrence. Papers. Joint University Library, Vanderbilt University, Nashville.

Page, Thomas Nelson. Papers. Special Collections, William R. Perkins Library, Duke University, Durham NC.

Pierce, Bessie Louis. Papers. Joseph Regenstein Library, University of Chicago.

Pittman, Thomas Merritt. Papers. Special Collections, William R. Perkins Library, Duke University, Durham NC.

Ramsdell, Charles W. Papers. Eugene C. Barker Center, University of Texas, Austin.

Rippy, J. Fred. Papers. Southern Historical Collection, University of North Carolina, Chapel Hill.

Robinson, Joseph T. Papers. Special Collections, University of Arkansas Library, Fayetteville.

Roosevelt, Franklin Delano. President's Official Files. Franklin Delano Roosevelt Presidential Library, Hyde Park NY.

———. President's Personal Files. Franklin Delano Roosevelt Presidential Library, Hyde Park NY.

———. President's Secretaries Files. Franklin Delano Roosevelt Presidential Library, Hyde Park NY.

Roper, Daniel C. Papers. Special Collections, William R. Perkins Library, Duke University, Durham NC.

Schmitt, Bernadette E. Papers. Library of Congress, Washington D.C.

Seymour, Charles. Papers. Sterling Memorial Library, Yale University, New Haven CT.

Sheib, Edward E. Vertical File. Louisiana and Lower Mississippi Collections, Louisiana State University, Baton Rouge.

Smith, Thomas V. Papers. Eugene C. Barker Center, University of Texas, Austin.

Snowden, Yates. Papers. South Caroliniana Library, University of South Carolina, Columbia.

Stephenson, Wendell H. Papers. Special Collections, William R. Perkins Library, Duke University, Durham NC.

Thayer, William Roscoe. Papers. Houghton Library, Harvard University, Cambridge MA.

Tugwell, Rexford. Papers. Franklin Delano Roosevelt Presidential Library, Hyde Park NY.

Turner, Frederick Jackson. Papers. Henry E. Huntington Library, San Marino CA.

———. Houghton Library, Harvard University, Cambridge MA.

University of Chicago Board of Trustees Minutes. Joseph Regenstein Library, University of Chicago.

Villard, Oswald Garrison. Papers. Houghton Library, Harvard University, Cambridge MA.

Virginia Agricultural and Mechanical College Board of Visitors. Minutes. Virginia Polytechnic Institute and State University Archives, Blacksburg.

Virginia Agricultural and Mechanical College Unofficial Board of Trustees. Minutes. Special Collections, Virginia Polytechnic Institute and State University Library, Blacksburg.

Virginia Executive Records: Governor Westmoreland Davis. Virginia State Library and Archives, Richmond.

Virginia State Board of Education. Minutes. Virginia State Library and Archives, Richmond.

Webb, Walter Prescott. Papers. Eugene C. Barker Center, University of Texas, Austin.

White, John Campbell. Papers. Library of Congress, Washington D.C.

Woodfin, Maude H. Papers. Virginia Historical Society, Richmond.

Yale Review. Papers. Beinecke Library, Yale University, New Haven CT.

UNPUBLISHED UNITED STATES CENSUSES

Seventh United States Census, 1850: Johnston County, North Carolina, Population Schedule.

Seventh United States Census, 1850: Wake County, North Carolina, Population Schedule.

Eighth United States Census, 1860: Johnston County, North Carolina, Population Schedule.

Eighth United States Census, 1860: Johnston County, North Carolina, Slave Schedule.

Eighth United States Census, 1860: Wake County, North Carolina, Population Schedule.

ARTICLES BY WILLIAM E. DODD

"Y.M.C.A." *Gray Jacket* 1 (1892): 55–56.

"Young Men's Christian Association." *Gray Jacket* 1 (1892): 74–75.

"The Place of Nathaniel Macon in Southern History." *American Historical Review* 7 (1902): 663–76.

"The Status of History in Southern Education." *Nation* 75 (1902): 109–11.

[Untitled response to C. Meriwether], *Nation* 75 (1902): 150.

"The Principle of Instructing United States Senators." *South Atlantic Quarterly* 1 (1902): 326–32.

"Karl Lamprecht and *Kulturgeschichte*." *Popular Science Monthly* 63 (1903): 419–26.

"Some Difficulties of the History Teacher in the South." *South Atlantic Quarterly* 3 (1904): 117–22.

"Freedom of Speech in the South." *Nation* 84 (1907): 383–84.

"Chief Justice Marshall and Virginia, 1813–1821." *American Historical Review* 12 (1907): 776–87.

"Democracy and Learning." *Nation* 89 (1909): 430–31.

"The Fight for the Northwest, 1860." *American Historical Review* 16 (1911): 774–88.

"History and Patriotism." *South Atlantic Quarterly* 12 (1913): 109–21.

"Profitable Fields of Investigation in American History, 1815–1860." *American Historical Review* 18 (1913): 522–36.

"Economic Interpretations of American History." *Journal of Political Economy* 24 (1916): 489–95.

"The Social Philosophy of the Old South." *American Journal of Sociology* 23 (1918): 735–46.

"Josephus Daniels." *The Public* 21 (1918): 791.

"British-American Difficulties." *The Public* 22 (1919): 572–74.

"Roosevelt." *The Public* 22 (1919): 1140.

"The Dilemma of Democracy in the United States." *Virginia Quarterly Review* 1 (1925): 350–63.

"When Washington Tried Isolation." *American Mercury* 4 (1925): 344–52.
"Napoleon Breaks Thomas Jefferson." *American Mercury* 5 (1925): 303–13.
"The Making of Andrew Jackson." *Century Magazine* 109 (1926): 531–38.
"Andrew Jackson and His Enemies." *Century Magazine* 111 (1926): 734–45.
"A Document That Changed the World." *New York Times*, 4 July 1926.
"The Rise of Abraham Lincoln." *Century Magazine* 113 (1927): 569–84.
"Lincoln or Lee." *Century Magazine* 113 (1927): 661–73.
"Samuel J. Tilden—A Prophet Unheeded." *New York Times*, 17 April 1927.
"Lincoln's Last Struggle." *Century Magazine* 114 (1927): 46–61.
"Epic of the Embattled Farmer." *New York Times*, 24 July 1927.
"Shall Our Farmers Become Peasants." *Century Magazine* 116 (1928): 30–44.
"Our Ingrowing Habit of Lawlessness." *Century Magazine* 116 (1928): 691–98.
"The Great Wilson Adventure." *New York Times*, 2 December 1928.
"The Passing of the Old United States." *Century Magazine* 119 (1929): 39–51.
"The Epic of Wilson: Again It Resounds." *New York Times*, 27 December 1931.
"The Emergence of the First Social Order in the United States." *American Histori-cal Review* 40 (1935): 217–31.

BOOKS WRITTEN BY WILLIAM E. DODD

The Life of Nathaniel Macon. Raleigh NC, 1903.
Jefferson Davis. Philadelphia, 1907.
Statesmen of the Old South; or, From Radicalism to Conservative Revolt. New York, 1911.
Expansion and Conflict. Boston, 1915.
The Cotton Kingdom: A Chronicle of the Old South. New Haven CT, 1919.
Woodrow Wilson and His Work. New York, 1926.
Lincoln or Lee. New York, 1928.
The Old South: Struggles for Democracy. New York, 1937.

Edited with Ray Standard Baker
The Public Papers of Woodrow Wilson. 6 vols. New York and London, 1925–27.

BOOK REVIEWS BY WILLIAM E. DODD

The Life of James Madison, by Gaillard Hunt. *New York Times,* 21 March 1903.
The American Republic and Its Government, by Albert Woodburn. *New York Times,* 4 April 1903.
The Cambridge Modern History: The United States, vol. 7, edited by A. W. Ward, G. W. Prothero, and Stanley Lenthes. *New York Times,* 15 August 1903.
Zur jüngsten Vergangenheit, by Von Karl Lamprecht. *American Historical Review* 9 (1904): 394–97.
Seventy-five Years in Old Virginia, with Some Accounts of the Life of the Author and Some History of the People against Whom His Lot Was Cast, by John Herbert Claiborne. *American Historical Review* 10 (1904): 219.

History of the United States from the Compromise of 1850, by James Ford Rhodes, vol. 5. *New York Times*, 31 December 1904.

The Political History of Virginia during the Reconstruction, by Hamilton James Eckenrode. *American Historical Review* 10 (1905): 700–701.

Reminiscences of Peace and War, by Mrs. Roger A. Pryor. *American Historical Review* 10 (1905): 924–25.

Forty Years of Active Service, by Charles T. O'Ferrall. *American Historical Review* 10 (1905): 925–26.

Memoirs with Special Reference to Secession and Civil War, by John H. Reagan. *American Historical Review* 12 (1907): 679–80.

The Old Dominion: Her Making and Her Manners, by Thomas Nelson Page. *American Historical Review* 14 (1908): 182–83.

Virginia's Attitude toward Slavery and Secession, by Beverley B. Munford. *American Historical Review* 15 (1910): 631–33.

J. L. M. Curry: A Biography, by Edwin Anderson Alderman and Armistead Churchill Gordon. *American Historical Review* 17 (1912): 854–55.

John Harlan, by Johnson Brigham. *American Historical Review* 19 (1914): 693.

Early Life and Letters of General Thomas J. Jackson, "Stonewall Jackson," by Thomas Jackson Arnold. *American Historical Review* 23 (1918): 414–15.

The Life of John Caldwell Calhoun, by William M. Meigs. *American Historical Review* 23 (1918): 874.

REVIEWS OF BOOKS BY WILLIAM E. DODD

Review of *The Life of Nathaniel Macon*. *New York Times*, 19 December 1903.

Review of *The Life of Nathaniel Macon*. *Nation* 78 (1904): 3.

Peirce, Paul S. Review of *The Life of Nathaniel Macon*. *American Historical Review* 10 (1904): 191–92.

Review of *Jefferson Davis*. *New York Times*, 15 February 1908.

Review of *Jefferson Davis*. *Nation* 86 (1908): 556.

Adams, Charles Francis, Jr. Review of *Jefferson Davis*. *American Historical Review* 13 (1908): 878.

Corwin, Edwin S. Review of *Woodrow Wilson and His Work*. *American Historical Review* 27 (1922): 334–35.

Buck, Paul H. Review of *The Old South: Struggles for Democracy*. *Saturday Review of Literature* 17 (30 October 1937): 7.

Thomas, David Y. Review of *The Old South: Struggles for Democracy*. *Journal of Southern History* 4 (1938): 99–101.

Nettles, Curtis. Review of *The Old South: Struggles for Democracy*. *American Historical Review* 44 (1938): 138–39.

NEWSPAPERS

New Orleans Picayune, 1903.
New Orleans Times-Democrat, 1903.

New York Times, 1917, 1920, 1933, 1936, 1938, 1939, 1940, 1942.
Richmond News, 1902.
Richmond Times, 1902.
Richmond Times-Dispatch, 1902, 1911.

OTHER BOOKS AND ARTICLES

American Historical Association. *Annual Report of the American Historical Association for the Year 1903.* 2 vols. Washington D.C., 1904.
———. *Annual Report of the American Historical Association for the Year 1910.* Washington D.C., 1912.
———. *Annual Report of the American Historical Association for the Year 1912.* Washington D.C., 1914.
———. *Annual Report of the American Historical Association for the Year 1914.* Washington D.C., 1916.
———. *Annual Report of the American Historical Association for the Year 1915.* Washington D.C., 1917.
Bancroft, Frederic, John H. Latane, and Dunbar Rowland. *The Attempt to Seize the American Historical Review: Rejoinder to Professor Albert Bushnell Hart [and] An Open Letter to Professor Andrew C. McLaughlin, Chairman of the Committee of Nine.* N. p., 1915.
Bassett, John Spencer. "Stirring Up the Fires of Racial Antipathy." *South Atlantic Quarterly* 2 (1903): 297–305.
———. "The Task of the Critic." *South Atlantic Quarterly* 3 (1904): 297–301.
Branson, L., comp. *The North Carolina Business Directory.* Raleigh, 1872.
Catalogue of the Virginia Agricultural and Mechanical College, 1891–92. Richmond, 1892.
Catalogue of the Virginia Agricultural and Mechanical College, 1892–93. Richmond, 1893.
Catalogue of the Virginia Agricultural and Mechanical College, 1893–94. Richmond, 1894.
Catalogue of the Virginia Agricultural and Mechanical College, 1894–95. Lynchburg, 1895.
Catalogue of the Virginia Agricultural and Mechanical College and Polytechnic Institute, 1895–96. Lynchburg, 1896.
Childers, Henry Herbert. "A Friend's View of Colonel House." *North American Review* 103 (1916): 553–58.
Christian, George L. *The Confederate Cause and Its Defenders: An Address Delivered before the Grand Camp of Confederate Veterans of Virginia.* Richmond, 1898.
———. "Official Report of the History Committee of the Grand Camp, C. V., Department of Virginia." *Confederate Veteran* 12 (1904): 161–69.
Craven, Avery O. "William E. Dodd: As Teacher." *University of Chicago Magazine* 32 (1940): 7–8.

Cussons, John. *United States "History" As the Yankee Makes and Takes.* Glenn Allen VA, 1900.

Dodd, William E., Jr., and Martha Dodd, eds. *Ambassador Dodd's Diary, 1933–1938.* New York, 1941.

Donnan, Elizabeth, and Leo F. Stock, eds. *An Historian's World: Selections from the Correspondence of John Franklin Jameson.* Philadelphia, 1956.

"The Fiftieth Anniversary Meeting." *American Historical Review* 40 (1935): 423–38.

Historical News. *American Historical Review* 31 (1925): 185–217.

Hull, Cordell. *The Memoirs of Cordell Hull.* 2 vols. New York, 1948.

Ickes, Harold L. *The Secret Diary of Harold L. Ickes.* 3 vols. New York, 1954–55.

Jameson, J. Franklin. "The Meeting of the American Historical Association at Richmond." *American Historical Review* 30 (1925): 451–77.

Jones, J. William. *Fiske's False History: Its Errors and Intentional Untruths Exposed.* N.p., 1898.

Mabry, W. Alexander, ed. "Professor William E. Dodd's Diary, 1916–1920." *John P. Branch Historical Papers of Randolph-Macon College*, n.s., 2 (1953): 9–86.

McGuire, Hunter H. "School Histories in the South." *Confederate Veteran* 7 (1899): 500–509.

McGuire, Hunter H., and George L. Christian. *The Confederate Cause and Conduct in the War between the States As Set Forth in the Reports of the History Committee of the Grand Camp, C. V., Virginia and Other Confederate Papers.* Richmond, 1907.

"The Meeting of the American Historical Association at New Orleans." *American Historical Review* 9 (1904): 437–55.

Minutes of the Eleventh Annual Reunion of the United Sons of Confederate Veterans. Nashville, 1907.

Munford, Beverley B. *Virginia's Attitude toward Slavery and Secession.* 1909. New York, 1910.

Nixon, Herman C. *Lower Piedmont County.* 1946. Reprint. Freeport NY, 1971.

Proceedings of the Thirty-fifth Annual Meeting of the Virginia State Bar Association. Richmond, 1924.

Roosevelt, Theodore. *The Letters of Theodore Roosevelt.* Ed. Elting E. Morrison. 8 vols. Cambridge MA, 1951–54.

Ross, Elizabeth E., and Ray King, eds. *Marriage Records of Johnston County, North Carolina.* Clayton NC, 1986.

Shirer, William L. *Berlin Diary: The Journal of a Foreign Correspondent, 1934–1941.* New York, 1941.

Sledd, Andrew M. "The Negro: Another View." *Atlantic Monthly* 90 (1902): 65–73.

Tansill, Charles C. *Backdoor to War: The Roosevelt Foreign Policy, 1933–1941.* Chicago, 1952.

"Their Excellencies, Our Ambassadors." *Fortune Magazine* 9 (1934): 108–22.

The University of Chicago Annual Register, 1907–08. Chicago, 1908.

The University of North Carolina Catalogue, 1901–1902. Chapel Hill, 1902.

U.S. Department of State. *Documents on German Foreign Policy, 1918–1945.* 4 vols. Washington D.C., 1949–51.

———. *Foreign Relations of the United States: Diplomatic Papers, 1933.* 5 vols. Washington D.C., 1948.

———. *Foreign Relations of the United States: Diplomatic Papers, 1934.* 5 vols. Washington D.C., 1951.

———. *Foreign Relations of the United States: Diplomatic Papers, 1935.* 4 vols. Washington D.C., 1951.

———. *Foreign Relations of the United States: Diplomatic Papers, 1937.* 5 vols. Washington D.C., 1954.

Virginia Division, U.D.C., Minutes of the Thirteenth Annual Convention. N.p., 1908.

Wilson, Woodrow. "Mr. Goldwin Smith's 'Views' on Our Political History." *Forum* 16 (1893): 489–99.

———. *The Papers of Woodrow Wilson.* Edited by Arthur S. Link et al. 58 vols. to date. Princeton, 1966–.

Secondary Sources

Ash, Stephen V. "Poor Whites in the Occupied South, 1861–1865." *Journal of Southern History* 57 (1991): 39–62.

Bailey, Fred Arthur. *Class and Tennessee's Confederate Generation.* Chapel Hill, 1987.

———. "Free Speech and the 'Lost Cause' in the Old Dominion." *Virginia Magazine of History and Biography* 103 (1995): 237–66.

———. "Free Speech and the Lost Cause in Texas: A Study in Social Control in the New South." *Southwestern Historical Quarterly* 47 (1994): 453–78.

———. "The Textbooks of the 'Lost Cause': Censorship and the Creation of Southern State Histories." *Georgia Historical Quarterly* 75 (1991): 507–33.

———. "A Virginia Scholar in Hitler's Court: The Tragic Ambassadorship of William Edward Dodd." *Virginia Magazine of History and Biography* 100 (July 1992): 323–42.

———. "William Edward Dodd: The South's Yeoman Historian." *North Carolina Historical Review* 66 (July 1989): 301–20.

Beard, Charles A. *American Foreign Policy in the Making, 1932–1940: A Study in Responsibilities.* New Haven CT, 1946.

Billington, Ray Allen. *Frederick Jackson Turner: Historian, Scholar, Teacher.* New York, 1973.

———. "Tempest in Clio's Teapot: The American Historical Association Rebellion of 1915." *American Historical Review* 78 (1973): 348–69.

Blum, John Morton. *Woodrow Wilson and the Politics of Morality.* Boston, 1956.

Boles, John B., and Evelyn Thomas Nolen, eds. *Interpreting Southern History: Historiographical Essays in Honor of Stanford W. Higginbothan.* Baton Rouge, 1987.

Burton, Orville Vernon. *In My Father's House Are Many Mansions: Family and Community in Edgefield, South Carolina.* Chapel Hill, 1987.

Clark, Blanche H. *Tennessee Yeomen.* Nashville, 1942.

Cobb, James C., and Charles R. Wilson, eds. *Perspectives on the American South: An Annual Review of Southern Politics and Culture.* New York, 1987.

Cole, Wayne S. *Roosevelt and the Isolationists, 1932–1945.* Lincoln NE, 1983.

Cooke, Jacob E. *Frederic Bancroft: Historian.* Norman OK, 1957.

Dallek, Robert. *Democrat and Diplomat: The Life of William Edward Dodd.* New York, 1968.

Dierenfield, Bruce J. *Keeper of the Rules: Congressman Howard W. Smith of Virginia.* Charlottesville, 1987.

Dow, Earl W. "The Features of the New History: Apropos of Lamprecht's 'Deutsche Geschichte.'" *American Historical Review* 3 (1898): 431–48.

Drummond, Donald F. *The Passing of American Neutrality, 1937–1941.* New York, 1968.

Eaton, Clement. "Class Differences in the Old South." *Virginia Quarterly Review* 33 (1957): 357–70.

Escott, Paul D. *After Secession: Jefferson Davis and the Failure of Confederate Nationalism.* Baton Rouge, 1978.

———. *Many Excellent People: Power and Privilege in North Carolina, 1850–1900.* Chapel Hill, 1985.

Findling, John E., ed. *Dictionary of American Diplomatic History.* Westport CT, 1980.

Gelfand, Lawrence E. *The Inquiry: American Preparations for Peace, 1917–1919.* New Haven CT, 1963.

Genovese, Eugene D. "Yeomen Farmers in a Slaveholders' Democracy." *Agricultural History* 49 (1975): 331–42.

George, Alexander L., and Juliette L. George. *Woodrow Wilson and Colonel House: A Personality Study.* 1956. Reprint. New York, 1964.

Green, Edwin L. *A History of the University of South Carolina.* Columbia, 1916.

Hahn, Steven. *The Roots of Southern Populism: Yeomen Farmers and the Transformation of the Georgia Upcountry, 1850–1890.* New York, 1984.

Hamilton, William Baskerville. *Fifty Years of the South Atlantic Quarterly.* Durham NC, 1952.

The Heritage of Johnston County Book Committee. *The Heritage of Johnston County, North Carolina.* Winston-Salem NC, 1985.

Hofstadter, Richard. *The Progressive Historians: Turner, Beard, Parrington.* New York, 1968.

Holme, John G. *The Life of Leonard Wood.* Garden City NY, 1920.

Larsen, William E. *Montague of Virginia: The Making of a Southern Progressive.* Baton Rouge, 1965.

Link, Arthur S. *Wilson: The Road to the White House.* Princeton, 1947.

McDonald, Forrest, and Grady McWhiney. "The Antebellum Southern Herdsman: A Reinterpretation." *Journal of Southern History* 47 (1975): 147–66.

Mowry, George E. *The Era of Theodore Roosevelt and the Birth of Modern America, 1900–1912*. New York, 1958.

Mulder, John M. *Woodrow Wilson: The Years of Preparation*. Princeton, 1978.

Murray, Robert K. *Red Scare: A Study in National Hysteria, 1919–1920*. 2d ed. New York, 1964.

Neu, Charles E. "In Search of Colonel Edward M. House: The Texas Years, 1858–1912." *Southwestern Quarterly* 93 (1989): 25–44.

Owsley, Frank L. "Defeatism in the Confederacy." *North Carolina Historical Review* 3 (1926): 445–56.

———. *Plain Folk of the Old South*. Baton Rouge, 1949.

Owsley, Harriet Chappell. *Frank Lawrence Owsley: Historian of the Old South*. Nashville, 1990.

Paludan, Phillip S. *Victims: A True Story of the Civil War*. Knoxville, 1981.

Reed, Ralph E., Jr. "Emory College and the Sledd Affair of 1902: A Case Study of Southern Honor and Racial Attitudes." *Georgia Historical Quarterly* 72 (1988): 463–92.

Roark, James L. *Masters without Slaves: Southern Planters in the Civil War and Reconstruction*. New York, 1977.

Roper, John Herbert. *U. B. Phillips: A Southern Mind*. Macon GA, 1984.

Scanlon, James Edward. *Randolph-Macon College: A Southern History, 1825–1967*. Charlottesville, 1983.

Shelton, Charlotte Jean. "William Atkinson Jones, 1849–1918: Independent Democracy in Gilded Age Virginia." Ph.D. diss., University of Virginia, 1980.

Shirer, William L. *The Rise and Fall of the Third Reich: A History of Nazi Germany*. New York, 1960.

Shugg, Roger W. *Origins of Class Struggle in Louisiana*. Baton Rouge, 1939.

Stephenson, Wendell H. *Southern History in the Making: Pioneer Historians of the South*. Baton Rouge, 1964.

———. *The South Lives in History: Southern Historians and Their Legacy*. Baton Rouge, 1955.

Tatum, Georgia L. *Disloyalty in the Confederacy*. Chapel Hill, 1934.

Thomas, Emory M. *The Confederacy as a Revolutionary Experience*. Englewood Cliffs NJ, 1971.

Weaver, Herbert. *Mississippi Farmers, 1850–1860*. Nashville, 1945.

White, William Allen. *Woodrow Wilson: The Man, His Times, and His Task*. Boston, 1929.

Wiebe, Robert H. *The Search for Order, 1877–1920*. New York, 1967.

Williams, Jack K. "A Bibliography of the Printed Writings of William Edward Dodd." *North Carolina Historical Review* 30 (1953): 72–85.

Woodward, C. Vann. *The Burden of Southern History*. New York, 1960.

Index

Minds of the New South

Robert F. Martin
HOWARD KESTER AND THE STRUGGLE FOR SOCIAL JUSTICE IN
THE SOUTH, 1904–77

Janis P. Stout
KATHERINE ANNE PORTER: A SENSE OF THE TIMES

Wayne Mixon
THE PEOPLE'S WRITER: ERSKINE CALDWELL AND THE SOUTH

Mark Royden Winchell
CLEANTH BROOKS AND THE RISE OF MODERN CRITICISM

Fred Arthur Bailey
WILLIAM EDWARD DODD: THE SOUTH'S YEOMAN SCHOLAR